A PRENTICE HALL SMALL BUSINESS GUIDE

FINANCING *the* SMALL BUSINESS

LAWRENCE W. TULLER

Prentice Hall
New York • London • Toronto • Sydney • Tokyo • Singapore

Prentice Hall General Reference
15 Columbus Circle
New York, NY 10023

A J.K. Lasser Book

J.K. Lasser, Prentice Hall and colophons are
registered trademarks of Simon & Schuster, Inc.

Manufactured in the United States of America

1 2 3 4 5 6 7 8 9 10

Library of Congress Cataloging-in-Publication Data

Tuller, Lawrence W.
  Financing the small business/by Lawrence W. Tuller
    p. cm.
  Includes index.
  ISBN 0-13-322116-4
  1. Small business—Finance. I. Title.
HG4027.7.T85 1991   91-3166
658.15'92—dc20   CIP

Dedication

To Charles, Susan and Barbara

Other Books By The Author

The Battle-Weary Executive: A Blueprint for New Beginnings

Getting Out: A Step-by-Step Guide to Selling a Business or Professional Practice

Buying In: A Complete Guide to Acquiring a Business or Professional Practice

Going Global: New Opportunities for Growing Companies to Compete in World Markets

Recession-Proof Your Business: How to Boost Cash Flow and Make it Through Tough Times with Ease

When The Bank Says No! Creative Financing for Closely Held Companies

Tap The Hidden Wealth In Your Business: Use Your Closely Held Company to—Increase Personal Cash, Maximize Retirement Income, Build Estate Assets . . . All Legally!

Contents

CHAPTER 1

The Banking Industry and Its Language

We all use banks. We write checks, make deposits, buy short-term investments, perhaps use a safe deposit box. At one time or another, most of us have borrowed from banks, either personally or for business reasons. We take out loans for a new car, a house, major appliances, or furniture. Businesses borrow for working capital, to purchase a new machine, or to expand facilities.

We trust banks. After all, doesn't the federal government guarantee that we'll get our money back regardless of how inefficiently a bank may be managed? And as for loans—when we borrow money we execute a loan agreement, clearly spelling out how much we must pay back on specific dates. What could be simpler or easier to understand?

But all is not as it appears in the banking industry. Banks are not in business to promote society's well-being—to help people and businesses in need of cash, to be a secure custodian of our family and business jewels, to bail out the federal government, or to assist in the growth of our nation. Banks are in business to make money. Pure and simple. Just like every other business. And when banks don't make money, they fail. The big difference between bank failures and other business failures is that the greater the number of banks that fail, the higher the probability that our deposits will be lost and that our loans must be repaid immediately.

Because so many misconceptions about banks proliferate in the business community and because—in spite of their difficulties—banks remain the cornerstone of business finance, it is difficult to make intelligent financing judgments without a basic understanding of the banking industry and some of its problems.

CURRENT STATUS OF THE BANKING INDUSTRY

According to the Federal Reserve Board, approximately 13 thousand banks operate in the United States, far and away the largest number of nongovernment-owned banks in any country in the world. Although commercial banks have failed at

1

the rate of over 200 per year since 1987 and the S & L disaster took its toll, new banks continue to open.

Why so many? One reason dates back to the beginning, when our nation was still rural. People from predominantly European heritage fleeing oppression and rigid class structures distrusted any large concentration of power—be it political, religious, or financial. In their new nation, our forefathers wanted no part of the substantial financial power European banks held over political bodies, as well as individuals. However, the settlers eventually needed a place to deposit cash and to borrow money for new businesses and farms; therefore, rural banks were born. These small, locally-owned banks dotted the American landscape for years.

Gradually, as the federal government grew to need its own financing and as businesses outgrew the capability of rural banks, large city banks developed. These city banks eventually blossomed into what today are referred to as money center banks, with vast hordes of resources. Contrary to the dreams of our ancestors, money center banks have now become more powerful than the European banks the settlers disdained. The Federal Reserve estimates that nine money center banks control over 50 percent of all U.S. banking assets.

Major changes have taken place in the banking industry during the last two years that directly affect smaller businesses. More can be expected in the future as American and foreign banks become increasingly competitive in each other's backyard. Recognizing this globalization of the banking industry and in an effort to prevent banks from overextending their loan portfolios, the Bank for International Settlements implemented an interim set of guidelines for bank capital. These guidelines state that in 1991 banks must have capital equal to a minimum of 7.25 percent of their assets. Their full force hits in 1993 when the ratio goes to 8 percent.

The Bank for International Settlements (BIS) was founded to coordinate the collection and rescheduling of German reparations after World War I. It is no longer involved with settlements but has survived as sort of a central bank for the central banks (e.g., the Federal Reserve Bank) of its 10 member countries. The BIS serves a useful purpose in that it functions objectively as an international financial ombudsman. It has a fully qualified multinational staff and is held in high esteem by its member central banks as a standard-setting body.

In 1986 the BIS published a volume titled *Recent Innovations in International Banking,* prepared by a study group of representatives from each of the member banks. This publication alerted the world financial community that a dangerous slippage had occurred in capital ratios of major banking institutions, both in America and abroad. The enormous errors made by banks in lending to Latin American countries contributed in no small measure to this deterioration. The Federal Reserve and the other member banks agreed to implement standardized, stepped, minimum capital ratio regulations beginning in 1987 and extending over the ensuing five years. The 1993 step will be the final jump.

These regulations had a profound effect on American money center banks, which in turn affected the entire banking system. Even small rural banks feel the pinch. Although American money center banks already boast some of the best ratios in the world, they now must raise additional capital just to maintain their present balance between assets and liabilities. Over the next several years, this could cause a funding crisis in the banking industry.

This shake-up in the banking industry has a profound effect on smaller and mid-size business borrowers. Any moves on the part of the money center banks ripple down to regional, state, and local banks. Since many of these banks already share the same problems as their bigger cousins, the impact is double barreled. These smaller banks must first get their own houses in order before they can cope with restricted borrowings from the big banks.

Why should you worry about bank capital and ratios? It's fine for bankers and regulators to pay attention to these matters, but what impact do they have on financing smaller businesses?

Like manufacturers, retailers, and service firms, banks need capital (cash) to operate their businesses. In addition, however, they must satisfy federal regulators who take orders from the Federal Reserve and the Comptroller of the Currency. Maintaining a minimum 7.5 percent to 8 percent capital ratio means that banks must hold this amount of money in reserve as a cushion against losses. This, in turn, determines how much they can lend. If a bank has insufficient capital, it has two choices: either get more capital or make fewer loans. And therein lies the rub. As banks contract their lending activity to strengthen their own balance sheets, small businesses get left in the cold.

THE REGULATORS STEP IN

One fall-out of the S & L debacle has been an increasing panic on the part of federal regulators. They claim that the BIS guidelines represent a bare minimum applicable only to the bluest of blue-chip banks. Non-performing Latin American loans were bad enough. With the collapse of the real estate market in 1990, however, non-performing property loans rose by $4.3 billion or 31 percent at the big banks.

Regulators insist that capital be reserved against these loans, but so far banks have been unable or unwilling to bite the bullet. The ratio of reserve provisions to non-performing loans at money center banks fell from 89 percent in October 1989 to 65 percent a year later. This caused the Fed to institute a measure claimed to be stricter than that imposed by the BIS core capital ratio.

The Fed now insists that the "tangible common equity" (common equity less intangibles, divided by total assets less intangibles) must equal at least 4 percent of a bank's total assets. Salomon Brothers estimates that by mid-1990 nine of the biggest banks were $6.8 billion short of that mark. Figure 1-1 sets out actual ratios as compiled by Salomon Brothers.

Figure 1–1

CAPITAL RATIO FOR NINE LEADING BANKS

As of 6/30/90

	Percent
Bank of New York	3.93
Chase Manhattan	3.16
Chemical Bank	2.81
Citicorp	2.61
Manufacturers Hanover	2.92
Bank of Boston	3.80
Continental Bank	3.54
First Interstate	3.62
Security Pacific	3.89
Composite	3.16

Most large American banks are holding companies; that is, they operate divisions and subsidiaries engaged in non-banking businesses: credit cards, mortgages, asset-based lending, and so on. Foreign bankers claim that if American bank holding companies were allowed to include their complete balance sheets, the Federal Reserve ratios would be unnecessary. Appendix A compares ratios of the top 20 American banks using both the Fed's definition and that of the BIS. Nevertheless, the Fed rules persist, and in the long run may turn out to be the most prudent.

THE SOLUTION

Banks can meet the Fed's capital ratio tests by taking one or a combination of five steps:

1. Raise additional capital by selling subordinated debt issues, preferred stock, or other instruments on the open market. But in late 1990, average bank shares were trading at three-quarters of book value and the bigger banks at two-thirds. Also, Standard & Poor's reduced the credit ratings of more than 35 banks in 1990, leaving only the venerable J.P.Morgan with a credit rating better than AA. These conditions effectively close the market to new issues.

2. Sell assets. These assets would have to be solid, premier loans; non-performing loans won't attract many buyers. But selling premium loans only increases a bank's ratio of non-performing loans to total assets, in turn creating the need for even more capital.

3. Cut dividends. Obviously, cutting dividends results in a further deterioration in share trading value, in turn exacerbating the problem of raising new, outside capital.

4. Slash operating costs. Since personnel costs are the biggest and the easiest to cut, most banks have chosen this option as a quick fix. Chase is shedding 5,000 jobs, although the figure could be much higher in the end. Citicorp is heading toward a reduction of 10,000 jobs. Many banks already slashed payroll by a combined total of more than 50,000 people in 1990.

5. Merge with another bank. According to industry estimates, the elimination of redundancies achieved through merging several big banks could save billion of dollars. However, strong power bosses heading most of the big banks make the likelihood of sharing control remote.

In the end, the most likely solution will include a portion of each of these steps. Regardless of how banks choose to deal with their problem, the inevitable result will be fewer loans and higher collateral requirements for small businesses. Long before the federal government admitted to a recession, business borrowers felt the pinch of a vicious credit crunch. They found banks calling short-term loans, insisting on timely debt service payments, and refusing to grant either extensions or new loans. Trends point to a worsening condition in the years ahead.

Bankers who in the past were amenable to working with businesses suffering short-term cash problems are suddenly adamant that loans be repaid on time. New loans for the acquisition of facilities or equipment have become scarcer and more difficult to qualify for. Start-up businesses find that substantial personal collateral must now be pledged. For all but the most secure businesses, leveraged buyouts have dried up. High-flying investment banks, asset-based lenders, and venture capitalists of the 1980s have pulled in their reins.

Although the banking industry is beginning to examine new philosophies leading to more prudent business practices, billion dollar errors in judgment can't be rectified overnight. The likelihood of another round of easy business credit in the foreseeable future seems remote. Every indicator points to a continuance of these conditions for several years. This means that entrepreneurs, businessowners, and managers must become smarter, tougher, and more creative in financing future start-ups or expansions. They must learn how to play the financial game, according to the rules laid down by the banking fraternity.

DIFFERENT TYPES OF BANKS

A variety of banks have proliferated on the American business scene. The Federal Reserve Bank is the American central bank. It acts as a bank for non-government banks and clears inter-bank transfers of funds. It processes checks written on banks throughout the country and debits and credits the accounts of both the payer and the payee banks.

Large money center banks represent the private sector equivalent of the Federal Reserve Bank. With banking deregulation, money center banks branched out into a variety of financial services ranging from investment banking to credit cards to foreign lending to clearing houses for international money transfers. Most have branches scattered throughout the world. Their primary activities, however, haven't changed. They continue to act as depositories, lenders, and purchasers of government securities.

Large banks may be further divided between retail banks and wholesale banks. Retail banks, such as Citicorp, Chase, and Chemical, concentrate on deposits, loans, and money manipulations for individual and business customers. Wholesale banks, such J.P.Morgan, Bankers Trust, and Morgan Guaranty, specialize in acting as banks for other banks. Although they also get involved in retail banking and investment transactions, they primarily act as wholesalers, borrowing and lending funds from other banks.

Next in line in the banking hierarchy, large regional banks such as Mellon, First Chicago, Norwest, and Crocker, function regionally in a fashion similar to money center banks at a national level. Federal and state laws prohibiting interstate banking encouraged the growth of banks to meet the needs of large regional businesses. Heretofore limited by city or county lines, recent legislation in several states has allowed these banks to expand statewide, and to acquire banks in other states. Large regional banks also have become involved in foreign loans and many have staffed multinational personnel to handle international accounts. Money center banks act as correspondents for regional banks.

Below the large regional banks, local federal and state licensed neighborhood and rural banks dot the landscape. In terms of pure numbers, these banks continue to make up the bulk of the more than 13,000 banks throughout the country. Most are strictly retail banks, loaning money to individuals and smaller businesses and acting as depositories. Because smaller businesses find it much easier to establish personal relationships with this size bank, most deal exclusively with them, leaving the larger banks to larger companies. Local banks use regional banks as correspondents. When a customer requires services beyond their scope, they merely funnel the transaction through their regional correspondent.

Specialized banks go by a variety of names: trusts, savings banks, savings and loan associations, thrifts, private banks, and so on. In addition, other financial institutions get involved in business finance to a greater or lesser extent: asset based lenders, commercial and industrial finance companies, credit unions, and so on. Many money center or regional banks incorporate these specialties as divisions or subsidiaries.

The Federal Deposit Insurance Corporation (FDIC) insures deposit accounts up to $100,000 in all federally licensed banks. A closer look at the problems of the FDIC and potential changes in FDIC regulations can be found in Chapter 2.

FOREIGN BANKS

In addition to American-owned banks, a great many foreign banks now maintain branch operations in the United States. Many of these are full-service banks competing head-on with money center, regional, and local American banks. According to the Fed, all U.S. branches and affiliates of foreign banks (including those U.S. banks acquired by foreigners) account for less than 10 percent of total banking assets in the United States. Although that isn't a very high percentage, it continues to grow. By contrast, a much greater percentage of European banks are owned by foreigners; some estimates reach 20 percent.

The FDIC does not insure deposit accounts in foreign-owned banks. Neither are foreign banks subjected to the stringent new capital ratio requirements of the Fed, although they are obliged to follow BIS guidelines. Foreign banks also operate under different accounting rules than their U.S. counterparts, allowing greater freedom and creativity.

The American Institute of Certified Public Accountants (AICPA), the Securities and Exchange Commission (SEC), and the General Accounting Office (GAO) make certain that U.S. banks abide by the uniform accounting practices set down by these groups. Generally, American banks follow the same conservative accounting principles that apply to any publicly listed company. Assets must be recorded at the lower of cost or market and liabilities recorded as soon as they are recognized. Off-balance sheet financing instruments are frowned upon. Stringent audit procedures ensure that banks comply with these rules.

Foreign banks, on the other hand, follow the accounting practices dictated by their home country. Certain American standards of reporting must be adhered to, however, and when they are not, the foreign bank gets into trouble (e.g., the 1990 laundered drug money case involving the Florida branch of the Arab-owned Bank of Credit and Commerce International). Excluding practices that endanger national security or that are clearly against public policy, foreign banks can do pretty much as they please. Many European banks follow off-balance sheet practices for letters of credit. Japanese banks are famous for recording certain assets at market value.

Many times a foreign bank makes a loan when an American bank won't. Especially now with bank regulators clamping down, a foreign bank might very well be the only avenue for financing business expansion. It's even possible to interest a foreign bank in first-stage financing, especially if the products lead to eventual exports. When a new bank opens its door in a city or neighborhood, new accounts are eagerly solicited. A newly opened branch of a foreign bank is no different. Very often you can get financing from one of these when the American bank next door says no.

Foreign banks are accustomed to dealing with standby letters of credit (L/C) and other creative performance guarantees. For example, contractors often find a foreign bank willing to post a standby L/C against a contractor's performance when a normal surety bond is unavailable or too expensive. Foreign bank standby L/Cs can also be used as payment guarantees to third party bank loans.

As competition from foreign banks increases, with any luck federal regulators and the accounting profession will reconsider now outdated accounting and reporting practices and allow American banks to compete on an equal footing. Until then, however, it makes sense to consider a foreign bank as a viable alternative source of funds.

CHOOSING THE RIGHT BANK

With the many types of banks and continually shifting bank portfolios and loan policies, it can be extremely difficult to sift out the right bank for a specific project. Yet, that is exactly what you must do to be certain of getting the right financing for the minimum cost.

Shopping for a bank is no different than shopping for a car. We wouldn't think of buying the first car we see in the showroom even if the dealer does happen to be located next door. We investigate, compare, evaluate, and finally choose the type of car we want. Then we search out and negotiate the best deal we can get, often with more than one dealer.

Probably because of the general mystique associated with banks and money, we seldom apply the same selection procedures when choosing a bank. Far too often we choose a bank because it is close, or because we know the name. More often than not, we choose a bank simply because we are happy to get a loan from any bank and jump at the first opportunity. Nine times out of 10, this route leads to higher costs and less desirable payback terms than necessary. Invariably, it also leads to eventual disagreement with the bank and a falling out. Then, trying to interest another bank becomes significantly more difficult.

The checklist/questionnaire in Figure 1-2 presents the type of questions that should be answered satisfactorily before signing up with any bank.

Figure 1–2
CHECKLIST/QUESTIONNAIRE FOR CHOOSING A BANK

BANK OWNERSHIP/STRUCTURE
 1. Is the bank's stock publicly traded?
 2. Who owns controlling blocks of shares?
 3. Foreign ownership or American?
 4. Is the bank licensed by the federal government or a state?
 5. Are deposits covered under FDIC?
 6. What is the current capital to assets ratio?

7. What is the current tangible common equity ratio?
8. What is the percentage of non-performing loans to total loans outstanding?
9. What was the current year's loan loss provision?
10. What is the dividend record over the past three years, including current year?
11. What percentage of outstanding loans are to Latin American/Third World nations?
12. What percentage of outstanding loans are secured by real estate?
13. Will the bank provide financial statements for the prior three years?

SERVICES OFFERED
14. Does the bank offer the following types of loans:
    a. Operating line of credit? Secured by receivables? Unsecured?
    b. Term loans for machinery, equipment, vehicles? For what period?
    c. Real estate mortgage? For what period?
15. What interest rate does the bank charge for each type of loan?
16. What down payment is required for term loans and mortgages?
17. Does the bank handle leases for equipment and autos? For what period?
18. Does the bank have an international department?
19. Does the bank have a finance company or asset-based lender division?
20. Does the bank have an investment banking division or an SBIC?
21. What short-term investment instruments are available? Overnight repos? Eurodollar accounts? Weekly certificates of deposit?
22. What are the monthly service charges?

LOCATION/CORRESPONDENTS
23. What branches exist nearby?
24. Where are loan officers located?
25. What regional banks are correspondents?
26. What money center banks are correspondents?

LOAN POLICIES/PORTFOLIOS
27. Will the bank provide working capital loans for a business start-up? Terms?
28. What is the smallest loan the bank will make for a start-up?
29. How much equity does an entrepreneur need for a start-up?
30. What type of personal guarantees are required? Co-signers?
31. How high will the bank go for an operating line?
32. Does the bank provide business acquisition funding?
33. Will the bank loan against an SBA guarantee? Terms?

CUSTOMERS/REFERENCES
34. What other accounts does the bank have in the same industry?
35. What experience does the loan officer have in this industry?
36. What percentage of loan portfolio is dedicated to small business accounts?
37. Which other businesses in the area use this bank?
38. Can the bank provide three references from other customers?

BANKING LANGUAGE

The banking industry has its own cadre of terms seemingly designed to confound non-bankers. Banking language adds a significant level of complexity to relatively simple transactions. This often leads a borrower to agree to rules and conditions grossly misunderstood from the very beginning.

Some of these terms are clearly necessary to describe instruments, situations, and conditions unique to banking. Others seem to have been injected as a way to encase banking in a cloak of mysticism, thereby elevating the industry above the mundane business world. Not dissimilar to special terminology concocted by lawyers, physicians, and other professionals, many complex banking terms describe simple, everyday events.

As a starting point, financiers speak of four stages of business financing: seed money, first-stage, second-stage, and third-stage. Funding the acquisition of a going business is often referred to as merely acquisition financing.

Seed money refers to the cash required in the preliminary stages of starting up a business. Typically, amounts run less than $20,000. Budding entrepreneurs require seed money to build a model or prototype of a new product with the expectation of bringing it to market. Seed money buys materials, pays rent and utilities, and funds market research. Except in unusual cases, banks do not make loans for seed money without iron-clad guarantees of repayment from a third party, such as the SBA.

First-stage financing is used to actually start a business. It may be used to meet payroll and other operating expenses, to purchase materials, or to acquire machinery, equipment, tools, and facilities for the production of products or services. First-stage financing occurs after a product or service has been selected and preliminary market research completed.

Second-stage financing relates to raising capital for expansion beyond the initial start-up phase. Perhaps a company needs an additional building for a new production line or inventory storage, or as a distribution warehouse. Second-stage financing also funds the purchase of additional equipment, machinery, or delivery vehicles. Rapidly increasing sales might necessitate a larger line of credit. Maybe a company needs financing to manage an export program.

Second-stage financing also is frequently used to refinance original loans from the first stage, converting short-term debt to longer terms. Typically, second-stage financing occurs between the second and fifth years after a company begins business. Beyond five or six years, it should be firmly established. Any additional financing is then referred to as third stage.

Third-stage financing usually involves larger amounts than either the first or second stage. A company might decide to float a public stock issue to raise equity capital for liquidating debt. It could use third-stage financing for establishing an overseas facility.

Third-stage capital also finances the acquisition of another business, branch plants, or warehouses. It funds the replacement or upgrading of machinery and equipment. It provides the cash to make major facilities renovations. Third-stage financing nearly always relates to major expansions, refinancing, or very expensive purchases of hard assets. At this stage in its maturity, a company should not have to go to the capital markets for additional working capital, except for overseas start-ups.

Most of the recommendations, ideas, and sources covered in this book relate to first- or second-stage financing. Since an overlap always occurs, a few third-stage sources will, of necessity, be included. Chapter 14 focuses on methods to raise third-stage capital for refinancing original debt, for major expansions, and for restructuring management incentive programs.

In order to intelligently assess the desirability of entering into bank agreements and, in fact, to judge the advisability of even doing business with a specific bank, a person needs a minimum understanding of banking vernacular. Literally hundreds of special bank terms will never be used by businesspeople and, therefore, should not be relevant. Some, however, must be used to communicate with bankers. Following are the most widely used and the most widely confused banking terms that come in handy in the mystical world of business finance.

Bank Instruments

A bank instrument is merely a document or agreement that evidences a specific indebtedness. Most people know about corporate or U.S. Treasury bonds, preferred or common stock, and debentures. Four other bank instruments used by smaller businesses may not be as familiar.

Demand Note

A demand note is merely a promissory note from a company to a bank. The note spells out the principal amount of the loan and the interest rate. It also may identify a due date for the final liquidation of the loan. But in all cases, a demand note specifies that the entire loan must be paid back on demand by the bank. In other words, regardless of any mutually agreed due date, the bank has the right to call for the entire payment at any time it wishes, unilaterally, without consent of the borrower.

Letter Of Credit

A letter of credit, commonly referred to as an L/C, is also a popular bank instrument. This document states that the bank has granted the holder an amount of credit equal to the face amount of the L/C. In international trade, the holder of the L/C presents it, along with other authenticating documentation, to the drawer's bank and demands payment of the face amount.

Domestically, letters of credit frequently serve as a guarantee that the payee will perform an act or make a payment. Used in this manner, it is called a "standby L/C." The term "standby" means that the holder cannot draw against the L/C unless the payee fails to perform or pay as agreed upon by contract. The construction industry uses standby L/Cs in place of surety bonds. They also are frequently used as back-up guarantees to a revenue bond issue or to secure loans from a large money center bank.

Junk Bonds

During the madcap 1980s, many companies large and small raised capital for third-stage financing through the use of junk bonds. The term "junk bond" indicates instruments rated below investment grade by credit rating agencies. Such a rating represents a very high risk for investors. Junk bonds are seldom secured by any collateral and because of their high risk to investors carry a very high interest rate.

Banker's Acceptance

A banker's acceptance (BA) is a time draft countersigned or "accepted" by the bank. Both documentary and clean BAs are used extensively in export trade to evidence that bank credit has been extended. Banker's acceptances can be discounted. This means that when presented by the drawer, the bank actually pays less than the face amount of the draft. This reflects the market discount plus the bank's acceptance commission. In the past BAs have not been used widely in the United States, although with the increasing number of foreign banks doing business in this country who do use BAs, competitive forces undoubtedly will encourage American banks to meet the challenge.

TYPES OF LOANS

Once again, most businesspeople are very familiar with the standard types of bank loans—mortgages, lines of credit, installment loans, and so on. New terminology that might not be so familiar evolved during the past 10 years: revolver, term loan, mezzanine debt, and non-performing loans.

Revolver

In banking parlance a revolver is not a gun, although many business owners believe bankers use it as such! A revolver describes short-term loans secured by receivables and inventory. The term "revolver" was coined because as the loan against one customer account is paid off from the collection of that account, another loan automatically takes its place with the next shipment. Individual loans against shipping invoices and collections keep revolving so that the outstanding loan balance continually changes. Exactly the same principle applies for loans against inventory.

Term Loan

Loans granted for a specific period of time, generally beyond one year, are frequently called term loans. When refinancing, short-term revolvers often get converted to three-to-five-year term loans. Typically, term loans provide for monthly or quarterly payments against principal and monthly payment of interest. Interest rates on term loans generally run two to three percentage points more than revolvers. Long-term assets secure term loans.

Mezzanine Debt

Used principally for financing the acquisition of a going business, mezzanine loans bridge the gap between term loans and equity contributions. Mezzanine debt is considered temporary, with terms running from one to three years. Within that time frame the borrower either liquidates the debt or refinances it with another term loan. Interest rates on mezzanine debt normally run one to two percentage points above term loans. The loan may be secured by a second position on long-term assets or it can be unsecured.

Non-Performing Loans

The term non-performing loan applies to a bank's balance sheet. A loan falls into this category if interest payments are more than 90 days in arrears. Federal regulators require that these loans be classified as high risk and provisioned against. Once a loan gets classified as non-performing, the bank may not accrue interest income from it.

Loan Security

Very few smaller businesses can borrow money without offering some type of collateral against the loan. As Chapter 2 points out, a bank's primary concern is getting the loan paid back. To ensure this, the bank requires a borrower to secure the loan with assets at least equal in value to the balance of the loan.

Liquid Or Soft Assets

Liquid assets or soft assets can readily be converted into cash in the event the borrower defaults. Such assets typically include current receivables, raw material and finished goods inventory, cash in bank accounts, certificates of deposit and other short-term bank instruments, and marketable securities. Liquid assets secure short-term debt due within one year such as revolvers.

Hard Assets

Machinery, equipment, buildings, land, automobiles, furniture, and fixtures are considered hard assets. Hard assets cannot be readily converted into cash. In the event of default, they must be sold by the lender to recoup the loan balance. These assets secure term loans, mezzanine debt, installment loans, and other long-term debt. Because hard assets can depreciate in value over time, lenders frequently demand that the market value of such assets at the execution of the loan exceeds the loan balance.

Cross Collateral

The term cross-collateral applies to assets of one company used to secure a loan to another company. If one company defaults on its loan payments, the lender can seize the assets of the second company as satisfaction. This typically occurs when more than one company has common ownership, such as when a businessowner personally owns the building housing the business that borrows the money. Cross-collaterization also applies between the assets of the business borrowing the money and the personal assets of the businessowner. To perfect a claim, the lender files a lien against the assets of both parties under the Uniform Commercial Code.

Guarantees

Lenders often insist on third-party guarantees as additional collateral. If a borrower defaults, the lender looks to the guarantor to repay the balance of the loan. It is not unusual for a lender to file a UCC lien against the assets of the guarantor as well as the borrower. A third-party guarantor may be the businessowner personally, a spouse, a relative or friend of the owner, another company, or a third-party financial organization such as the SBA or another bank. Obviously, to have any value the guarantee must be supported by assets sufficient to liquidate the defaulted loan.

INTEREST RATES

In America, interest rates are usually based on the prime rate. The interest rate on short- and long-term loans is quoted as prime plus so many points. The rate may be fixed; that is, the interest rate established at the execution of the loan remains the same over the term of the loan, regardless of what happens to prime. The rate may also be variable; that is, it varies with prime, based on the point spread established when executing the loan.

Prime Rate

Bankers define prime rate as the rate of interest they charge their best commercial customers. They claim that they base this rate on a complicated cost formula that takes into account the bank's cost of money (interest it pays out), its operating expenses (salaries, supplies, telephone, etc.), and its housing expense (rent, depreciation, and so on). Theoretically, this cost *plus* a reasonable profit margin *equals* prime rate.

But, this is not true. The large money center banks establish a fictitious interest rate called prime, based on what the traffic will bear. All correspondent banks around the country then follow suit, regardless of what their specific cost structure may be. Obviously, it doesn't cost a bank in rural Wyoming as much to operate as a bank in mid-town Manhattan. Yet they both use the same prime measure to establish interest rates.

It should be clearly understood that the Federal Reserve Bank does *not* set the prime rate. It has nothing to do with it. Prime rate is established by money center banks as a measuring base against which to calculate customer interest charges.

Basis Points

One hundred basis points equal one percentage point of interest. Basis points measure the market in corporate bonds. The phrase "spread over Treasuries" is used by bond issuers and traders to discuss the bond market. They measure the rate earned or charged by the number of basis points over a comparable maturity U.S. Treasury benchmark security. Companies utilizing municipal revenue bonds pay interest based on basis points plus or minus interest percentages against the prime rate.

Libor

The London Interbank Offered Rate, referred to as LIBOR, is the European equivalent of the U.S. prime rate, although it is not calculated the same way. LIBOR represents the base lending rate between banks in the London Eurocurrency market. With increasing frequency, the globalization of the financial system forces U.S. lenders to quote interest rates based on LIBOR rather than prime. Generally, LIBOR runs slightly less than prime. Borrowers approve of LIBOR because it represents an actual rate charged by one bank to another bank, not a fictitious estimate.

OTHER BANKING TERMS

A few other banking terms might cause confusion. Since the financial community continually originates new phrases, words, terminology, and concepts, it is impossible to stay attuned to the entire spectrum. Currently, however, some terms are so universally used that it helps to have a basic understanding of what they mean.

Leveraging

Everyone has heard of leveraged buyouts or LBOs. A business or an individual uses a small amount of equity as a down payment to buy a company. Using the target company's assets as collateral, loans make up the difference in the purchase price. The theory behind LBOs is that the earnings from the company can then be used to repay the loan, thus 'leveraging up' or increasing the value of the owners equity contribution. Most of us practice leveraging when we buy a house or condo with a small down payment and a mortgage. As the mortgage gets paid down and the value of the dwelling appreciates, our equity multiplies geometrically.

Working Capital

Accountants define working capital as current assets less current liabilities. In business finance, a working capital loan is used to fund increasing receivables and inventory purchases as the business grows. Cash must be expended before sales can be collected and working capital loans provide the bridge. Working capital loans can be revolvers or lines of credit.

Globalization

Globalization is a relatively new term in banking circles that has come about as a result of the growth in international trade. Money flows freely across national borders. As companies expand overseas they need to finance this expansion with local funds. Globalization provides the means to do this. In simple terms, globalization is the process of interlinking financial markets in different countries into a common, worldwide pool of funds to be accessed by both borrowers and lenders. Foreign banks operating in the United States bring globalization to our doorstep.

Debt To Equity

Lenders of all varieties use a company's debt to equity ratio to judge the safety of a loan. The higher the debt to equity ratio—that is, the more debt a company has relative to its net worth—the less secure the loan. Smaller companies should try to keep this ratio at no more than one dollar of net worth for every three dollars of debt. Although lenders prefer a lower ratio, most will consider a loan if the resultant ratio hovers around 3 to 1. In prior years, LBOs frequently created debt to equity ratios closer to 9 to 1!

TYPES OF LENDERS

Commercial banks and their foreign equivalent—clearing banks—are the most common sources of first- and second-stage financing, but they by no means represent the only sources. A variety of other financial institutions, federal and state agencies, and private organizations stand ready to provide financing assistance during both stages. These sources may charge less than banks or, as in the case of asset-based lenders, significantly more. In other circumstances, a commercial bank may not be interested in financing a specific project, requiring other sources regardless of cost.

The remainder of this book emphasizes the importance of using the right source for a specific application of the funds. Where a choice exists between two or more sources, the advantages and disadvantages of one over the other is pointed out. Where no choice exists, and only one source of funds will handle a specific project, that is also disclosed.

Although more complicated and less popular sources exist—especially when sourcing funds overseas—the 12 most readily accessible domestic non-bank financing sources are:

1. Private financial institutions
   a. Venture capital funds
   b. Small Business Investment Companies (SBIC)
   c. Small investment banks
   d. Finance companies
   e. Foreign merchant banks
2. Federal and state agencies
   a. Small Business Administration (SBA)
   b. Small Business Innovative Research (SBIR)
   c. Export-Import Bank (Eximbank)
   d. State development agencies
3. Other sources
   a. Pension funds
   b. Insurance companies
   c. Private foundations

PRIVATE FINANCIAL INSTITUTIONS

Venture capital funds come in all sizes and shapes. Some have an investment portfolio of less than $50,000; others measure close to one billion dollars. Some are privately owned. Large corporations or banks own others. Still others trade in public markets. Small Business Investment Companies are venture capital firms funded in part by the SBA.

Venture capital funds originally invested equity and debt in small, start-up companies with high-tech products. As we all know, venture capital firms practically built Silicon Valley. The wave of new, high-tech opportunities eventually tapered off in the late 1970s and early 1980s. By this time, venture capital firms that had grown along with their investments, began branching out.

Although some continue to restrict themselves to high-tech start-ups, most now get involved in financing first-, second-, and even some third-stage expansion. In addition, the high-flying financial markets of the middle and late 1980s encouraged venture capitalists to look beyond high-tech companies to more mundane, slower-growth industries.

Today, venture capital firms of all sizes hold both equity investment and debt in large and small companies in a wide range of industries. First-stage financing remains the preference of most. Venture capital firms also handle second-stage financing for companies in which they already have a vested interest. Several will entertain proposals for second-stage financing from other companies, however, providing they are in rapid growth industries.

Two overwhelming conditions characterize venture capital financing: equity capital represents at least part, if not all of the funding, and the return to the venture capital firm must range between 25 and 40 percent per year. Obviously, this precludes many companies from attracting venture capital funds. There aren't too many small companies that can afford to pay out 25 to 40 percent of their earnings to investors. Venture capital firms also expect a company to go public within five years of making the initial investment. In this way they recoup their appreciated investment and expect to make a significant capital gain.

Small investment banks are really venture capital funds that have branched out into stable industries. They prefer to think of themselves as investment banks because the term connotes less risky investments.

Finance companies are also called asset-based lenders. They loan money to high-risk companies that commercial banks won't touch. They normally require less equity from the owner than commercial banks. Finance companies charge very high interest but will amortize a term loan over five to seven years. They can also be difficult to work with if business conditions begin to deteriorate.

Foreign merchant banks represent the foreign equivalent of large American investment banks. However, most will finance small and mid-size companies where large investment banks won't. British merchant banks are especially easy to work with. In addition to providing financing themselves, merchant banks can be of enormous assistance in locating other financial institutions to package a financing deal.

FEDERAL AND STATE AGENCIES

The Small Business Administration (SBA) is probably the best known federal agency for helping start-up businesses find capital. Every major city and many smaller communities boast SBA offices, and applications for financing assistance are easy to complete.

The SBA offers two types of financial assistance: direct loans and guarantees for bank loans. Because of federal budget constraints, direct loans are more difficult to arrange than guarantees, but still available as a last resort. To get SBA assistance, a company's loan application must be turned down by at least two commercial banks.

The Small Business Innovative Research program (SBIR) was specifically designed for small businesses engaged in the research and development of new products. Capital funnels down from the federal government through various state small business development agencies. Awards are made on competitive applications. For a start-up venture the amount cannot exceed $50,000.

Companies wishing to begin an export program find the Eximbank the best source of funding. Although the SBA does support a small export program, the agency has been relatively inactive in this area for several years. The Eximbank, however, under prodding from Congress, has recently become more attuned to the needs of small businesses. Similar to the SBA, the Eximbank offers both direct loans and bank guarantees, with the latter taking precedence.

Several state development agencies actively assist small businesses in getting started. Most operate through a local development company (LDC) or bureau. Many provide a modest amount of direct loans as well as bank guarantees. Opportunities for state assistance depend entirely on the state of business residence and the current condition of state finances.

Other Sources

A variety of non-bank, non-government funding sources exist. Pension funds and insurance companies are excellent sources for major expansion capital. Although these behemoths are difficult to contact directly, working through an investment bank or a venture capital firm often brings good results.

Several private foundations operate specifically to assist small businesses develop socially beneficial products or projects. Most of these foundations grant awards rather than loans, although a few also make low-interest loans. The size of the loan or grant is not large, however. Most range between $5,000 and $15,000; a few go as high as $50,000.

The following chapters examine the pros and cons and the methods of obtaining capital from each of these sources, as well as others. No two businesses are alike;

neither are capital sources. When looking for capital, several conditions determine the best source:

- Size and type of the business.
- Geographic location.
- Whether funds are needed for first-, second-, or third-stage financing.
- The application of the funds.
- The economic condition of the financial markets.

Very often loans, grants, and equity from several sources must be combined to raise enough capital. In almost all cases, however, a commercial bank should be the first stop in the search for money. Even when other sources are ultimately used, it frequently pays to begin with a bank. On the assumption that the best offense in the financing game is to understand the rules under which bankers play, the next chapter explores the various conditions affecting a bank's decision-making process.

CHAPTER 2

Understanding Bankers

What's so unique about bankers? Nothing. Bankers are no different than manufacturers, retailers, or service people. Banks are in business to make a profit just like IBM, Macy's, or the New York Yankees. On the other hand, bankers do have unique ways of judging the viability of a business transaction that differ markedly from those used in other industries.

It doesn't make any sense to buy a new car without understanding the difference between makes and models. And it certainly doesn't make any sense to take the car out of a dealer's showroom without first learning how to drive. Nearly every adult American knows a little bit about cars and how dealers expect a person to negotiate a price lower than the sticker price. But the same individual that spends days, maybe weeks, researching cars and negotiating the best deal, tends to fall apart when applying for a loan. Why? Because bankers use a different set of criteria for making a business decision than other business managers, and this throws us off balance.

This chapter describes the major criteria banks use to evaluate loan applications, sorts out the level of importance attached to each, and identifies sales tactics that bring the best results.

LOAN CRITERIA

Every bank weighs the merits of a loan against its current portfolio requirements as well as against other elements peculiar to that specific bank at that specific time. However, all banks attach a high priority to the following eight factors:

1. Relationship between the bank and the applicant
2. Management ability of the business owner
3. References from other banks
4. Credit history
5. Amount of equity capital
6. Collateral to secure the loan

7. Cash flow to repay the loan

8. Economic trends

Scoring high in all of these categories automatically assures you of getting the capital you need from virtually any financial institution. Conversely, a single negative can kill a deal. Low scores in more than one category nearly always means rejection.

RELATIONSHIPS

Even though banks rent a product—money—and therefore are *not* strictly a service business, most bankers like to think of themselves as selling services. This mentality is relevant to a borrower because, as in any service business, personal relationships between the buyer and seller often determine whether a business transaction closes.

Your company is not a buyer when applying for a bank loan; it is a seller. A sales campaign must be mounted early enough to lay the groundwork for the loan. And as in any sales campaign, direct, one-on-one relationships between seller and buyer usually result in the best opportunity for making the sale.

Of the eight primary loan criteria, the strength of relationships between borrower and lender stands head and shoulders above the rest. Irrational as it may appear, if a banker likes you and feels comfortable with you, any shortcomings in other criteria are often overlooked—or at least minimized. That being the case, it makes sense to get on the good side of bankers long before you need their money.

Romance them. Take them to ballgames. Ask them out for lunch. Show interest and compassion for their personal lives. Bend over backwards to make the relationship a positive force. Other tactics can be just as powerful. The following have been used successfully time and time again, but they must be done long before applying for a loan.

Borrow When You Don't Need The Money

We all know the common maxim: "When you don't need money banks are eager to lend it. When you do need it, they are no where to be found." That being the case, establish a record before you need the money. If you plan to start a business, take out a small loan at least six months before the start-up. Use a car, CDs, or some other personal asset as collateral. If already in business, borrow against the business assets.

In either case, be sure to pay the loan back in full before you need a legitimate loan. This establishes a lender/debtor relationship and gives a banker confidence that you do in fact fulfill your obligations.

Give The Bank Financial Statements

Bankers love to look at balance sheets and income statements. If you are already in business, volunteer your company's financial statements from last year or last month. Explain any unusual items. Clarify any apparent problem areas. A forecast for next year also helps.

If you are just starting a business, volunteer a personal financial statement that shows your assets and liabilities. Giving a banker financial statements well in advance of needing a loan accomplishes two purposes: it illustrates that you have nothing to hide and are in fact a solid citizen, and it demonstrates that you know the value of financial statements and how to read them.

Hire A Public Accountant And Lawyer Known To The Bank

Hiring outside accountants and lawyers when you really don't need them costs money. On the other hand, it clearly demonstrates that you value professional assistance, which bankers like to see. Ask your banker for recommendations. Try to ferret out which CPA or lawyer the bank feels comfortable with. Conversely, find out from CPAs and lawyers what they think of the bank. If you are already in business, a certified audit increases a bank's confidence that you care about good internal controls; something they also love to see.

MANAGEMENT ABILITY

Finance companies know how to liquidate assets and seldom hesitate to foreclose when borrowers default. Commercial banks are different. They are not equipped to liquidate a company's assets and therefore avoid foreclosure whenever possible. For this reason, bankers regard the strength of your background and that of any management personnel in your company as crucial to the decision process. Banks want to be as certain as possible that the people in charge can, in fact, manage the business and do everything in their power to pay back the loan.

This shouldn't be a problem with a business already up and running. Company financial statements, market acceptance of products or services, and competitive position provide a good indication of your managerial capabilities. The bank can rest assured that your technical and managerial acumen has already been proven.

Starting a new company or acquiring a going business requires a different tack. Prior employers may be asked to verify your management abilities. If you have owned other businesses, customers or suppliers may be asked to substantiate credentials. Proving technical proficiency when coming from the professions or the education field should be a snap. Professional recognition, such as engineering or accounting certification or scientific awards, provide concrete evidence.

Regardless of the means employed, you must be able to satisfy the bank that your business will be professionally managed and, therefore, that the loan will be repaid. References carry more weight than any other element for verifying management ability.

REFERENCES

Without solid references you won't get to first base with a bank. The best ones come from other bankers. References from business associates and professionals are also helpful, especially if the bank knows them. References are especially important for building relationships with a bank you haven't done business with before. References don't have to be elaborate. Just enough to show the banker that you are reliable, honest, and hopefully, a capable manager.

References should be in letter form—one or two paragraphs. They should be on appropriate letterhead and recently dated. All reference letters should carry a telephone number so that the banker can confirm or clarify any points.

The best references come from other banks with whom you have done business—preferably borrowing money and paying it back. This gets tricky, however, and invariably raises the question: Why not get the loan from the bank with which you already have a good relationship? Bankers are sensitive to loan-shoppers. They like to feel that once a relationship has been established you will never seek loans elsewhere. Soliciting a new bank raises a red flag. A loan officer immediately assumes that something went wrong with your first relationship. This can easily kill any chances for a new loan.

Two possible approaches get around this problem; the choice depends on your relationship with the first bank. The best way is to ask the first bank to explain in the reference letter why it cannot consider your new loan request. A full portfolio, different location, or the wrong type of loan satisfies most bankers. A second, but less preferable way, is to explain to the new bank why you would rather do business with them than with the first bank. This can backfire, however. Being critical of the first bank only leads to trouble. Solid relationships still get top billing. Bankers get suspicious of anyone changing banks because of personality clashes or policy disagreements. Getting over this hurdle requires tact, diplomacy, and salesmanship. The best approach plays up to the banker's ego!

Reference letters—basically character references—also should be obtained from owners of other businesses, business partners, or anyone known to the bank or whose reputation can be verified. A reference from a CPA, lawyer, investment advisor, or anyone in a financial services business or profession carries the most weight.

COLLATERAL

Collateral is next in order of importance. Banks always look first at the security of their loans. They want to be certain of getting their money back. Federal bank examiners regard adequate collateral as a top priority in judging a bank's financial stability. As Chapter 1 pointed out, current problems in the banking industry can be directly attributed to non-performing loans to foreign governments, commercial real estate developers, and leveraged buyouts that were made without sufficient collateral.

Although banks earn a good portion of their income from loans, the profit motive takes second place to getting their money back. This is the primary difference between banks and other businesses in a free enterprise system. Profit motivates everyone else. Loan repayment motivates banks. Regardless of the profitability your business enjoys, without adequate collateral, forget about getting a loan from a commercial bank. This more than any other reason spawned the venture capital industry and the junk bond market, and has allowed foreign banks to gain a strong foothold in America.

What does a bank regard as sufficient collateral? For working capital loans, banks accept receivables less than 90 days old, easily resalable raw material inventory, and marketable finished products. For term loans, they require hard assets—machinery, equipment, vehicles, buildings, and land. Banks make loans based on a percentage of the cash they estimate can be recovered from an asset on a forced liquidation.

For instance, banks commonly loan 80 to 85 percent of the face amount of qualified receivables and 20 to 40 percent of the resale value of qualified inventory. Those willing to grant term loans base the amount on approximately 60 to 80 percent of the amount of cash they could get if forced to sell hard assets at an auction.

CAPITAL

Banks regard capital as the amount of equity an owner has in a business. This capital, when compared to the amount of the loan, results in the debt to equity ratio described in Chapter 1. Although during the 1980s many financial institutions loaned acquisition funds against very little equity—frequently without any equity from the owner—times have changed. Today most commercial banks lend a maximum of three times the amount of capital in a business. However, other financial institutions continue to loan on a much higher ratio as later chapters point out.

The more capital you commit to the business, the more amenable a bank will be. Bankers believe that if and when the business gets in trouble, an owner with a significant amount of personal capital committed is *less* likely to default on loan payments, and certainly *less* likely to file for bankruptcy.

Banks frequently require additional capital for first-stage and very often for second- and third-stage financing, too. This usually takes the form of personal guarantees or pledges of personal assets. Of course, banks hope they will never have to force collection against these assets; but they also believe that psychologically an owner is more committed to repaying the loan if personal assets could be jeopardized.

If you don't have sufficient personal assets to satisfy the bank, co-guarantors or personal assets pledged by relatives or other third parties will be necessary. Banking mentality dictates getting as much of a commitment as possible, regardless of the source. The more they can get, they happier they are. And of course, the more collateral they can show the bank examiner, the less criticism they endure.

Cash Flow

The projected cash flow of the business is the third area a bank looks at in determining the likelihood of repayment. Even though a bank has liens against all assets of the company, liens against an owner's personal assets, and personal guarantees from the owner and perhaps others, a loan will not be made unless the bank is comfortable that enough "free cash" exists to repay the loan and interest when due.

A bank defines "free cash" as the amount of cash remaining in a company's bank account after all expenses and obligations are paid, except for two elements: the owner's cash draw and debt service payments. Banks exclude compensation to businessowners because they expect owners to make sure the bank gets paid before taking out any personal cash. If cash flow projections show sufficient free cash to make debt service payments, banks don't care what you do with the balance.

Cash flow projections come from a formal set of financial statements—balance sheets and income statements—projected into the future over the term of the loan. When applying for a loan, a cash flow projection becomes an integral part of the financing plan described in Chapter 3. Of course projections always change. Therefore, after granting a loan, banks expect borrowers to furnish updated versions of cash flow projections periodically. This enables the bank to monitor the progress of the business.

Banks are extremely conservative when judging the likelihood of loan repayments. When applying for a loan, don't expect a bank to believe your projections. Banks always reduce projected cash flow by some factor—ranging the gamut from 20 to 60 percent. The best way to keep this discounting to a minimum, assuming you have an operating company, is to base the projection on the current cash flow being generated. From this base, assumptions can be made of increased volume or improved margins resulting from the new loan.

Regardless of the procedure used, however, banks rarely believe what loan applicants present. Therefore, always ask for more money than you really need. Banks need some point to negotiate down from. Recognizing this in the beginning saves a lot of time and increases the chances of getting what you need.

CREDIT HISTORY

Assuming you satisfy a bank with adequate collateral, capital, and cash flow, and that the banker feels you can run the business, the next hurdle will be your credit history. Credit ratings play second fiddle to the other criteria, unless you have been through a personal or business bankruptcy. Then, all of a sudden, credit history becomes the dominant criteria.

Although the bankruptcy laws were formulated to allow an individual or a company a second chance, banks don't look at it that way. From a bank's perspective, there is no such thing as a second chance for borrowing money. If a person has defaulted once, banks assume that it could happen again. Even though bankruptcy laws give secured creditors precedence over all others (including wages owed employees and taxes due the U.S. government), and adequate collateral ensures that banks very seldom lose a penny in a bankruptcy filing, the stigma still exists. This stigma is very difficult, if not impossible, to overcome. If you have a bankruptcy blemish on your credit history, don't even try to get a loan from a commercial bank, regardless of how successful you may have been since it happened.

One way around this insurmountable hurdle is to place the ownership of your company in the hands of outsiders—friends, business associates with a clean record, distant relatives, or even a trust. Taking this route also means placing the official management of the company in other hands. Pragmatically you still run the company, but officially someone else is in charge.

Most businessowners or entrepreneurs just starting out, who face a bankruptcy credit history, have more success raising capital from sources other than commercial banks.

Other than with a bankruptcy stigma, credit history doesn't mean too much. You can be a slow payer to suppliers and government agencies and still get a loan, provided you have good explanations. The only non-bankruptcy stigma impossible to overcome is a previous default against a bank loan, regardless of which bank held the paper. Once again, banks believe that if you default once, you could again. Since prior bank reference letters are practically a necessity, defaults will be readily revealed, regardless of what a credit bureau report shows.

ECONOMIC CONDITIONS

The final bank criteria are current and near term projected economic conditions. Although bankers may not be astute economists, they do read the newspapers. They also listen carefully to prognostications from the Fed.

Three economic conditions affect a bank's willingness to loan money: the current status of the banking industry, the condition of the general economy, and the trend in the borrower's industry. The first set of conditions, the current status of the banking industry, takes precedence.

With the relaxation of federal regulations, banks expanded into a variety of financial services previously avoided. Unfortunately, they expanded into services without sufficient knowledge of the markets. Banks acquired or started asset-based lenders, SBICs, mortgage lending departments, international departments, investment banking divisions, credit card divisions, and a variety of other financial services. Some banks succeeded admirably in mastering the techniques and management procedures for these new ventures. Others have been notably unsuccessful.

One fallout of this expansion was not foreseen in most of the banking community—that economic factors different from those influencing pure banking activities affected these new ventures. Strict federal regulations and FDIC insurance insulated banks from violent economic swings, as long as they stayed in their traditional businesses. But with expansion, economic curves affecting property values, business profitability, the stock market, international exchange rates, and a variety of other conditions that impact other businesses, suddenly hit bankers where it hurts: on their balance sheets.

These new economic pressures had an enormous effect on bank loan policies. Chapter 1 elaborated on the increased capital requirements mandated by the Fed. With unprotected loan losses resulting from businesses little understood by bankers, the industry has suddenly started scrambling to return to more traditional activities. Many banks have either closed or are in the process of selling the same businesses they acquired over the past decade. Finance companies, investment banking divisions, and mortgage loan portfolios are rapidly finding new homes.

As this trend continues, the banking industry will eventually right itself and probably once again become a protected monopoly. In the meantime, however, small businesses must be even more careful than in the past to choose a bank that will survive and meet their capital needs. Regardless of collateral, relationships, references, or other criteria, a bank in the throes of severe economic contraction will not be interested in extending small business loans. Economic conditions in the general economy and in the borrowers' industry are also important, but certainly not as critical as the economic vicissitudes of the banking industry.

When the country or your region falls into a recession, banks become more choosy about loan collateral. They want a higher capital base and a tighter debt to equity ratio. And projected cash flow receives much closer scrutiny.

An industry on the skids has little chance of near term growth. This makes borrowing from a bank practically impossible. You are much better off either waiting for the cycle to turn or raising capital from non-bank sources.

THE FEDERAL DEPOSIT INSURANCE CORPORATION

The Federal Deposit Insurance Corporation (FDIC) is a federal agency that insures deposits in federally-licensed banks up to a maximum of $100,000 per account. Inaugurated as a result of the Great Depression, the FDIC has been and remains the underpinning of the American banking system. With the FDIC in the background, depositors rest assured that their money remains safe even if a bank fails.

Literally thousands of depositors have already collected or are waiting to collect from the FDIC's sister agency, the Federal Savings and Loan Deposit Insurance Corporation (FSLDIC). As many depositors learned, however, with the FSLDIC itself bankrupt, it may be several years before all claims get settled—and then with taxpayers' money.

Critics of the FDIC system claim that by insuring accounts, the government takes one more rung out of the competitive ladder in the banking industry. Banks attract depositor's money regardless of the efficiency and prudent investment policies of their managements. Knowing that the FDIC will always bail out their customers, banks pay little attention to the basic management principles that are necessary for survival in the rest of the business world.

These critics attribute most of the difficulties currently experienced in the banking industry to this lack of competitive management initiative. They argue vociferously that the financial system would be much healthier by completely abandoning the FDIC.

The FDIC is nearly bankrupt already and unless effective corrective measures surface quickly, the critics will have their way. At the end of 1987, the FDIC fund had a reserve balance of $18.3 billion. Two years of bank failures reduced this reserve to $13.2 billion by the end of 1989. Continued bank failures in 1990 depleted the fund to $9 billion. Expected failures in 1991 will bring the fund down to $4 billion. Federal regulators estimate complete FDIC bankruptcy by early 1992, unless Congress acts.

Existing laws call for the FDIC to have $1.25 in reserves for every $100 in bank deposits. However, it has been at least 5 years since the fund was in compliance. The General Accounting Office (GAO) estimates that the FDIC will lose between $5 billion and $6 billion a year for the next three years as a result of an estimated 600 to 700 additional bank failures.

The federal budget office has voiced concern that the fund's low level might encourage federal regulators to give banks more time to work out their problems. They did this with the S & Ls, and we all know the disastrous results from that action.

Rather than doing away with the FDIC completely, as recommended by free-market advocates, several proposals have been advanced to change the rules. Two proposals have received the most attention: either limit the number of accounts per depositor that can be insured under the FDIC to three, or increase the amount of insurance premium banks must pay into the fund from 12 cents to 19.5 cents—the highest amount permitted by law. Naturally, the American Banking Association (ABA) opposes both of these ideas as well as all others that have been advanced.

Some of the other proposals are to:

- Require the owners of banks that wish to expand into traditionally non-banking areas, such as securities brokerage and insurance underwriting, to increase their own capital investments in their banks.

- Give federal regulators the power to curb risky bank activities permitted under some state laws.

- Limit "pass-through" insurance for pension funds and other large institutional investors. Under current law, a deposit by a pension fund with 100 members has protection equal to 100 times the $100,000 limit or $10 million!

- Force regulators to crack down on weak banks before they fail.

- Require annual, on-site audit examinations of large banks as well as those that are ailing.

Early in 1991 the American Banking Association, together with three other banking industry trade organizations, offered their own proposal to save the FDIC. The banking industry would loan the FDIC money to bring its balance in line. This proposal, however, fails to consider that the government would then have to borrow more money from banks that are already near collapse to pay interest on their loan!

It seems clear that, regardless of the path chosen, the dire straits of the banking industry will cause Congress to make radical changes in how depositors' accounts are protected and what this protection will cost banks. The ABA notwithstanding, it seems likely that these changes will be piecemeal over the next several years. Changes in depositor protection, together with repeal or modification of the Glass-Steagall and McFadden Acts, will undoubtedly change the structure of the American banking industry. Hopefully, such changes will introduce more free-market characteristics into the system, which in turn should make American banks more competitive in the world financial market.

APPROACHING A BANK FOR A LOAN

Regardless of how good bank relationships may be, it always works best to be totally prepared when first applying for a loan. First impressions are important when borrowing money, even more than in normal business activities. Knowing who you will be meeting and what position the loan officer holds in the bank hierarchy makes a good starting point.

KNOW THE LOAN OFFICER

If at all possible, try to get an appointment with at least a senior vice president of the bank. If you use a branch bank, the branch manager will have to do. It's important to know what authority the loan officer has in the loan approval process. Lower echelon loan officers merely shuffle paper. They meet with a prospective borrower, make sure all the paperwork gets completed, and then shuffle the loan application package further up the ladder for review and approval (or rejection). Some banks use loan committees to make the final decision, while others delegate this authority to a senior bank officer.

When you deal with lower echelon bankers all the work of establishing a good relationship is wasted. Decisions are made higher up by people you have never met and who don't know you from the next applicant. Some bank officials estimate that under these conditions more the 75 percent of loan applications get turned down. Without a personal relationship, loan decisions are made purely on the numbers, and frequently the numbers cannot tell the whole story.

A second problem arises when efforts have been made over a period of time to establish a good rapport with a banker only to learn that when you apply for a loan, the banker has moved on to a new assignment or a different branch office. Personnel turnover in the banking industry is phenomenal. Six to 12 months in one job seems to be about the average tenure, except for top executives.

Bank executives argue that relationships should be established with a bank, not a specific banker. That's great in theory, but it just doesn't work. How can anyone establish a personal relationship with a corporation? Dealing with low echelon loan officers without decision-making authority and high bank personnel turnover are two of the greatest drawbacks in trying to do business with a bank. No easy solution exists. If you plan to borrow from a bank, the best you can do is research the decision-making status of loan officers and then choose a bank that offers the best internal structure.

DOCUMENTATION

Notwithstanding the difficulties of dealing with impersonal loan committees, come to the first meeting fully prepared with all the data and documents necessary to move the decision process along. You will have to complete a bank loan application form and probably translate your personal financial statement to the bank's format. Aside from these simple steps, the following documentation should be on hand:

1. Reference letters—at least one from another bank that knows you.
2. Personal financial statement showing both assets and liabilities.
3. Recent credit report from a reputable credit agency for both the company and yourself.
4. Financing plan (the next chapter describes its content).
5. Minutes from your board of directors authorizing the borrowing (if you have a corporation) or partnership memorandum executed by all partners (if you have a partnership).
6. Certificate of incorporation and corporate seal if you run a corporation; a partnership agreement for a partnership.
7. Complete documentation of any other outstanding business loans, including real estate mortgages.

QUESTIONS BANKERS ASK

Coming prepared with complete documentation shows the banker that you are serious about the loan, that you understand what information banks need to make a decision, and that you are, in fact, a professional manager with sound financial acumen. Right away the banker should be alerted that you are not interested in banking platitudes and that you want a quick answer—yes or no.

In addition, complete preparation forestalls a great many useless and time-consuming questions. Unfortunately, regardless of how well prepared a person may be, bankers seem obliged to ask the same questions over and over again. The following standard questions get asked by all bankers:

1. How will you pay the loan back?
2. When will you pay the loan back?
3. What assurances can you give that you will pay it back on time?
4. What evidence can you give that you know how to run the business?
5. Who is your competition and what are they doing in the market?
6. Why is your business better than the others?

7. How much money can you put in?

8. Will you sign a personal guarantee?

9. What are the assets in your business worth?

10. What collateral can you provide?

11. What are your plans for growing the business in the future?

Will your relationship with a banker be sustained over a long period of time? That's hard to guess. Current bank philosophy stresses the need and the desirability of long term relationships, both for the bank and for the customer. Yet, banks prevent long-lasting friendships from developing by continuing to move personnel around and changing internal policies.

As silly as it might sound, your ability to sustain a relationship with a banker over a period of time has virtually nothing to do with your business or the bank. Sound relationships, those that endure for years and enable a borrower to rely on a banker and a banker to rely on a borrower, are based on personal synergisms. Time and again, in those rare instances when a banker remains in the same job or at the same location for several years, borrowers fervently advocate what a great bank they deal with and how wonderful the bank personnel are. Unfortunately, rapid personnel turnover makes the reverse condition far more prevalent.

Several years ago when the small business segment of my consulting practice was at its peak, I took a poll of over 275 past and present clients asking what they considered to be the most important elements for staying on the good side of their banker over a period of years. I was surprised at the answers, although I probably shouldn't have been. Overwhelmingly, they gave the following reasons in this sequence:

1. Belong to the same golf club, tennis club, or other athletic club.

2. Belong to the same religious denomination.

3. Belong to the same social or civic organizations.

4. Have children in the same school.

5. Graduated from the same college or graduate school.

6. Originally came from the same hometown.

7. Share the same political views.

MONITORING A LOAN

Getting a loan in the first place is only half the financing equation. Keeping your bank happy during the loan payback period is the other half. Because of a bank's preoccupation with recovering its money, expect one or more bank auditors and loan officers to keep close tabs on your on-going business. Frequent audit reviews, meetings with loan officers, submission of financial statements, regular evaluation of cash balances on deposit, and a variety of other yardsticks enable a bank to monitor compliance with loan covenants and, at the same time, look for warning signals that your business is faltering. If these signals get too strong, count on your bank getting even deeper into your business.

Here are the major signals that raise a red flag:

1. Failure to meet debt service payment.
2. Being late or hesitant to provide financial statements and other financial data required in the loan agreement.
3. Steadily shrinking bank balances.
4. Overdrafts and returned checks.
5. Turnover of key management personnel.
6. Personal financial difficulties of the businessowner or principals.
7. Hesitancy in accepting or extending social invitations from or to bank officials.
8. Inventory levels increasing without corresponding sales increase.
9. Reluctance to permit bank auditors and other bank officials to view the property or to examine the company's record.
10. Failure to make regular meetings with bank officials.
11. Lawsuits against the company.
12. A slowdown in accounts payable turnover.
13. Slipping accounts receivable collections.
14. Large equipment or facilities purchases without prior bank notification.
15. Increasing debt to equity ratio.

If one or more of these conditions occurs, it's best to inform your bank in advance, before information comes from other sources. By so doing, at least you have an opportunity to offer logical explanations before your banker forms personal, and often erroneous, judgments. Bankers hate surprises. If they form their own judgments without your input, regardless of the accuracy of their data or perceived reasons, chances are very high that relationships will quickly deteriorate.

ADVANTAGES AND DISADVANTAGES OF BORROWING FROM A BANK

Certainly a business is better off operating with its own cash. Interest expense can be an enormous burden and eat into profits that could otherwise be used to grow the business. On the other hand, the American free enterprise system has been built on credit. In rapidly growing companies without a significant cash reserve there is virtually no way to meet payroll and buy materials without using borrowed money. When that time comes, some definite advantages exist for choosing a commercial bank over other sources of capital. There are also some glaring disadvantages. A few of the big ones—six on the plus side, six on the minus side—follow.

ADVANTAGES IN USING BANK DEBT

1. Banks are conveniently located. Usually a branch will be located down the street from your business or at least within an easy drive.
2. Banks normally charge lower interest rates than other financial institutions.
3. A good credit rating established through a bank is about as good a reference as you can get anywhere.
4. Banks are easy to locate and, with publicly available financial information, easy to research.
5. Once established with a bank, many other services become available (e.g trust department, payroll preparation, customer credit checks).
6. A commercial bank must be used for financing export sales.

DISADVANTAGES IN USING BANK DEBT

1. Bankers are notoriously poor businesspeople. Your banker probably won't know anything about your industry or business. Bankers frequently give bad operating advice.
2. Long-lasting personal relationships are nearly impossible because of high bank personnel turnover.
3. Banks demand excess collateral for loans, including personal guarantees.
4. Banks do not like to lend long-term money.
5. Nearly all bank loan agreements are unilateral—that is, the bank has the right to call the loan on demand, any time it wants to, regardless of whether or not debt service payments have been made on time.
6. Banks are non-competitive. With the FDIC in the background, a bank does not have to be managed efficiently to attract customers. With abundant federal regulations, one bank cannot offer significantly different services from another bank.

Although commercial banks remain an important segment of the financial community they are not the only nor necessarily the best source of funds. Other financial institutions specialize in different types of loans for various purposes. One common element exists between banks and other financing sources, however; this is the need to establish and then maintain solid personal relationships. Dealing in money creates a natural distrust between parties. Although this may never be completely overcome, honest relationships between creditor and debtor can go a long way toward easing the pain of borrowing and repaying money.

RELATIONSHIPS WITH OTHER FINANCIAL INSTITUTIONS

The eight criteria governing loans from commercial banks are not much different from those used by other financial institutions; yet, distinct differences in emphasis do exist.

For reasons already stated, commercial banks continue to be the most conservative institutions in the financing spectrum. The responsibility for maintaining public confidence in our entire financial system falls, for better or for worse, on the shoulders of the commercial banking industry. With this responsibility comes a natural conservatism. Although not always practiced, it exists nonetheless. Free from this public responsibility, other financial institutions concentrate more on making a profit rather than on being repaid.

ASSET-BASED LENDERS

Asset-based lenders (nee finance companies), when freed from the yoke of commercial bank parents, fall at the far end of the risk-debt spectrum. These lenders, fully capable of foreclosing and liquidating assets to recoup their investment, charge exorbitant rates for the risks they take. Asset-based lenders focus more intently on the underlying value of asset collateral and are more interested in the ability of the business to make money.

Managers of asset-based lenders tend to have a much stronger background in general business management than their commercial bank cousins. Because of this broader background, a different approach must be used to establish working relationships. Relationships with asset-based lenders can only be developed and nurtured after the fact, not months or years before making a loan application.

As businesspeople, these executives want the relationship to be on a purely business level. They expect to be kept regularly informed—sometimes weekly—of how the business is doing. They don't care much for the romancing and the ballgames. They don't want to be entertained, but they do want to be treated as professionals. Being heavy risk-takers, asset-based lenders keep a close rein on the operation of the company. The relationship is more of a master/servant arrangement—with the borrower always the servant.

VENTURE CAPITAL FIRMS AND SMALL INVESTMENT BANKS

At the other end of the financial spectrum, venture capital firms and small investment banks expect substantial appreciation on their equity investment and a high average annual return. Venture capitalists and investment bankers are themselves businesspeople, not bankers. Most possess knowledge in a wide range of industries. Their primary interest is to see a company grow and eventually become profitable enough to go public.

Venture capital firms and small investment banks concentrate on equity investments rather than debt. They also provide mezzanine financing to bridge the gap between bank debt and their equity contribution. Because they concentrate on equity, these financiers actually become investors in the company. The relationship follows that of a partnership rather than a purely debtor/creditor arrangement.

Unless a personal friend happens to be a venture capitalist or the executive of a small investment bank, the likelihood of forming a close relationship prior to negotiating a deal is very remote. Once the deal closes, the relationship becomes very close, including shared board decisions. At times, operating decisions also will be made jointly. These financiers know financial statements and *pro forma* forecasts and expect the businessowner to be equally knowledgeable.

Whether raising capital from a bank, an asset based lender, a venture capital firm, or a small investment bank, preparation remains the key to success. Those who take the time to prepare a professional looking financing package and make the effort to anticipate the questions inevitably asked, always stand a better chance of getting what they need. The following chapter takes you through the next steps for raising capital, and explores how and when to prepare and then present a completely documented loan application.

CHAPTER 3

Preparing to Borrow From a Bank

A bank's decision to accept or reject a loan application for first-stage financing is primarily based on a borrower's personal ability to repay the loan. As a company grows into its second stage, a clean record of loan payments causes banks to shift gears. Now they place more weight on the business and less on your personal aptitude and integrity. Personal assets and individual financial standing remain important, but by this time banks expect the business to generate enough cash to repay the loan and look to you only as a fall-back source. Each year that a business improves its earnings and cash flow performance, owners become further distanced from repayment obligation. Nevertheless, management ability, personal integrity, and financial stability remain important ingredients for sound bank relations.

Regardless of the financing stage, however, banks want to see hard facts in addition to these personal attributes. This chapter examines the documentation and supporting evidence necessary to obtain a bank loan for all three financing stages, although the emphasis stays on the first stage.

"The more money you need, the easier it is to get" is a general rule of thumb in the financing game. Naturally exceptions exist. The SBA, for example, has maximum limits beyond which it cannot go. The value of collateral must be sufficient for any size loan. Experience has shown, however, that given the proper collateral, it's much easier to raise $10 million than $500,000; and it's easier to raise $500,000 than $50,000. So if you have an option, go for broke, even if you turn around and quickly repay the excess.

THE FINANCING PACKAGE

A financing package consists of assorted documents that, when properly assembled, present a complete picture of the business owner, the business, and the market. Although the degree of importance attached to each segment varies with the financing stage and with the proposed use of the funds, the same data must be included in all cases.

A financing package consists of two broad sections and several detailed segments within each section. The first section covers material related to the individual who owns a business or who wishes to start or acquire a business. It presents the best possible picture and includes four sub-headings:

- Personal background
- Business experience
- Financial status
- Reference letters

The second section covers information about the business under the following sub-headings:

- Company structure and history
- Product/service characteristics
- Market status
- Financial performance

BUSINESSOWNER'S QUALIFICATIONS

Nearly all bankers rank management ability at or near the top of the priority ladder, especially for a new business without a market track record. Because start-ups are such a high risk, bankers must rely almost exclusively on their perception of the applicant's management ability to produce the product and capture a market. With this in mind, personal background and experience may, in the end, be the most important criteria for judging the efficacy of making a loan. And all smart bankers know this.

PERSONAL STATISTICS

The first item on the agenda should be a written description of personal statistics—residential address and phone number, education (including any academic awards), family status, condition of health, and even though it smacks of discrimination, age. Whether we like it or not, the financial community continues to harbor traditional misconceptions that must be dealt with head-on at the first meeting.

Banks in different parts of the country and of different sizes hold onto different prejudices. Some feel that a woman raising children has no business applying for a loan to start a business, or that an unmarried man or woman represents a higher risk than one who is married. Others feel that a man or woman past the age of 55 won't be around long enough to pay the loan back. Still others regard young applicants as lacking the experience necessary to make a business prosper. Even race and religion continue to play a part in some banks' decisions. On the flip side, in an effort to remain unbiased, many banks have adopted anti-discrimination policies that effectively create reverse discrimination by giving minorities, women, young people, or the elderly preferential treatment.

Obviously, none of these practices are made public. If they were, a hue and cry would be raised and the bank could suffer irreversible damage to its public image. But discrimination exists nonetheless. To pretend otherwise only wastes time and money trying to accomplish something that isn't doable in the first place. We may not sanction discrimination, but the fact remains that prejudices do exist. We can't hide from reality.

To prevent wasted time and effort, it makes sense to discreetly search out how a specific bank regards your unique situation before going to the trouble of preparing and presenting a financial package. Although formal acknowledgments won't be forthcoming, it doesn't take long to intuitively judge where you stand after interviewing two or three bankers. If you sense you will be discriminated against, you might as well be pragmatic about it and search out another bank rather than try to fight city hall. If you do win the battle, chances are high you won't have much of a relationship after the loan is granted, and that only brings trouble and a lot of heartache.

BUSINESS EXPERIENCE

Banks also want to know what work experience qualifies a borrower to operate the business. A banker looks at work experience from two vantage points: management experience and technical experience. Don't expect a banker to understand the specific talents required to operate your business. It would be pure coincidence to find one with first-hand knowledge of your specialty.

However, that doesn't deter them from expecting you to have concrete work experience in the same or similar type of business that you plan to go into. The evidence of this experience comes from previous jobs, technical certification, expertise in a hobby, or from previous ownership of a similar business.

Regardless of the specific type of experience, managerial talent and technical capability must be conclusively demonstrated. If a banker can't be satisfied that you can handle both the managerial and the technical aspects of your new business, it's impossible to get a loan.

Banks also want to know your business objectives. Why do you want to get into this business? What do you hope to accomplish over the next 5, 10, or 15 years? These objectives should clearly reflect a long-term commitment to the business. Banks frown on short-term goals. Many potential businessowners fail to attract a bank's interest merely because they misstate their objectives.

The proper answers to these questions are: that you expect to build the business into a viable market competitor; that you expect to continue gaining market share; that eventually your company will be a major force in the marketplace; and most important of all, that you will stay with the company for the rest of your working career. No banker wants to hear plans about eventually selling the company and recouping large capital gains. That may be a viable personal objective, but *never* admit it to a bank.

FINANCIAL STATUS

Banks are interested in two aspects of a borrower's personal financial status: how much capital will be contributed to the business and what assets and liabilities does the borrower own. The first question is easy. Anyone starting a business must have some amount of cash equity. Maybe only $5,000 or $10,000. Whatever the amount may be, banks want it to be a significant portion of your cash reserves. From a bank's perspective, the higher the proportion of personal cash and assets committed to a business, the less likely a person will be to throw in the towel and walk away when the going gets tough.

Full financial commitment to the business is absolutely essential. More than any other criteria, an owner's financial commitment controls the likelihood of raising outside capital for any purpose. As long as a bank, or any other lender or investor, believes that you would suffer substantial personal financial damage if the business goes under, they should look favorably at the other criteria. If they don't believe this, then the other criteria means nothing.

Two types of documentation substantiate financial commitment: a personal statement of financial condition and personal tax returns. A personal statement of financial condition lists all personal assets at their current market value, and all debts and obligations owed to non-family creditors. Later in the chapter we'll take a look at the steps for preparing such a statement.

Tax returns for the previous three years won't verify your cash balances, but they do show the bank how much income was earned. From this a bank can easily estimate what your cash reserves should be.

REFERENCES

Chapter 2 described references as one of the key criteria for loan approval. Although valid references are important for second-stage financing and occasionally for third-stage, they are crucial when going after first-stage money. Include as many quality reference letters as possible.

They must be from qualified and preferably well-know sources, however. It won't do any good to get a letter of commendation from your neighbor or friend stating what a great person you are. This goes straight to the trash barrel. On the other hand, reference letters from previous employers attesting to your honesty, integrity, and management acumen can be invaluable. So are references from partners in law firms or national public accounting firms.

Any reference letter you can get from a well-positioned executive in a bank or financial institution counts twice as much. Investment bankers, finance company executives, senior executives from other banks, and officers of securities houses rank the highest. References from high government officials such as senators, congressional representatives, well-known officials from the executive branch, or governors are always impressive. These individuals may not know you too well, but the mere fact that you have their support adds political clout to your effort.

ESTABLISHING CREDENTIALS

In the banking industry, reputation means everything. You can successfully own and operate a manufacturing company or a retail business without your customers, competitors, or even neighbors knowing you personally. The business is successful not because of any public knowledge of who you are or how great a manager or technician you may be, but because the marketplace accepts its products.

Within the financial community, such is not the case. Although thousands of people work in the industry without ever being recognized as outstanding citizens or possessing extraordinary financial acumen, those who rise to the top attribute their success in no small measure to their unblemished reputation. The same principle holds true when applying for a loan. Establishing a public reputation as an expert in a specific field nearly always eases the way toward favorable action.

The big question for most of us is how to establish credentials as an expert in our field? Certainly reference letters from others in the same line of work help. But this is not the same as a public reputation. Although no sure-fire way exists to become publicly known, the following ideas have worked for others.

1. Run for public office.
2. Write a book.
3. Speak before a trade group.
4. Appear on a television talk show.
5. Publish articles in a professional journal or trade magazine.
6. Achieve recognition as a community supporter.
7. Teach at a university.
8. Hold office in a trade organization.
9. Start a business newsletter.
10. Speak before a banking or other financial group.

It doesn't seem to make much difference which path you choose. Just do something in the public sphere that attracts attention to your expertise. Even if you can't achieve instant recognition, a copy of a public review of your work included as part of the financing package carries significant weight with most banks as well as other lenders and investors.

PERSONAL STATEMENT OF FINANCIAL CONDITION

Every loan application includes a personal statement of financial condition and a summary of income sources. Each bank uses a slightly different format, but the content remains the same. It helps to prepare your own statement of financial condition in a format that emphasizes your best points and to include it in the financial package. Most banks want it redone on their form but that's just a copy job. The inclusion of such a statement in the financial package immediately demonstrates an understanding of the loan process and, in turn, impresses bankers.

Figure 3-1 outlines the structure of a statement of financial condition, including the listing of income sources.

Figure 3–1

STATEMENT OF FINANCIAL CONDITION

As of date _____

A. ASSETS
    1. Cash in checking and savings accounts
    2. Cash equivalent investments—CDs, money market accounts, etc.
    3. IRAs, Keogh plan accounts, SEPs, and other retirement accounts
    4. Marketable securities—traded stocks, bonds, mutual funds, etc. (at current market value)
    5. Cash surrender value of life insurance policies
        Total cash and cash equivalents
    6. Investments in privately-held companies or public companies whose stock is not traded
    7. Investment in limited partnerships
    8. Investments in commercial or rental real estate (current market value)
    9. Collectibles—stamps, coins, antiques, jewelry, art, etc. (current market value)
   10. Investment in land (current market value)

11. Other non-liquid investments
     Total non-liquid investments
12. Residence (current market value)
13. Second or vacation home, cottage, villa, etc. (current market value)
14. Automobiles (current market value)
15. Personal property at estimated market value—furniture; hobby equipment (i.e., woodworking tools); library; boat; airplane; other personal property.
     Total personal property
16. Other assets
     <u>TOTAL ASSETS</u>

B. LIABILITIES
   1. Notes and other loans payable to banks (list bank and amount)—
      #1
      #2
      #3
   2. Loans against the cash surrender value of life insurance
   3. Current credit card balances
   4. Other bills payable
      Total current debt
   5. Mortgage on residence (current balance and monthly payment amount)
   6. Mortgage on other property (current balance and monthly payment amount)
   7. Loans from family members, friends, etc. (balance and due date)
   8. Other loans, debts, and obligations (list)
      <u>TOTAL LIABILITIES</u>

C. NET WORTH (EQUITY) (SUBTRACT TOTAL LIABILITIES FROM TOTAL ASSETS)

D. INCOME   *Monthly*   *Annual*
   1. Interest
   2. Dividends
   3. Pension
   4. Annuities
   5. Rentals
   6. Other investment income
   7. Spouse's wages
   8. Other income   _____   _____
      <u>TOTAL INCOME</u>   _____   _____

The income shown does not reflect any salary or draw from the business. A banker wants to see how much income will be available outside the business in the event it must be used to repay the loan. Also, the statement of financial condition should not be prepared in an accounting format. Asset values should be listed at their current market value, not at cost. Obviously, some market values will have to be estimated. In those instances, inflate the assets to a reasonable replacement cost.

This statement reflects only personal assets and liabilities. It has nothing to do with the business. Therefore, include financial statements for the company in the business section of the package.

In addition to personal information, the financial package must include a comprehensive explanation of the business being financed. This section of the package is referred to as a "financing plan."

BUSINESS "FINANCING PLAN"

The financing plan consists of four main sections, each dealing with separate segments of the business: history, product or service, market, financial. In some cases, especially for third-stage companies, the financing plan incorporates the personal section described above. For first- and second-stage funding, however, banks prefer to keep the two sections separate.

A financing plan describes how the outside capital will be used in the business and how it will be repaid. It also becomes a commitment that the business will be operated to achieve specific results. Lastly, it serves as a documented promise to repay the loan on schedule.

Whereas a financing plan may be similar to a business plan, several important differences stand out. A financing plan emphasizes the financial performance of the business rather than product or market growth. It accents cash flow instead of profitability. A financing plan must be prepared in bank language. It must be conservative enough to ensure a high probability of being achieved.

Banks, finance companies, venture capitalists, government agencies, and private financial sources each require slight variations in the format of the plan. Variations also apply for loans at different financing stages. This makes it impossible to lay out a universal format.

The following sections, however, describe universal elements. These elements appear in plans for first-, second-, or third-stage bank financing. Raising third-stage capital through non-bank sources, such as public markets, necessitates the use of formats in accordance with prescribed regulations and custom.

Financing plans begin with a preamble, a description of how much money you need and what it will be used for. This introductory section highlights products or services offered for sale, market niches that the business serves, how the borrowed money will be used, and one paragraph describing when and how the loan will be repaid. The preamble should be short (no longer than one page), succinct, and give the banker a quick synopsis of the rest of the plan. The next section of the plan, company history, begins to describe the details of the business.

Company History

For a start-up business there isn't any history except the product development and market research phases. Presumably, however, a company has already been formed and, therefore, a complete description of its ownership and capitalization should be set forth. For an S corporation include the names, relationships, and ownership percentage for each of the shareholders. If the business has been operating for several years, describe any company name changes and variations in ownership percentages. Identify any outstanding debts to banks, to other institutions, or to individuals. Two pages should be more than adequate for this section.

Products or Services

The next section includes a brief description of a company's products or services. Avoid technical specifications, but include enough information to give an unknowledgeable banker a reasonable idea of what the company sells. Also include enough market statistics to prove that market demand exists for the product or service. An elaborate market analysis looks like overkill. Simple statistical trends from government files or trade associations are sufficient.

The most important item in this section is a description of why your particular product or service is better than the rest; why it is unique. Both lenders and investors are well aware of the number of new businesses that fail after one or two years. Many times failure results from trying to sell a product or service that does not offer the market anything different or better than already established competitors. If you can't come up with a better mousetrap, don't borrow money to bring it to market.

Markets/Competition

Include three sub-sections in the markets/competition segment: market size, growth potential, and company share; existing and potential new competition; and opportunities for export sales or other foreign market penetration. Market size will probably have to be estimated, especially if you are selling into one or more niche markets. However, base estimates on as many factual statistics as possible.

Most trade associations maintain statistics compiled from member companies and extrapolations to your niche market shouldn't be too difficult. Otherwise, the federal Department of Commerce stocks reams of trade information by virtually any Standard Industrial Classification (SIC) code. Don't guess. Base your judgment on statistics that can be verified by the bank.

Once you find a source of information about market size, this same source usually furnishes estimates and projections of market growth—at least nationally.

Obviously, you will have to adjust these national projections for local or regional markets. Calculate market share from your sales forecast.

Research competition very carefully. What companies sell into your market niche? How big are they and how long have they been in the market? Can you compete with price, or must you rely on service or superior quality? What is the potential for new entrants over the succeeding five years? Don't get into elaborate explanations and analysis. A banker will never understand it and probably won't read it anyway. Limit the competitive analysis to a few simple and succinct sentences.

Every lender or investor gets excited about foreign sales potential. Be sure to include a paragraph stating how you plan to exploit foreign markets over the next five years. Whether you really plan to do so or not is irrelevant; it looks good.

FINANCIAL

Financial data is the one section bankers understand completely, or at least they should. If your company has at least two years of operating results, include annual balance sheets and income statements for three years. Annual audits by certified public accountants carry a lot of weight with all lenders and investors. Even if you can only get the most recent year audited, it's well worth the money.

Business start-ups, of course, don't have this luxury. You can't do much about this except to include statements for current year-to-date results. Even those prepared by yourself are better than nothing.

Also include business tax returns for the past three years. For unincorporated businesses this means Schedule C from your personal return. Corporations and partnerships, of course, have their own tax forms.

The second segment of this section is the most important of the entire financing plan. It lays out pro forma, or projected, financial statements for the next five years. This becomes the final proof that the company can generate sufficient cash to repay the loan. Although you must include balance sheets and income statements, pro forma cash flow schedules are the most important. A start-up company, without history upon which to base projections, must use market size, market growth, and market share projections to arrive at the sales forecast. Other companies can extrapolate from historical data.

PACKAGING THE PLAN

Package the plan in the most professional way possible. Showmanship is the essence of any successful sales campaign; getting a loan requires the same sales tactics employed when selling a product. The "right look" goes a long way toward capturing the attention of even the most jaundiced banker.

The financing plan forms an integral part of the total presentation but should be packaged separately. Most financing plans should not be more than 20 or 25 pages. The best and most convenient packaging can be done with a plastic spiral binder popular for internal reports. The pages should be numbered, with a table of contents and section dividers. Be sure the cover and back are laminated. First class quick-print shops have the capability to do this binding for a nominal price. Get about a dozen copies right in the beginning. It's a lot cheaper than going back for more later on.

Regardless of the packaging technique, if the financing plan looks professional, it will be regarded with professional interest and add immeasurably to the reception given the total package. Time and again, bankers peruse a professionally prepared plan cover to cover, whereas one that is sloppily prepared or poorly presented gets tossed in the trash barrel.

FINANCING PLAN VARIATIONS

The general content of a financing plan remains the same regardless of the type of business or the amount of the loan. However, different emphasis on particular sections can add impetus for certain types of businesses. Whether you are going after first-, second-, or third-stage financing also makes a difference.

Any start-up business should emphasize the uniqueness of the product or service to be sold. The more evidential detail included in this section, the greater the likelihood a bank will understand why the loan is important. Competition and marketing plans also carry heavy weight. With little or no financial history, it's difficult to convince a bank of the efficacy of pro forma forecasts. They are still an important piece of the plan, but carry less weight than if the business has been operating for several years.

Conversely, the longer a business has been operating, the more important past performance becomes and the greater relevance pro forma forecasts assume. Unless you go after research and development funding, the uniqueness of the product has already been established in the marketplace.

Plans for second-stage financing accent the need for additional capacity to handle increased business. This means placing greater emphasis on proving the assumptions used to forecast increased sales. Management structure and potential changes in the capability of supervisory and technical personnel also play more important roles.

Banks have a difficult time understanding the need for multiple or tiered corporations. If your business includes more than one corporation or both corporate and partnership (or limited partnership) structures, take more space in the first section to describe the reasons for this hierarchy.

Increase the amount of space dedicated to discussions of employee efficiency, inventory control, and product costs for manufacturing businesses. Service businesses need to emphasize the technical abilities and skills of both the owner and key employees. Concentrate on describing pricing, sales promotional efforts, and customer service for retail establishments.

The secret in preparing a winning financing plan is to keep in mind what banks do and don't know about your business and then emphasize those aspects that could be confusing or misunderstood. Bankers need all the help they can get to grasp the essence of a business. They must feel comfortable that they understand the business well enough to monitor it, or you will never get the loan.

PERSONAL GUARANTEES

As mentioned in Chapter 2, be prepared to execute a personal guarantee as additional collateral, especially when applying for a start-up loan. Personal guarantees are always dangerous; but beginning entrepreneurs usually don't have any choice. Foreclosure procedures against personal assets fall under state laws, however, not federal, making them difficult to enforce. Therefore, the likelihood of a bank actually collecting against a guarantee remains remote. On the other hand, personal guarantees create a heavy psychological burden.

If a bank or other creditor does get a court-awarded judgment against your personal assets, the only way out may be to declare personal bankruptcy. Never a palatable solution, personal bankruptcy laws prevent creditors from seizing your assets until you work out a repayment plan. If a plan cannot be negotiated, creditors can force a liquidation of your assets to settle claims.

Laws governing both personal and business bankruptcies are extremely complex and follow an entirely different set of legal principles than those we live under every day. Only a competent bankruptcy attorney can provide the facts. However, every businessowner, or potential businessowner, should learn the basics of bankruptcy law as soon as possible. You may never need to file bankruptcy, but knowing the same rules the bank knows puts you on an even footing when negotiating loan collateral.

The decision to declare personal bankruptcy should be based on what assets you own that could be seized. Obviously, without liquidatable assets in your name a creditor can't satisfy a judgment. Therefore, the question of who has title to personal assets makes all the difference in the world. Methods do exist to protect personal assets from banks and other creditors. Chapter 8 describes three ways to transfer assets out of your name that have worked for others.

If transferring title to your personal assets isn't feasible, a less satisfactory way makes it so complicated for a bank or other creditor to seize the assets that the cost of doing so exceeds the value of the assets. Four popular scenarios are used. Assets can be transferred to:

1. Several corporations, each with different ownership structures.
2. Several corporations located in different states.
3. Revocable trusts located off-shore.
4. Off-shore corporations in a safe-haven country.

If the judgment is large enough and the assets have a high enough value, these methods won't be foolproof. Corporate shields can be pierced by court action. Transfers of assets to revocable trusts can be invalidated under certain circumstances. Most owners of small businesses, however, find these methods sufficient to deter all but the most aggressive creditors. My book, *Tap The Hidden Wealth In Your Business,* points out more sophisticated ways that may be necessary for complete protection.

GAINING THE EDGE WITH BANKS

If banks and bankers all had the same capabilities and the same loan criteria, it would be a simple matter to come up with a list of action steps to ensure success. Such is not the case, however. Every bank puts different emphasis on each of the criteria. Each banker comes from a different background. Each has different career aspirations. Each possesses a different intellectual capability. Every bank stresses a different portfolio mix of working capital loans, term loans, mortgages, and other types of income-producing investments. And each bank's capital ratio faces different pressures from regulators.

WHEN APPLYING FOR A LOAN

Nevertheless, certain approaches seem to work better than others to give borrowers an edge. They are not sacrosanct; and they certainly don't guarantee the approval of a loan application. Most beginning, as well as established, business-owners, however, find that following 10 simple rules usually allows them to take the offense rather than the defense when dealing with banks.

1. Work hard at establishing a good rapport with a bank official high enough in the organization to have clout. Make the time to get to know your banker and to allow your banker to know you.
2. Build management and technical credentials. Develop a high profile in your industry or a recognizable technical skill.
3. Shop for the right bank. Interview bank officials, examine bank financial statements, and become familiar with bank loan policies.

4. Build a reputation for honesty and integrity with other financial institutions and in your community/industry. Try to get another bank to give you a good reference.

5. Come to the first loan application meeting prepared with a complete, well-documented, professional-looking financing package. Keep it as simple as possible.

6. Demonstrate that you understand your banker's concern about getting the loan repaid. Offer collateral, capital, and guarantees before the banker asks.

7. Know your own business well enough to clearly describe its uniqueness in the marketplace. Thoroughly understand competitors' positions.

8. Always play the "nice guy/gal" role. Be professional in appearance and demeanor.

9. Treat bankers with TLC (tender loving care). Bankers don't expect borrowers to care about their personal and professional well-being. Demonstrate that you are different.

10. Walk away from the deal if it doesn't feel right. Don't beg for a loan or argue with a banker.

Step #3 is especially important. Just as each bank is different from another, each borrower has different needs. Do enough research to be sure that the financial institution you choose makes the type of loan you need. A lot of time and effort can be wasted trying to get a loan from the wrong source. The right source may or may not be a commercial bank.

CLOSING THE DEAL

The second phase of getting a loan is making sure that the final loan agreement contains provisions you can live with. All too frequently, with the euphoria of success clouding our minds, we gloss over the fine print in loan agreements. Invariably this leads to eventual disagreements with bank officials and major obstacles to sound bank relations. It's not overly difficult to read a contract, but if you don't understand the implications of each provision, get a lawyer to translate.

Over the years I have negotiated many loan agreements for my own businesses and for clients. I have found that abiding by three basic principles seems to be the best way to stay out of trouble.

1. Don't hesitate to state your objections to any of the terms in the agreement at the time they are being negotiated. Banks expect knowledgeable customers to take exception to some of their boilerplate language. Most are willing to make modifications if pressed. Once you execute the agreement it's too late to disagree.

2. Insist that every condition you agree to is translated into writing. In the heat of battle, clauses or terms are agreed to verbally. When good personal relationships exist between you and your banker, it's very easy to let it go at that. This invariably leads to misunderstandings and problems later on. Personnel turnover in the banking industry is high. Your very friendly banker will likely move on to a different job before the loan gets fully repaid. The loan agreement is with the bank, not the banker.

3. Look at the long-term effect the loan provisions will have on your business and on your personal life. You will probably be living with this bank for several years. Even if you desperately need the cash right now, if the covenants might hurt your business next year or beyond, it isn't worth the gamble. Also, be aware of any provisions that affect you personally. Two provisions cause the greatest personal harm: clauses that obligate you personally, or your estate if you die, to pay off the loan balance; and those that restrict the amount of compensation you can withdraw from the business.

Purchasing new equipment, developing an export program, acquiring a going business, implementing a research and development program, or adding another facility can probably be financed easier and at less cost by using non-bank sources. Very often better terms and conditions along with higher amounts of capital can be raised through sources other than commercial banks.

The next chapter develops standards based on the financing stage and the application of funds that can be used to attract non-bank capital. Carefully executed, these standards reduce the search time necessary to locate funds. They also lay the groundwork for assessing which funding source is the right one for your particular needs. The next chapter also analyzes the benefits and drawbacks applicable to each of these sources.

CHAPTER 4

Choosing The Right Financing

We all know the danger of using short-term loans to purchase equipment or real estate. The loan must be paid back before the asset generates cash. We also know that the reverse happens when we use term loans to finance working capital. The heat of battle, however, creates a strong temptation to ignore these basic matching principles and raise capital anywhere we can, regardless of its use. Going down this road, we eventually learn that capital becomes increasingly difficult to raise, interest rates are higher than they should be, and exorbitant debt service saps our cash.

Raising capital from the right sources and in the right form to meet specific objectives is the primary goal of intelligent financing. This chapter sets the standards for determining the best funding sources for each of the major uses of business capital:

1. To start a business.
2. To acquire a going business.
3. To build receivables and inventory during growth periods.
4. To purchase machinery, equipment, and other tangible assets.
5. To expand facilities.
6. To develop a new product.
7. To start an export program.

STARTING A BUSINESS

Every day, hundreds of dream-filled entrepreneurs in virtually every conceivable industry become businessowners. A frighteningly high percentage fall by the wayside. Starting a business without sufficient capital resources continues to be the primary cause of failure. In finance parlance, the capital needed to originate a business is called "seed money."

Seed money might be $1,000, $5,000, or more. It pays the rent, purchases materials, buys or leases small pieces of equipment, and funds market research.

More often than not, seed money also pays the entrepreneur's living expenses during this start-up period.

A business start-up might take two months or two years. During this time it is difficult, if not impossible, to borrow money from a commercial bank or any other financial institution. Seed money generally comes from savings, relatives, or friends. No one else will take the risk.

A few exceptions to this rule do exist, however. As described in Chapter 6, financing a research project or a business dedicated to social improvement can be arranged through private foundation grants, the Small Business Innovative Research program, or even the SBA, although the latter tends to shy away from funding seed money. Occasionally, entrepreneurial friends gamble small amounts of seed money to get a new business going. Venture capital firms have also been known to contribute seed money for high-tech product development. By and large, however, initial funding must come from your own pocket.

First-Stage Financing

Although at times it's hard to differentiate between seed money and first-stage financing, the finance industry likes to think of the latter as coming into play after completing the market research and initial development effort. First-stage funds can be used to acquire production machinery and equipment, to rent or purchase production space, to purchase production materials, to pay employees, and to meet all other operating expenses of getting a business going. For service and retail businesses not requiring product development expenditures, first-stage financing and seed money are essentially the same.

Money spent for further product development beyond the initial model building or prototype stage also falls into first-stage financing. Separate resources from the Small Business Innovative Research program and from private foundations fund such advanced product development.

Financing a first-time business acquisition requires separate consideration because of the unique sources of such funds. Financing the acquisition of a franchise also demands special tactics. Both acquisitions involve decision-making processes distinct from those used for traditional first-stage financing.

Risk Analysis for Business Start-Ups

From the perspective of a lender or investor, financing a new business always carries more risk than lending to or investing in a going enterprise. Many uncertainties in a start-up vanish once the business establishes a track record.

Does the businessowner have enough savings to pay personal expenses while developing the business? A good rule of thumb states that a business takes three years to generate enough ongoing income for a living wage. During those three years, personal living expenses as well as equity capital for the business must come from the owner, not a lender or investor.

Does the businessowner have the management acumen to build a profitable, self-sustaining business? A person may have all the necessary credentials on paper and still not master the nuts-and-bolts skills to bring a new company to fruition. Technical skills could be more than sufficient as an employee. They may not be sufficient to handle the day-to-day problem solving necessary to start a business.

Will competitive forces allow a new entrant into the market? Market research may point to a logical opening but as soon as you start making sales calls and need orders to sustain the business, the market dries up. Competitors can be very protective of market share. Price cutting, advertising, and promotion gimmicks quickly restrict the new entrant's marketing program. This happened in spades in the long-distance telephone business as soon as AT & T decided to stop the expansion of MCI and Sprint.

Does the new product or service fill a market demand? Starting a business to fire-proof cars might sound like a great idea. Certainly people need this protection. But do they really want it? Are they willing to pay for it?

These are the types of questions financiers worry about when lending or investing in start-up businesses. This also contributes to the popularity of franchise businesses. Franchises already have market acceptance, product design, and competitive position. The only remaining question is whether the franchisee has the management acumen to succeed.

All lenders and investors are risk-takers. The money game has always been a risky business and probably will continue to be forever. Of course, different levels of risk exist. And, as in every other business, the higher the risk, the more money costs and the more stringent the terms.

In the hierarchy of risk-taking, commercial banks continue to be far and away the most conservative; venture capital firms occupy the other end of the spectrum. Finance companies, government agencies (such as the SBA), and private foundations fall between these two extremes. For comparison purposes, small investment banks can be grouped with venture capital firms.

Figure 4-1 provides a handy reference to match the funding for various start-up businesses with the most likely sources of financing.

Figure 4–1

MOST LIKELY FINANCING SOURCES FOR START-UP BUSINESSES

	Bank	Venture Capital	Finance Company	Gov't. Agency	Private Foundation
Manufacturing/assembly					
High-tech product		X	X		
Low-tech product			X	X	X
Retailing					
Health care	X	X			
Food products	X				
Clothing				X	
Hardgoods and electronics			X		
Business services				X	
Service					
Consumer		X			
Business	X	X			
Professional	X				
Social services					X
Distribution					
Mail-order		X		X	
Warehousing			X		
Delivery			X		

Regardless of which institution makes the actual loan or investment, commercial banks eventually get involved. As pointed out in Chapter 6, it's almost impossible to operate a business requiring working capital loans without interfacing with a bank. Therefore, even though first-stage financing can come from the government, venture capitalists, or any other non-bank source, it pays to establish bank relationships right in the beginning. You'll need a bank later on. Also, with a bank in the background, other financial institutions feel more secure and willing to go the extra inch to round up the necessary money.

ACQUIRING A GOING BUSINESS

For a variety of reasons, many potential entrepreneurs believe that buying a going business is a better way to own a company than starting one from scratch. A going business certainly has advantages, not the least of which is immediate cash flow. Financing an acquisition requires a different approach than financing a business start-up, however.

With an existing customer base, established market acceptance, and knowledgeable employees, an operating business carries significantly less risk to financiers than a business start-up. The potential for a quicker return on investment or faster pay back of loans also opens doors closed to start-ups.

Conversely, however, because assets and customer goodwill already exist, the price to get into a going business ranges much higher than the cost of starting one. This tends to encourage a consortium of financing players rather than a single financial institution. It also discourages commercial banks, traditionally bound to short-term loans and high-collateral value, from participating in acquisitions of other than very small companies.

Financing choices for business acquisitions vary by the size of the deal. The seller normally finances very small acquisitions with a purchase price of less than $50,000, although commercial banks traditionally provide working capital loans once the deal closes.

Acquisitions with purchase prices between $50,000 and $1.5 million attract small venture capital firms or small investment banks. Asset-based lenders specializing in loans secured by machinery, equipment, and real estate like to participate in deals with purchase prices between $2 million and $8 million. If the purchase price exceeds $8 million, a combination of investment banks or venture capital firms, asset-based lenders, and foreign merchant banks normally handle the acquisition financing, while a commercial bank picks up the working capital line.

Three major criteria other than purchase price influence the source of acquisition financing: expected cash flow over a five year period, the target company industry, and the type of hard asset collateral.

EXPECTED CASH FLOW

Small investment banks or venture capital firms specializing in non-high-tech deals look closely at the expected cash flow from the acquisition over the ensuing five years. Companies that show promise of returning an average of 30 to 40 percent per year on the investment bank's or venture capital firm's investment stand an excellent chance of getting the entire financing package from one of these sources. Since these firms prefer equity investments, or a combination of mezzanine debt and equity, to straight term loans, they look at return on investment as opposed to a high-interest rate.

Increasingly, especially with the general economy stable or in a downturn, small investment banks and venture capital firms try to invest in companies that produce more mature products rather than high-flying, glamour businesses. Few companies in stable industries have the ability to generate a 30 to 40 percent return per year, however. Consequently, on a downward cycle, high cash flow assumes a less critical role, although it remains an important criteria.

THE TARGET'S INDUSTRY

If an acquisition target cannot be expected to offer high cash returns the industry it services might still influence an investment bank or venture capital firm to invest. In this case, the major criteria becomes a judgment of whether the company can be taken public within a five year period and what price the stock will bring. If they can't get a high cash return through operations, these financiers look toward recouping a significantly appreciated investment through public trading. Once again, the most important criteria continues to be return on equity investment, not interest income.

HARD-ASSET COLLATERAL

An acquisition target in a manufacturing business that has a substantial amount of machinery and equipment, or owns valuable real property, attracts asset-based lenders as the most likely source of funding. These institutions are interested in two things: a high interest rate and high liquidation value of hard assets. If an acquisition candidate meets these prerequisites, long-term loans should be available from asset-based lenders. These institutions require very low down payments.

Chapter 8 examines the entire subject of financing your first acquisition in greater detail. It also highlights the advantages and risks of using different funding sources.

STARTING UP A FRANCHISE

Franchising has become as popular as apple pie and baseball. The Department of Commerce lists thousands of franchise businesses that have sprung up over the past 40 years: everything from fast food to dude ranches to car washes to business brokerages.

A franchise start-up takes on yet a third dimension in financing criteria and sources. Some franchisers offer to assist the franchisee in locating appropriate financing. Others leave you to fend for yourself. In either case, the financing criteria standards and risk analysis stay the same as with other sources.

Banks are more eager to fund a franchise start-up than a business from scratch and for good reason. A reputable franchise should already have market acceptance. More important, performance statistics from other franchisees in the same business can be easily obtained. These figures substantiate how much income and cash flow can be expected in the first, second, and often the third year. This gives banks a lot of comfort.

Many franchisers also control the location of the facility, its layout, equipment configuration, and even participate in and direct advertising campaigns. As long as the franchisee follows directions and maintains a reasonably prudent approach, managing the business should not be a mystery. This also gives lenders confidence.

Finally, some franchisers require the purchase of new equipment and other operating assets. New hard assets with a good market value also minimize a lender's risk. All in all, financing a franchise start-up takes less effort and time than funding a business from scratch. Chapter 7 examines alternative financing programs to fund franchise start-ups.

EXPANDING A BUSINESS

Second-stage financing generally occurs after a business has been up and running for a couple of years, but before it becomes a mature competitor in the marketplace. Seed money brought the product concept to the production stage. First-stage funds brought it to market. Now it's time to expand operations either by adding personnel and inventory, acquiring additional machinery and equipment, or branching out into additional facilities. Perhaps foreign markets look attractive and an export program makes sense. Or the market seems ripe to accept a new product or product line.

By the time you reach this stage, financing risk normally diminishes to a reasonable level. Banks or other financial institutions that financed the first stage should now feel comfortable that the decision to take the gamble was a good one. By this time, they should recognize that the business has established a market niche, its products competitive, its managers capable, and the financial credibility of the owner proven. When the time comes to expand, lenders and investors concentrate more on the risk of growing the business and less time worrying about managerial capabilities.

Still, many businesses falter during this stage of their development. Overzealous product introductions during the first couple of years, unforeseen technological developments, new market competition, and many other factors contribute to failure. Financial institutions are well aware of these possibilities and continue to play a cautious role. Nevertheless, second-stage financing is usually much easier to arrange than first-stage.

FUND WORKING CAPITAL

Commercial banks play a major role in working capital loans. As pointed out in Chapter 6, demand notes, as well as receivables and inventory, secure most working capital loans. As long as the business grows and short-term loans can be used to fund payroll, material purchases, and operating expenses while waiting to collect receivables, commercial banks are the way to go.

However, small service businesses that operate on a cash basis—contractors, repair shops, pick up and delivery businesses, and so on—find it nearly impossible to attract commercial bank interest. Customer progress payments normally fill the gap when a service contract extends over a period of time. Otherwise, plan on getting all your working capital from receivables.

The most difficult part of financing working capital requirements has always been determining both how much and when outside capital is needed. Succumbing to the temptation to borrow as much as banks will lend leads to horrendous mistakes. More than one businessowner has sunk a company by borrowing to the hilt, using what was needed in the business, and taking the balance home. Short-term loans should only be used to fund business growth. If it isn't needed for that, don't borrow it.

Purchasing hard assets with borrowed funds might also lead to future cash problems. If anticipated increased sales materialize, extra cash should be generated in the future to pay back the loan. If not, cash flow from the same level of sales will have to be used. In effect, the loans funding payroll and material purchases have been wasted. The company remains saddled with debt service payments without enough cash generated to handle them.

Purchase Hard Assets

Financing the purchase of hard assets to expand a product line or to support increased market demand should be accomplished with one of the many forms of long-term debt or equity. Foreign banks, small investment banks, asset-based lenders, mortgage lenders, and a few of the larger commercial banks are the best sources. The financial risk of expanding hard assets rests with the probability of generating more sales and, therefore, more cash flow with these assets. To the extent this occurs, everyone wins—the lender or investor, as well as the company. If it doesn't occur, theoretically the lender or investor can seize the hard asset collateral as repayment and still come out whole.

The choice of long-term debt or equity financing depends on the type of expansion, the amount of money required, anticipated cash flow, and the existing profitability of the company. The same principles applied by investment banks and other equity investors for acquisition financing apply to the purchase of hard assets. If the anticipated cash flow yields sufficient return on investment or if the company stands a reasonably good chance of going public within five years, equity investors can always be found.

Theoreticians speak of the high cost of equity financing. This is certainly true for larger corporations that must rely on dividend payments to attract investors. Non-deductible dividends result in cash payments to investors that are

50 percent higher than paying interest (at an effective 35 percent corporate tax rate).

Equity financing for smaller companies, however, can frequently be structured to avoid dividend payments and, thus, double taxation. Arrange with the investment bank or other equity investor to convert a portion of the funds to unsecured mezzanine debt. Pay interest on this the same as with any other debt obligation, except in this case set the interest rate high enough to cover at least part of the investors expected return. Structure the return on the balance of the investment to be escrowed over a four or five year period until the company goes public. At the time of the public offering, the investors get paid off. Income earned on the escrowed funds can be added to the appreciation gain when the investor cashes in.

Hard assets can also be financed with long-term debt. Commercial banks normally don't like to lend long-term money, except with installment loans secured by automobiles, office equipment, trucks and other hard assets that are easily liquidated. And understandably so. Effective interest charged on installment loans typically averages more than 18 percent per year!

In spite of this exorbitant interest charge, consumers and businesses alike use installment loans for everything from machinery to trucks to furniture. Outstanding installment debt currently runs about $800 billion in the United States. Cynthia Latta of DRI/McGraw-Hill estimates this level remaining constant for the next two to three years, in spite of contracting credit markets.

Asset-based lenders (or finance companies), mortgage lenders, and other institutions that specialize in long-term, hard asset lending present alternatives to commercial banks. They all charge high-interest rates, but offer amortization terms much longer than banks.

For equipment, machinery, and vehicles, asset-based lenders require less down payment than anyone else. As with acquisition funding, asset-based lenders are more concerned with the underlying value of collateralized assets than with an owner's equity investment. Down payment requirements from mortgage lenders fluctuate with the supply of mortgage funds, but currently the range seems to run between 20 and 30 percent.

LEASING HARD ASSETS

Purchasing assets isn't the only way to go. Although it doesn't receive the publicity it has in the past, leasing remains a favorite way for many companies to finance expansion. The Revenue Act of 1986 materially changed the handling of leases for tax purposes, but many companies in the leasing business still do very well.

Leasing is probably the least risky way to acquire operating assets. Without a down payment you eliminate financial risk completely and conserve cash at the same time. It is also a low-risk venture for the leasing company. By retaining title to the assets it can seize them upon default without going through the expensive and complex process of foreclosure and holding an auction.

On the flip side, you will never own the assets and therefore, cannot use them to collateralize future loan requirements. In addition, since the leasing company must make a profit on the deal, lease payments are almost always higher than bank interest.

Chapter 11 explores the pros and cons of leasing versus buying.

FINANCING AN EXPORT PROGRAM

Exporting has become a popular way to expand a business base without incurring large expenditures. The number of small and mid-size companies engaged in exporting doubled in 1989, again in 1990, and projections call for another geometric increase in 1991. And with good reason. Global markets are booming in virtually every industry while American markets struggle from recessionary pressures.

Equally important, a company can engage in exporting without spending any of its own money. Properly structured, export financing provides 100 percent of the funds needed for working capital, to purchase machinery and equipment for the production of export products, and to ensure collections from customers.

Commercial banks must get into the export financing loop. However, because banks look at exporting as a higher risk than domestic trade, they do not lend money for either buyer credit or supplier credit without a third party guarantee. Therefore, financing an export program means beginning with the guarantee. Such guarantees may come from a third party bank or from a federal-government agency. The cleanest and certainly the fastest source of guarantees comes through the use of letters of credit (L/Cs). A foreign buyer issues L/Cs through its own bank. This bank guarantees your bank that it will pay for the shipment of goods upon presentation of the appropriate sale and shipping documentation. You can then use the L/C as a third party bank guarantee to collateralize working capital loans from your bank.

The Export-Import Bank (Eximbank) also guarantees working capital loans. Recent criticism has turned Eximbank from concentrating on multinational corporations to encouraging smaller companies to enter the fray. Eximbank offers several programs involving both bank guarantees and direct loans. These programs include working capital financing, term loans to purchase machinery and equipment for export production, and assistance to foreign buyers. The Federal Credit Insurance Association (FCIA) provides foreign commercial and political risk insurance.

A number of other privately and federally-sponsored programs help finance export production and sales. These include a variety of programs under the Caribbean Basin Initiative (CBI), the SBA (working with Eximbank), the Private Export Finance Corporation (PEFCO), and bureaus within the Departments of Commerce and Agriculture.

All Eximbank and other government financing programs work through commercial banks as intermediaries. A full examination of export financing is included in Chapter 12.

REFINANCING FIRST-STAGE DEBT

Whether starting a company from scratch, starting a franchise, or buying a going business, most businessowners find that once established, they can reduce debt service payments by refinancing original start-up debt. With market acceptance, proven product competitiveness, and a track record of three or more years of increasing sales and profitability, a person can usually negotiate much better terms than originally forced into. Lower interest rates, longer payout terms, and reduced collateral are all likely outcomes of refinancing original debt.

It might even be possible to substitute equity capital for debt, either with a private placement or through an initial public stock offering (IPO). The latter, considered third-stage financing, applies to companies well established in the market and sporting a progressively improving profitability record over several years. IPOs can be a viable refinancing possibility, provided the company has attractive market characteristics and the financial markets are strong. Generally, however, it works best to reserve IPOs for later needs. Chapter 14 discusses the pros and cons of public issues along with other refinancing methods.

Clearly, refinancing makes little sense unless a company can improve its lot. There isn't much to be gained by converting an outstanding term loan of $475,000 with three years to go into a new term loan for $500,000 for five years. On the other hand, converting it into a term loan for 10 years could materially reduce monthly debt service. And converting a $475,000 balance into a five year loan for $800,000 immediately adds $325,000 to cash reserves.

Refinancing can be a valid move in the third or fourth year if your business has experienced reasonable growth and profitability. Whether raising additional capital for expansion purposes, reducing interest expense, or dropping monthly debt service payments, refinancing original start-up debt nearly always makes sense.

Timing can be crucial, however. Falling interest rates could indicate you should wait. The same holds true when rates exceed those in your original loan. Financial markets should be bullish or steady, not contracting, with the general economy and industry curves indicating growth opportunities over the next three years.

The mood in the banking industry also affects the desirability of refinancing. Industry upheavals in 1989 and 1990 made these years a questionable time to seek out more advantageous financing. Pressures from falling real estate markets, collapsing LBOs, and capital pressures from the Fed caused many banks to contract their loan business. Not only did new loans become scarce, many banks called those already outstanding.

On the other hand, for every downturn there must be a recovery. New loans are the life-blood of the banking industry, just as new investments keep venture capitalists and small investment banks in business. The latter part of 1991 saw many banks and other financial institutions begin to open their coffers. Refinancing again became a viable course.

THIRD-STAGE FINANCING

Although exceptions certainly exist, third-stage financing generally refers to raising major expansion capital for an already established business. Such expansion includes opening a series of branch offices nationwide, positioning new distribution warehouses to take advantage of opening new markets, acquiring additional plant facilities, upgrading or expanding machinery and equipment capabilities, or entering the global marketplace.

Third-stage financing involves a significantly greater amount of capital than either first- or second-stage. Large amounts of new debt may distort a company's balance sheet or increase debt service beyond its capabilities. Perhaps equity infusions should be substituted for new debt. To enter overseas markets, a company might consider a joint venture with a foreign partner or the acquisition of a going business in a foreign land, both requiring new capital.

Raising third-stage capital involves a significantly different approach than that used previously. Now a company must seriously consider the tradeoffs in sharing ownership, either through a stock issue or through some form of partnership joint venture. Special development financing with revenue bonds might be applicable in certain circumstances. Although later chapters deal in detail with various methods for raising larger amounts of capital, this is probably a good place to review at least the common types of financing available for major expansions.

Although a clear demarcation doesn't exist between second- and third-stage financing, and certainly for some companies the distinction is meaningless, four major avenues exist for raising large amounts of capital:

- Public issues
- Revenue bonds
- International development banks
- Joint ventures

PUBLIC ISSUES

Selling company shares and floating long-term debt issues through public offerings is one of the most viable ways for profitable companies to raise a significant amount of outside capital. Both stock and bond issues can be offered through domestic markets, as well as through foreign stock exchanges, depending on where the funds will be applied.

Any public issue is a costly exercise. Securities and Exchange Commission (SEC) regulations must be followed. Audit fees, legal fees, and underwriter commissions and fees must be paid. Significant printing and distribution outlays always occur when filing complex SEC registration statements. Shareholder or bondholder relations add still more expenses.

Using foreign exchanges is even more complex. A myriad of complications and costs arise when meeting unfamiliar foreign securities registration and issuance laws. Overseas lawyers and accountants must be retained. Foreign accounting, tax, and legal requirements must be met. Whether issuing stock, bonds, or other instruments, costs can easily run in excess of $500,000. Obviously, it makes no sense to incur such costs unless you need a significant amount of new capital.

Revenue Bonds

Municipal revenue bonds have been and continue to be a favorite mechanism for raising significant amounts of capital for real estate development. Hotels, shopping centers, commercial and industrial buildings, hospitals, schools, and many other large-scale development projects can only be completed with large infusions of new capital, usually debt. To encourage private contractors to engage in such projects, and assuming the projects are socially beneficial to the community and meet somewhat rigid IRS criteria, municipal governments assist private-sector efforts with industrial or development revenue bonds.

Revenue bond issues typically range in excess of $10 million and frequently fall in the $50 million to $200 million range. Their attractiveness rests with the tax-exempt status of interest paid to bondholders. Not only does this tax-exempt status help sell the bonds to the public, it also reduces the interest rate paid by the company.

There is a catch, however. Unless the company has a high public bond rating from Standard & Poor's or another national rating service, it must provide the bond-issuing authority iron-clad collateral. This usually means securing the bonds with a standby letter of credit from a money center or other large bank. This, in turn, means that to attract such a guarantor, the company must maintain a high credit rating and be able to substantiate repayment of the bond principal and interest.

Clearly, revenue bonds are not for everyone. On the other hand, an established company with a record of growth and profitability should have little difficulty in meeting the bond criteria. Of course, as stated earlier, to carry tax-exempt status the project must be within a geographic area that the municipal authority wishes to develop; and, it must meet IRS criteria.

INTERNATIONAL DEVELOPMENT BANKS

International Development Banks (IDB) provide a convenient mechanism to finance overseas expansion, either by acquiring going businesses or by building manufacturing and distribution facilities. IDBs are financed and supported by one or more U.S. and foreign government agencies. Their purpose is to finance private sector business investments in developing nations.

There are four "super" IDBs supported by large groups of nations. The new European Bank for Reconstruction and Development in Eastern Europe, for example, boasts a membership of more than 34 nations. Local IDBs also exist in most developing countries. These local development banks draw funds from the "super" IDBs supplemented by contributions and guarantees from the local government.

To take advantage of IDB financing a company must either invest in a developing country with construction of a new plant and equipment or expansion of its existing facilities. Qualifying projects create jobs, add foreign currency through exports, develop local natural resources, or contribute to the infrastructure of the country. IDB financing comes in practically any amount. Small businesses, as well as large, utilize IDB financing for nearly every type of foreign investment.

IDBs are relatively easy to work with and application for assistance can be made directly with either the relevant "super" IDB or a local development bank. Ultimate funding usually comes from a local foreign bank. With guarantees from an IDB, companies have little difficulty qualifying.

Most small businesses find that a finance package combining assistance from an IDB with funding from a U.S. government agency, such as the Overseas Private Investment Corporation (OPIC), offers the most reasonable mix of interest cost and capital availability. In certain countries, financing through a local or "super" IDB also provides political and economic advantages for exporting goods back to the United States. Chapter 13 examines financing overseas expansion through IDBs as well as other government and private financing sources.

JOINT VENTURES

Although many smaller American companies remain unfamiliar with financing through joint ventures, foreign companies have used this avenue for years. A joint venture is nothing more than a business partnership between two or more operating companies, either foreign or domestic. Within the United States joint ventures have become popular as a means of financing expansion and as a method for spreading the risk of entering new markets. From a financing perspective, usually one partner manages the financing while the other brings marketing, production, or research strength to the table.

Within the United States many industry giants, as well as supporting business-es, have found that joint ventures with cash-rich foreign partners offer a feasible way to expand. The automotive companies have teamed up with Toyota, Mitsubishi, Nissan, and Renault. Large investment banks, universities, pharmaceutical compa-nies, and real estate developers suffering from a cash crunch have found the answer to new capital through domestic joint ventures with Japanese, Korean, German, French, Dutch, English, and Taiwanese companies.

Joint ventures are also a popular means of financing overseas expansion. In many countries, financing through local banks or government bureaucracies re-mains closed to foreign investors. By teaming up with a national partner, the combined joint venture circumvents these barriers and raises significant amounts of low cost capital. A joint venture with a cash-rich foreign company is especially attractive when entering a depressed economy, such as Eastern Europe or the Soviet Union. Local financing may not be available under any circumstances and the only way to enter a market is with internal cash supplied by a foreign partner.

Although an array of problems can and generally do arise with joint ventures, a carefully constructed contractual arrangement spelling out the responsibilities and contributions from each party can make the arrangement workable. Some compa-nies, however, especially those with closely guarded patents and proprietary technical expertise, find that by forming a joint venture they must share this technology with a partner. In some cases this means abandoning valuable assets. Later chapters explore some of the ways companies have found to get around this problem as well as additional opportunities and risks in using joint ventures for financing both domestic and foreign expansion.

SUMMARY

Raising new capital without a clear grasp of the fundamentals of matching financing sources and forms of capital with anticipated uses nearly always results in higher costs, weaker balance sheets, and greater loss of cash through debt service payments than necessary. Through the prudent planning and evaluation of alternate sources and forms of capital, small businesses can avoid the costly and inefficient process of refinancing unmanageable debt. The following summarizes the sources, forms, and uses of new capital.

1. *Starting a business.* Starting a business from scratch requires adequate seed money that the entrepreneur must raise from savings, friends, and family (in some cases through foundation grants) and first-stage loans or equity capital from outside sources. This outside capital may come from commercial banks, venture capital firms, finance companies, government agencies, or founda-tions. The source and form depends on the type of business being started and

the amount of seed money contributed. Short-term loans should be used for purchasing materials, paying workers, market research, advertising, renting space, and other working capital needs. Long-term debt and equity should be used to purchase equipment or facilities.

2. *Buying a going business.* Acquiring a going business is an alternative to starting a company from scratch. Various financing sources fund acquisitions. Small investment banks and venture capital firms work best for deals with a purchase price up to $1.5 million. Asset-based lenders like deals of $2 million to $8 million. Larger deals interest foreign merchant banks. Seller financing continues to be the most economical way to fund smaller business acquisitions with a purchase price of less than $200,000. In all cases, the assets of the business should be used to collateralize borrowed funds.

3. *Franchise businesses.* Starting a franchise business is another way to begin. Many of the larger, more reputable franchisers assist new buyers in arranging either equipment and facilities leases or commercial bank loans. Others force the franchisee to locate appropriate start-up funding. Commercial banks look more kindly on franchise start-ups because of the marketing, technical, advertising, and training support provided by the franchiser, limiting the risk of business failure.

4. *Expansion financing.* Financing second-stage expansions takes on a different structure. With an established market for its products or services and a successful management track record of overcoming initial start-up hurdles, companies at this stage find financial institutions more amenable to participating in both debt and equity funding. Short-term loans from commercial banks or finance companies secured by inventory and receivables should be used for expanded working capital needs. Long-term debt from finance companies, banks, investment banks, or venture capital firms fund the purchase of equipment, machinery, and facilities to be employed in the business for at least the length of the loan.

Equity capital from small investment banks might be cheaper long-term capital by eliminating interest charges, but the non-deductibility of dividend payments can easily wipe out this advantage. Also, equity investors often demand exorbitant returns which are impractical for many businesses. Leasing equipment, machinery, and facilities presents another viable alternative.

5. *Export financing.* Companies entering export markets can finance 100 percent of working capital and production equipment needs. Government agencies also provide guaranteed insurance against the non-collectibility of receivables. Commercial banks, both domestic and foreign, work closely with Eximbank in arranging funding and guarantees. A variety of other private- and government-sponsored programs offer financing for export trade.

6. *Refinancing first-stage debt.* Once a company has been in business for two, three, or four years and has proven its profitability, refinancing original start-up debt becomes a viable step. In most cases, refinanced debt will be less expensive, have longer payout terms, and require less collateral. Initial public stock offerings to replace original debt could be a possibility at this stage. The status of the economy and the outlook for financial trends by bankers and market analysts determines what structure to go after for refinancing.

7. *Third-stage financing.* As a company matures, broader financing sources open up. Public stock and bond issues result in substantial outside capital even though it means incurring significant issue costs and sharing the ownership of the business. Municipal revenue bonds form a likely source for real estate development projects. International development banks and joint ventures can be used effectively to expand operations overseas. Financing major expansions of facilities, markets, or product lines domestically through joint ventures is another possibility.

CHAPTER 5

Finding Professional Assistance For Raising First-Stage Capital

For obscure reasons, many banks and other financial institutions prefer to arrange financing packages through an intermediary rather than direct with the customer. It works the same way as buying a house. Real estate agents know which banks offer the best terms for a specific type of dwelling and frequently negotiate the entire transaction without buyer participation.

Business financing is almost that simple, but not quite. Because management ability and personal relationships are such important elements in a lender's criteria, it's difficult to delegate the entire process to an agent. At some point, borrower and lender must meet and get to know each other.

A competent financing advisor should be able to source the best combination of loans and equity capital. An advisor can also structure the most beneficial deal with the lead lender, or the sole source if the transaction involves only one lender or investor. Regardless of the amount of capital required and whether first-, second-, or third-stage financing, a professional advisor nearly always makes the job easier and faster, and arranges better terms than doing it yourself. For first-stage financing, however, because the business and its owner are unknown and unproven quantities, a professional advisor becomes paramount just to attract a lender's interest.

If any of four conditions exist you may not need professional advice, although it can still be very helpful:

1. You have an established personal relationship with the financial institution.
2. You need less than $20,000.
3. You borrow under an installment loan.
4. The value of readily marketable collateral is substantially in excess of the loan.

In all other cases, professional advisors make the task much easier and faster.

A variety of advisors stand ready to help. The most likely sources to assist with first-stage financing continue to be:

1. The local commercial bank that handles your personal checking and savings accounts.
2. The public accountant who prepares your personal tax return.
3. The Small Business Administration (SBA).
4. State and local development agencies.
5. Commercial real estate agents.
6. Local small business trade groups.
7. Franchisers.
8. Large CPA firms.
9. Management consultants specializing in financing.
10. Merger and acquisition (M & A) consultants and business brokers.
11. Money brokers.
12. Small investment banks.

The right choice depends upon: the amount and type of capital required; the type of business you own; whether it has been started from scratch, is a franchise, or is to be purchased; the company's location; and current economic conditions. During the start-up mode, the choice also depends on the stage of product development and how much seed money has already been raised.

PERSONAL BANK

A meeting with the manager of the bank that handles your personal checking and savings accounts can be a good starting point. If you need $5,000 to $10,000 and can offer collateral valued in excess of the loan, it might extend the loan itself. On the other hand, a small, independently-owned local bank will probably decline and suggest a larger correspondent bank in the area.

As previous chapters pointed out, soliciting a loan from a new commercial bank always requires a reference from your local bank anyway. It's usually a good idea to start here even if your loan request gets turned down. Even though another institution ends up making the loan, good relations with a local bank come in handy at one time or another. As long as you keep your personal bank informed of what you are doing and offer it the opportunity to participate, reference letters should never be a problem.

Your personal banker might not be with a small independent bank. Managers of regional branch banks can also be helpful. Most branch managers tend to be at the lower end of the management hierarchy. Given the opportunity to recommend a customer to another division of the bank, or even to another bank or finance company, boosts a manager's ego. It also shows superiors that the manager has the ability to promote business beyond branch capabilities. This nearly always leads to a bonus or even a promotion. Having boosted the career of a bank manager, you can be assured of instant cooperation when you go back for assistance later on.

A personal banker can also suggest other avenues of financing—perhaps the Small Business Administration (SBA) or the Small Business Innovative Research (SBIR) program. Venture capital firms always maintain close contacts with the banking fraternity. Many smaller consulting firms rely on commercial banks for referrals. Once your personal banker takes an interest in what you are trying to do, suggestions for capital sources and competent professional advisors nearly always follow.

Asking for assistance won't cost a penny. Not only are banks the least costly source of professional advice, asking for help establishes important relationships for later needs. Unfortunately, not all bankers have the qualifications to provide concrete professional assistance. Many are familiar only with the depository services typically offered to individual and small business customers. If qualified, however, assistance from a personal banker can certainly be the quickest, easiest, and cheapest way to go.

PERSONAL TAX ACCOUNTANT

Small public accounting firms represent another excellent source of professional assistance. With the complexity of tax laws multiplying, most of us use tax lawyers or public accountants to prepare our tax returns. Although lawyers seem to be of little help in sourcing business capital, public accounting firms maintain close contacts with the financial community. Many public accountants, especially sole practitioners and partners in local firms, also hold positions in venture capital firms, SBICs, or small investment banking companies.

Several advantages accrue from working through your personal tax advisor. Public accountants assume new financing will increase the size and complexity of your business, leading to higher fees for tax work and possibly additional audit or consulting work. Seldom, if ever, do they charge extra for this advice. Knowing your background, a public accountant can smooth the way when approaching capital sources—whether they be banks, venture capital firms, government agencies, or other institutions. An independent accountant's personal recommendation counts nearly as much as a bank reference. Not infrequently, this type of personal reference tilts the scales in favor of a loan even when other criteria falls short.

After identifying one or more sources, a financing plan must be prepared. The same independent accountant who provided sourcing assistance should be able to offer valuable help in this area. Since banks and other financing sources know that public accountants specialize in preparing financial statements and pro forma forecasts, any financing plan so blessed receives serious consideration.

Finally, because a personal accountant knows your tax status, help in planning a tax-advantaged capital structure can be invaluable. Without sufficient up-front planning, a capital structure that might seem appropriate from a cost and availability perspective could end up costing a substantial amount in excess taxes. A tax advisor can guide the structuring to minimize tax problems that could arise in later years.

SMALL BUSINESS ADMINISTRATION

The Small Business Administration (SBA) also offers financing advice. If your business doesn't qualify for an SBA loan or bank guarantee, or if for one reason or another you don't want to become involved with SBA financing, most SBA offices can still provide guidance.

Although the capability of SBA personnel varies considerably between offices, it doesn't take very long to ascertain whether their advice is a waste of time or not. Even if SBA officials can't help, most offices utilize free counseling services from retired business people. Volunteers from the Service Corps of Retired Executives (SCORE) help SBA applicants strategize their objectives, prepare financing plans, and assist as business consultants wherever their talents are needed. And they do this free of charge.

Unfortunately, most SCORE members have no consulting background. Many come from lower management positions in large and mid-sized companies. Although well intentioned, advice from these people tends to be superfluous at best and erroneous at worst. On the other hand, SCORE members might point you to financing options outside of the SBA. It certainly can't hurt to investigate SCORE as a source of professional assistance. It won't cost a dime.

Some 'volunteers" working through SBA offices are active consultants trying to get new clients. Starting a consulting practice, they see SBA applicants as potential new clients. They are quick to offer their services, and they do charge consulting fees. Unfortunately, most have no experience in the financing game and tend to lead clients down the wrong paths. It's generally best to stay away from them.

SBA offices also sponsor courses, conferences, and seminars for small businesses. Many are free, some involve a small charge. The conferences tend to be broad-based, covering several aspects of starting a business, including raising capital. Usually, qualified businesspeople from the community make presentations on specific topics. Occasionally, a banker or financing consultant volunteers time to give a speech or participate in a symposium. This can be an excellent way to identify a professional advisor. Also, these professionals normally provide referrals to qualified consultants, bankers, or public accountants with contacts in the financial community.

Later chapters describe forms of financing assistance available directly from the SBA and its sister organizations. These programs are set up to encourage direct application without going through an intermediary, although professional advice increases the probability of getting what you need.

STATE AND LOCAL DEVELOPMENT COMPANIES

Most communities have one or more locally sponsored development companies established specifically to help promote the development of small businesses. These development agencies get their funding from city, township, county, or state small business development departments. They conduct seminars on various business topics, provide financing assistance, and help small businesses locate technical advice.

In the financing arena, these development organizations help companies arrange revenue bond financing for commercial real estate development projects, government subsidized funding for research and development, labor training subsidies, and specific grants or low-cost loans for urban redevelopment projects.

Many of the coordinators and active leaders in these programs are, or have been in private business and know of professional consulting or accounting advisors. Most seem willing to help a small business raise capital, even though it may not be possible to do so through their program.

FEDERAL DEVELOPMENT PROGRAM ASSISTANCE

The federal government also plays a role through branch offices of the U.S. Economic Development Agency. A quick call to a local office could provide additional leads to private advisors, or even directly to sources of capital. However, the agency limits its direct funding to socially beneficial projects, such as urban redevelopment.

STATE DEVELOPMENT ASSISTANCE

State development agencies provide the same type of assistance. Many states have formed Small Business Development Companies (SBDC) specifically to help small businesses locate financing and get started in projects beneficial to the state and the community. Once again, if your business doesn't fit this mold, it's still possible to get leads through these agencies.

SPECIAL ASSISTANCE FOR WOMEN

The American Woman's Economic Development Corporation (AWED) has been established specifically to help women start businesses. Under the organization's Loan Literacy program, women planning to start a business receive help for locating appropriate lending sources. Ten private weekly counseling sessions help women prepare a well-thought-out financing plan and complete bank loan applications. The national offices of AWED can be reached at (212) 692-9100 or (800) 222-AWED.

COMMERCIAL REAL ESTATE AGENTS

Often overlooked as a viable source of financing assistance, commercial real estate agents by the very nature of their business maintain ready access to a host of financing sources. In addition to mortgage banks, commercial real estate companies keep tabs on the activities of Real Estate Investment Trusts (REIT), Real Estate Mortgage Investment Conduits (REMIC), real estate limited partnerships, foreign investment blocs, and a variety of other capital sources geared to real estate investments.

Assistance from real estate companies is limited to financing the acquisition or expansion of land and buildings, not working capital or equipment purchases. Larger commercial real estate brokerages handle projects over $100 million and cannot actively source funds for smaller deals. Even in this case, however, most will point the way to consultants or smaller real estate agencies for assistance.

Commercial real estate companies also maintain listings of domestic and foreign professional mortgage brokers. Although small businesses should approach mortgage brokers with great care, the competent ones do provide qualified services for sourcing mortgages.

Most of the time, however, mortgage amounts needed by smaller companies tend to be too low to warrant much attention. Mortgage brokers calculate their profits as a percentage of the financing package. They spend as much time and effort placing a mortgage for $1 million as one for $100 million and their earnings on the lesser amount just doesn't justify their time.

Also, a great many people who hold themselves out as mortgage brokers are nothing more than "quick-buck" artists, ready and willing to gouge the unsuspecting client without rendering agreed-to services. It's best to stay away from mortgage brokers unless you know who you are dealing with and can verify credentials.

Commercial real estate companies can be located in any large or mid-size city. Just check the phone book listings under "commercial real estate."

SMALL BUSINESS TRADE GROUPS AND TRADE ASSOCIATIONS

Small business trade groups can be found promoting the start-up and development of small businesses in nearly every community. These trade groups go under a variety of names and are generally associated with or sponsored by the local chamber of commerce. In addition to technical assistance, site selection advice, labor recruiting, and local market research information, these groups offer assistance to companies seeking start-up or expansion capital.

Although most small business trade groups do not have funds to invest or lend themselves, they work closely with local banks and other financial institutions to secure capital for local businesses. This assistance is always free of charge. Although the helpfulness of a trade group depends on the caliber of people involved in it, some are extremely competent. As a minimum, introductions to local bankers can be arranged. Even if you source capital elsewhere, over the long haul it helps to nurture these contacts.

Certain industry trade associations maintain listings of capital sources for small businesses. As with small business trade groups, trade associations can't help in the preparation of the financing plan or in the negotiation of the terms and conditions of a loan or investment. They can, and often do, however, provide guidance in locating appropriate sources of funds. Normally those trade associations representing industries boasting many small suppliers do the best job. Industry trade associations dominated by giants, such as steel, automotive, aerospace, or telecommunications are virtually useless to the small business. Other trade associations that represent industries such as machine tools, toys, sporting equipment, and automotive aftermarket products, can help to at least get you started down the financing road.

FRANCHISERS

As popular as franchising has become over the last 20 years the lack of financing assistance given to most new franchisees seems surprising. Some of the bigger name franchises do offer assistance in locating leasing companies. Others help in sourcing mortgage money. Generally, however, the financing of capital equipment or facilities is left up to the individual franchisee.

Nevertheless, rapidly changing conditions in many franchise industries have begun to swing the pendulum. High growth franchisers have started to offer financing guidance, although those in smaller, more stable industries continue to be reluctant to get involved. As a general rule, don't expect a franchiser to be of much help in sourcing either expansion or operating capital. Assistance for preparing financing plans isn't within their jurisdiction either.

LARGE PUBLIC ACCOUNTING FIRMS

Large public accounting firms offer a wide range of contacts in the financial community. All of the Big 6 firms—Arthur Andersen, Ernst & Young, Price Waterhouse, etc.—and many of the larger regional firms maintain close relationships with all of the money center and regional banks. They also stay in close contact with larger investment banks, venture capital firms, and finance companies. When you need significant amounts of capital, these professionals often maintain a broader range of financial contacts than any other advisor.

Services relating to the raising of capital usually fall under the jurisdiction of a management consulting department. Offices in major cities throughout the country staff consulting departments, although those in the larger cities offer the greatest range of assistance. An initial appointment is relatively easy: just call the local office and ask to meet with a management consulting partner. Usually one or two partners specialize in financing services. The meeting should be free, but expect to pay a substantial hourly rate for actual assistance. In East Coast offices, this fee ranges from $150 to $300 an hour.

It usually doesn't pay to use a large public accounting firm unless you need capital in excess of $5 million. The cost is just too prohibitive. On the other hand, when making a public stock issue professional advice from one of these firms can't be beat. Securities and Exchange Commission regulations require certified audits and complex registrations. In the eyes of the investing public, a large public accounting firm always carries more weight than a small firm.

Other than for a public issue, however, engaging a large firm to help prepare a financing plan is usually not economical. Although many offices try desperately to develop a small business clientele and jump at the opportunity to get a new client, they charge substantially more than equally competent smaller firms.

MANAGEMENT CONSULTANTS

Competent management consultants also charge much less than large accounting firms. Many consultants specialize in arranging financing either as a stand alone service or as part of a broader service base that includes restructuring, acquisitions, strategic planning, or small business advisory services. These specialists charge either hourly rates ranging from $120 to $180 per hour or retainers ranging from $1,500 to $3,000 per month. If you need a small amount of capital—say less than $1 million—an hourly rate usually ends up being cheaper. For larger amounts, or for a complex financing package involving several sources, clients usually come out ahead with a retainer.

Management consultants specializing in the various aspects of financing and refinancing must maintain constant contact with financial institutions, private investors, and government financial assistance programs. This puts them in the forefront of professional advisors with up-to-date information about who is doing what in the finance game. Such current intelligence enables the packaging of a variety of financing instruments to serve the needs of a vast array of clients of all sizes and in all industries. Of all the possibilities for obtaining financing assistance, management consultants specializing in this area offer the greatest probability of success in the shortest period of time.

Unfortunately, many management consultants hold themselves out as financing experts but are really novices. Since anyone can be called a management consultant without state or federal licensing and without professional association standards, small businesses must be extremely careful to choose the right one. A consultant without financing competency can cost a client a significant amount of money without delivering anything of substance. Even worse, unqualified consultants tend to recommend their favorite financial institution whether or not it may be the best for the client. If the bank or other institution turns down a loan request, these consultants frequently tell clients that money cannot be obtained from any source.

Three proven methods verify a consultant's qualifications. These are:

- References from prior clients;
- References from financial institutions; and
- Face-to-face interviews.

Avoid any consultant unwilling to offer at least three references from prior clients. All references should be thoroughly verified. Don't hesitate to ask probing questions. Find out specifically how broad a base of financing contacts the consultant maintains, the amount of assistance the consultant offers for the preparation and submission of the financing plan and loan application, and the degree of integrity and honesty portrayed not only to the client but also in dealings with financial institutions.

A competent financing consultant should provide at least three references from financial institutions. Ideally, one should be from a well-known commercial bank, one from a venture capital firm, and one from a government agency—preferably the SBA. Just as with client references, financial institution references should be verified directly.

The interviewing process is the catch-all phase of qualifying a management consultant. References from prior clients and financial institutions can check out perfectly but the consultant might still be the wrong choice for the job. In the financing game, personal rapport between client and advisor often makes the difference between a successful search and one that falls short. A consultant must understand your business well enough to sell your needs to financial institutions or investors.

The only way to be sure that a client-consultant relationship works is to ask the right questions at an initial interview. Meet at least two, and preferably three, consultants before choosing one for the job. The following list of interview questions has proven valuable for clients seeking a financing specialist.

1. How many financing deals have you put together in the past twelve months? (Should be at least three or four.)

2. When was the last time you arranged financing through a venture capital firm? An investment bank? A government agency? A foreign bank? (Should have done at least one deal through each of these sources within the past three years.)

3. Have you arranged multiple source financing packages? (Should be answered in the affirmative.)

4. What were the amounts of the financing packages you put together over the prior two years? (Should have done at least one with an amount similar to what you need.)

5. Will you help assemble a financing plan? (Obviously the answer must be yes.)

6. What is the content of financing plans that you prepare? (Should be close to the parameters set out in Chapter 4.)

7. How will you structure your fees? Hourly? Retainer? Project flat fee? Not to exceed? Percentage of financing package? (If the consultant answers with only one type of acceptable fee arrangement chances are good that a broad base of financing sources is not in his or her repertoire. The correct answer should be based on the amount of capital needed, complexity of the deal, the underlying assets of your company, company earnings record, type of business, and a variety of other criteria. Qualified consultants will answer that the fee structure depends on the type and complexity of the engagement.)

8. How much time will you devote to this engagement? (Should commit to a specific number of hours per week or month until the financing is arranged. One of the biggest dangers when working with consultants is that the consultant has so many simultaneous clients that the time committed to your work becomes minimal. Therefore, a consultant should be pinned down to a specific time commitment.)

9. Be sure to obtain and verify prior client and financial institution references.

Locating a qualified consultant is never easy. The good ones do not advertise. The best consultants for first-stage financing tend to be sole practitioners or partners in very small firms. Large consulting firms or consulting divisions of Big 6 accounting firms do not devote the attention to a small client necessary to structure the best financing package. Also, the fees charged by larger consulting firms are much too high. The best way to track down a qualified consultant is through a referral from your personal commercial banker or your independent accountant, both of whom should know of consultants they have worked with in the past. In some cities, SBA offices maintain a listing of consultants. The SBA might recommend a list of three or four to choose from, but that's as far as they go. The danger of going this route has already been described.

MERGER & ACQUISITION CONSULTANTS AND BUSINESS BROKERS

When purchasing a going business or product line, merger and acquisition (M & A) consultants and business brokers can be invaluable sources of financing advice. Business brokers handle smaller businesses such as retail stores and service shops. A business broker provides the quickest and most efficient way to buy one of these small businesses. Not only do brokers maintain extensive listings of a variety of companies for sale, they also have access to local funding.

Financing very small business acquisitions comes either from the seller or from a local commercial bank. Competent business brokers know which banks currently grant loans for this purpose. Usually at no charge to the buyer, business brokers advise where to go to get the money and how a financing package could be put together. They stop short of assisting with the preparation of a financing plan, however. Any city telephone directory lists business brokers active in that specific locale.

Larger business acquisitions can be handled best by M & A consultants. These professionals make a living sourcing buyers and sellers for privately held and smaller, publicly held companies. One of their services is to act as a professional financing advisor to the buyer.

Competent M & A consultants know that the hardest part of any business acquisition or sale is to arrange appropriate financing, either as a leveraged buyout (LBO) or a straight investment. Without adequate funding, deals never close. Therefore, to be successful in this field a consultant must stay alert to sources of funding for different types and sizes of acquisitions. Because of this close tie between sourcing buyers and sellers and locating appropriate financing, many M & A consultants specialize in financing or refinancing companies in addition to their acquisition and divestiture work.

When retaining an M & A consultant to assist in making an acquisition, no additional fee should be involved for arranging the financing. In addition, these consultants offer invaluable assistance in preparing and submitting financing plans, again as part of the overall acquisition fee.

Qualified M & A consultants are difficult to locate except by referral. Any mid-size or large bank works with these specialists and most will provide the names of two or three to choose from. Larger accounting firms and corporate legal practices also maintain relationships with M & A consultants. If all else fails, the National Association of Merger and Acquisition Consultants (NAMAC) can provide names of members in your area. Many qualified consultants do not belong to this association, however, so it's better to try banks and other referral sources first.

Chapter 8 describes how to work with M & A consultants throughout the acquisition phase.

MONEY BROKERS

Money brokers, or loan brokers as they like to call themselves, earn their living by matching financial institutions and other sources of funds with companies in search of capital. Money brokerage is a totally unregulated industry and unscrupulous charlatans proliferate in it, although not all money brokers fall into this category. Some very reputable individuals and small companies make a living in this business. Unfortunately, both the good ones and the crooks enter and leave the business so rapidly that it is impossible to list even a small number of them. Although banks welcome referrals from money brokers, more than one banker has referred to this breed as the "whores of the finance industry."

Many national and international money brokers advertise in the *Wall Street Journal* in the "Capital Available" section. They also place advertisements in big city newspapers and in trade and business magazines. Most consultants that specialize in arranging financing know of two or three money brokers to call upon if needed.

Some brokers have international connections. They place debt and equity money from nefarious foreign sources in secure American companies. Some of this money emanates from oil rich Arab investors. Some comes from international arms dealers, wealthy foreign families that do not wish to be identified, foreign government caches, and funds obtained illegally through drug and other cross-border transactions. In all fairness, seldom do international money brokers know the original source of capital they place. Most of it flows through two or more foreign banks before it ever reaches a money broker.

Reputable domestic money brokers place deals primarily through commercial banking channels. Most are straightforward brokerage deals and perfectly legitimate.

Money brokers usually charge a percentage of the loan or investment balance. This fee ranges from .5 percent to 5 percent, depending on the source and the amount of the money. Although commercial banks work through money brokers, most frown on them charging more than .5 to 1 percent.

A money broker only provides leads to capital sources. Don't expect any help in preparing a financing plan or negotiating a financing package. In fact, you seldom meet a money broker personally. Most conduct the entire transaction by phone. Money brokers can be most helpful for arranging difficult debt financing packages.

Since money brokers handle high-risk deals, expect to pay a considerable premium for funds, especially if the source is other than a commercial bank. Still, money brokers serve a market niche and should not be discounted. When money is scarce, they may provide the only means.

SMALL INVESTMENT BANKS

Small investment banks and some venture capital firms provide professional financing assistance in addition to other investment activities. Large investment banks also handle capital sourcing engagements but limit their clientele to large companies. In some respects, contracting with a small investment bank as your financial advisor can often be the most expedient way to raise larger sums of money, especially during first-stage financing when your company has little or no earnings history and few, if any, hard assets.

Later chapters describe how to use both investment banks and venture capital firms as active players in raising debt and equity capital, but here we are concerned only with their roles as financial advisors. Probably the greatest advantage in using an investment bank is that these professionals maintain a cadre of private equity investors eager to participate in growing companies.

As described in Chapter 4, traditional lending institutions often classify start-up or first-stage financing as high-risk business. This makes conventional short- and long-term loans hard to arrange. To get a business going, or to bring a new product to market, equity money might be the only recourse. With equity players standing in the wings, small investment banks become the logical choice to help arrange the package.

Expect to pay investment banks a sizable fee for their help. Most work on a flat percentage of the financing package—usually in excess of 2 percent—plus a monthly retainer that usually runs in excess of $10,000. Obviously at this price it doesn't make sense to use these services unless other professional advisors are unable to come up with your required capital. In this sense, investment banks, along with money brokers, become a "court of last resort." If, however, an investment bank participates directly in the financing package, as described in Chapter 8, it does not charge anything for financial advice.

CONTRACTUAL GUIDELINES

Getting financing assistance from commercial banks, government agencies, your independent accountant, franchisers, trade groups, trade associations, or local development companies never requires the execution of contractual agreements. Since these sources don't charge, no contracts are needed. When using other professional advisors who do charge a fee, a carefully worded contractual document must be executed to assure their compliance with your understanding of the assignment. These professionals also insist on a contract as evidence of your legal obligation to pay for their services.

Each consultant, large accounting firm, money broker, or investment bank has its own boilerplate contract for this purpose. Usually, you can't do much to materially alter its terms and conditions or the body of the contractual language. On the other hand, to the extent that you disagree with any of the clauses or believe them to be detrimental to your interest, you certainly have the right to try to negotiate changes. As a minimum, the following matters should be spelled out clearly and unequivocally in the contract.

1. Basis of fee structure—hourly rate, retainer, flat fee, etc.
2. Specific date of termination.
3. Any guarantees of performance the advisor is willing to grant.
4. Specific time per week or per month to be spent by the advisor on the engagement.
5. Activities to be performed in addition to raising the capital such as helping to prepare the financing plan or to negotiate the deal with a lender or investor.
6. Actions to be performed by you or your company such as arranging for an audit or producing financial statements or tax returns.
7. Whether you will be expected to execute a personal guarantee and if so, what parameters will the advisor insist be included.
8. If possible, a declaration by the advisor of the type of financing to be solicited—equity capital, long-term secured debt, short-term bank loans, private debt, etc.

SUMMARY

Choosing the right professional advisor to help arrange a financing package can be a crucial first step in the early stages of business growth. Structuring the wrong type of financing has caused the demise of more than one small business. Conditions surrounding the growth, potential profitability, and the potential need for hard assets varies with each business. A multitude of financing sources proliferate in the financial market place. For these reasons, it is almost impossible to get the job done right without the advice of an expert. Trying to raise capital on your own, especially for larger amounts, increases the probability that you will end up with the wrong capital structure, or not being able to raise the amount you need. Professional advisors fill a much needed role in helping a business grow to the next stage.

Professional advisors can be grouped into two categories: those whose services are free and those who charge. Advantages and risks exist in using each type. The amount of capital required, the type of business, general economic conditions, and location of the business all have a hand in determining which way to go.

In the "free" category, the following sources are ranked by major criteria:

1. **Local bank handling your personal checking and savings accounts.**
   Quality of advice: Fair to excellent
   Timeliness: Fair
   Assistance in preparing financing plan: None
   Certainty of results: Questionable

2. **Local accounting firm handling your tax and other personal financial matters.**
   Quality of advice: Good to excellent
   Timeliness: Good
   Assistance in preparing financing plan: Yes
   Certainty of results: Fair to good

3. **The Small Business Administration (SBA) and SCORE.**
   Quality of advice: Very poor to good
   Timeliness: Fair
   Assistance in preparing financing plan: Yes
   Certainty of results: Questionable for any except small amounts

4. **State and local development agencies.**
   Quality of advice: Good
   Timeliness: Good
   Assistance in preparing financing plan: No
   Certainty of results: Fair

5. **Commercial real estate agents.**
   Quality of advice: Good to excellent
   Timeliness: Fair to good
   Assistance in preparing financing plan: No
   Certainty of results: Questionable

6. **Small business trade groups and trade associations.**
   Quality of advice: Fair to good
   Timeliness: Poor
   Assistance in preparing financing plan: No
   Certainty of results: Poor to excellent

7. **Franchisers.**
   Quality of advice: Fair
   Timeliness: Good
   Assistance in preparing financing plan: No
   Certainty of results: Good

The following summarizes sources who charge for their services:

1. **Large public accounting firms.**
   Quality of advice: Excellent
   Timeliness: Good
   Assistance in preparing financing plan: Yes
   Certainty of results: Good to excellent
   Cost: High—$150 to $300 per hour

2. **Management consultants specializing in financing.**
   Quality of advice: Excellent
   Timeliness: Excellent
   Assistance in preparing financing plan: Yes
   Certainty of results: Good to excellent
   Cost: Moderately high—$120 to $150 per hour or retainer of $1,500 to $3,000 per month

3. **Merger and acquisition consultants and business brokers.**
   Quality of advice: M & A consultants—Excellent
                        Business brokers—fair to good
   Timeliness: Good to excellent
   Assistance in preparing financing plan: M & A consultants—Yes
                                         Business brokers—No
   Certainty of results: Good
   Cost: Business brokers—Low or free
         M & A consultants—Free if engaged for acquisition consulting

4. **Money brokers.**
   Quality of advice: Fair to good
   Timeliness: Fair to good
   Assistance in preparing financing plan: No
   Certainty of results: Questionable
   Cost: High—up to 5 percent of the financing package

5. **Small investment banks.**
   Quality of advice: Excellent
   Timeliness: Good to excellent
   Assistance in preparing financing plan: In some cases
   Certainty of results: Good to excellent
   Cost: Very high—in excess of 2 percent of financing package plus monthly retainer ranging upward from $10,000

These rankings are meant as guidelines only. The quality of advice, timeliness, certainty of results, and cost vary all over the lot and depend almost entirely upon the individual performing the work. The wrong choice of a financial advisor leads to disastrous results. The best approach is to carefully investigate all alternatives, obtain references for likely candidates, and then pick the one or two sources that seem to meet your objectives.

CHAPTER 6

Raising Working Capital For Starting A Business

A new business without sales or profit history needs working capital as much or more than a company that has been operating for a few years. Beginning entrepreneurs ask the same bewildering question: "How do I borrow money for payroll and materials when my business doesn't have any assets to use as collateral?"

During boom times, banks throughout the country advertise their desire to make loans. They spend billions on public relations campaigns to establish a "Big Brother" image standing ready and willing to encourage the entrepreneurial spirit in America's small businesses. Even in tough times, banks like to think of themselves a community minded, promoting their desire and ability to help struggling entrepreneurs.

Yet, when push comes to shove, few banks, if any, make working capital loans to start-up businesses. To purchase equipment or real estate, yes. To pay the bills, no. How then can you raise enough capital to bring your product or service idea to market? What sources will listen when the only collateral you can offer is a dream?

DETERMINING CASH REQUIREMENTS

Before approaching a bank or other financial institution for a working capital loan, or any capital for that matter, a financing plan as described in Chapter 3 must be prepared. A pro forma projection of cash is the key element, especially for first-stage companies. This cash flow projection estimates cash receipts from sales compared to operating cash expenditures by month. The monthly cash shortfall represents the amount that must be borrowed. The more detailed the estimate, backed by reasonable operating and market assumptions, the higher the likelihood of getting the loan and the greater the probability of arriving at the proper capital structure.

In addition to working capital, the financing of the purchase or lease of production equipment, delivery and production vehicles, automobiles, office equipment, and other hard assets occurs early in the game. (Chapter 9 describes appropriate financing sources and forms for these hard assets.) This chapter focuses exclusively on raising capital to pay for operating expenses.

Initial capital to start a business—seed money—nearly always comes from capital contributions of the businessowner and equity or loans from family and friends. As pointed out in previous chapters, banks and other financial institutions rarely lend seed money, unless, of course, you pledge sufficient non-business assets as collateral.

During the very early start-up phase, cash raised as seed money should be used to pay for market investigations, organization expenses, minimum office and research supplies, equipment and office lease expenses, prototype product development, and all other expenses necessary to determine the feasibility of bringing the product or service to market. In certain instances, feasibility study expenses can be funded through foundation grants and Small Business Innovative Research loans and grants as discussed later in this chapter; but, in most cases, seed money comes from the entrepreneur.

Once the market has been established and product prototype efforts completed, it's time to set up a company to start producing and selling the product or service, including arranging for the acquisition of facilities, equipment, personnel, and materials. Financing this first-stage development requires detailed estimates of what expenses will be incurred and what sales will be generated over the ensuing one to two years. As described in Chapter 3, these estimates then become the basis for a financing plan to support requests for working capital loans.

Many start-up businesses never get any further than the initial stage because they are unable to define in clear, concise terms what cash they need to move forward. Without succinct definitions of cash requirements, no bank or other institution will consider lending to a developing business.

The starting point for developing a first-stage working capital plan is to identify those expenses to be incurred over the ensuing 12 months. Once completed, this projection can be extended to a second 12 months. The next phase requires a conservative forecast of sales for each of the 12 month segments.

The construction of such a working capital plan differs slightly between manufacturing, retail, and service businesses, although each uses a similar format. Since estimating the cash requirements for manufacturing companies is the most complex of the three, this is a good place to begin.

A CASH PLAN FOR MANUFACTURING COMPANIES

Manufacturing businesses typically have 11 categories of cash expenditures. They need cash to pay for:

- Production materials and supplies
- Payroll, payroll taxes, group insurance, and worker's compensation

- Rent for production/warehouse/sales/administrative facilities
- Utilities and telephone
- Business insurance
- Transportation and freight
- Advertising and sales promotion
- Market research
- Product development
- Tools
- Other operating expenses to produce and sell the product or service

Although the format used to display forecasted cash requirements is not critical to a successful loan application, nearly all financial institutions accept the following standards:

1. Estimate cash expenditures for the shortest practical time period. Months are better than quarters; weeks are better than months. Estimates of daily expenditures, however, are impractical.

2. Project cash collections from credit sales conservatively. Very few companies meet trade payable obligations in less than 30 days. Estimate 30 to 60 days, on average.

3. Summarize weekly cash expenditures and receipts by month for one year.

4. Construct a separate inventory schedule showing expenditures for purchases and payroll and clearly identify corresponding sales of inventory. This is called an inventory flow schedule.

5. Estimate trade payable turnover conservatively. In other words, instead of using trade payables to finance working capital beyond 30 days, assume all payables will be paid within 30 days of receipt of the invoice. If you can extend credit beyond 30 days, that's extra cash.

6. Include all expenses necessary to produce and sell the product, as well as non-productive expenses such as occupancy and taxes.

7. Exclude any salary or draw for yourself.

8. Exclude expenditures for the purchase of production equipment, machinery, delivery vehicles, or automobiles. These items should be acquired with long-term funds, not working capital. However, include lease obligations for facilities, equipment, and automobiles.

Figure 6–1 illustrates one format for projecting a four-month cash flow for a small, start-up manufacturing company, using hypothetical amounts. A corresponding inventory flow schedule appears in Figure 6–2.

Figure 6–1

XYZ MANUFACTURING CORP.
CASH FLOW FORECAST

For the four months ended April 30, 19XX

	Jan.	Feb.	Mar.	Apr.	Total
Beginning receivables	0	0	50	110	0
Sales	0	50	100	125	275
Less: Collections	0	0	40	80	120
Ending receivables	0	50	110	155	155
Beginning trade payables	10	30	52	67	10
Purchases	20	40	50	50	160
Less: Payments	0	18	35	48	101
Ending trade payables	30	52	67	69	69
CASH RECEIPTS					
Collections from sales (15%)	0	0	6	14	20
Bank loans	280	43	85	106	514
Total receipts	280	43	91	120	533
CASH EXPENDITURES					
Principal payment of loans	0	0	34	77	111
Interest expense	3	3	4	4	14
Payment of trade payables	0	18	35	48	101
Payroll and payroll taxes	12	12	12	12	48
Employee health insurance and worker's compensation	3	3	3	3	12
Building rent	3	3	3	3	12
Electricity	2	2	2	2	8
Fuel	1	1	1	1	4
Water	2	2	2	2	8
Telephone	3	3	3	3	12
Business insurance	5	5	5	5	20
Operating supplies	7	7	7	7	28
Office supplies	3	3	3	3	12
Equipment lease payments	2	2	2	2	8
Transportation and freight	2	2	2	2	8
Advertising and sales promotion	7	7	7	7	28
Market research	6	6	6	6	24
Product development	10	10	10	10	40
Other operating expenses	2	2	2	2	8
Small tools	3	3	3	3	12
Total expenditures	76	94	146	202	518

Cash Surplus (Shortfall)	204	(51)	(55)	(82)	16
Less: Owner's salary/draw	4	4	4	4	16
NET CASH SURPLUS (SHORTFALL)	200	(55)	(59)	(86)	0
Beginning bank balance	5	205	150	91	5
Net cash surplus (shortfall)	200	(55)	(59)	(86)	0
Ending bank balance	205	150	91	5	5
BANK LOANS					
Term loan	280	280	280	280	280
Revolver:					
Beginning loan balance	0	0	43	94	0
New loans—85% of sales	0	43	85	106	234
Less: Principal payments—					
85% of collections	0	0	34	77	111
Ending loan balance	0	43	94	123	123
Total loan balances	280	323	374	403	403

Figure 6–2

XYZ MANUFACTURING CORP.
INVENTORY FLOW SCHEDULE

For the four months ended April 30, 19XX

	Jan.	Feb.	Mar.	Apr.	Total
Beginning inventory	0	32	59	71	0
Additions:					
Material purchases	20	40	50	50	160
Labor	12	12	12	12	48
Total additions	32	52	62	62	208
Cost of sales:					
Materials	0	20	40	50	110
Labor	0	5	10	13	28
Total cost of sales	0	25	50	63	138
Ending inventory	32	59	71	70	70

This example shows that the company needs two types of working capital loans: a one-year term loan; and, a working capital line of credit, or revolver, secured by a borrowing base of 85 percent of accounts receivable.

The term loan will be secured by a lien against inventory and a second position against all business equipment and vehicles, assuming such assets will be acquired with additional loans. A personal guarantee from the owner also will probably be required as additional collateral. Although some businessowners with a close personal contact at a commercial bank might be able to coerce the bank into granting an open line of credit, a revolving line is far more common.

Using a format that identifies sales and purchases on account and a corollary inventory flow schedule lays the groundwork for projected pro forma financial statements to be included in the financing plan.

Cash flow projections from the hypothetical XYZ Manufacturing Corp. demonstrate that if no loans were obtained, the company would have a shortfall for each of the four months of 73, 91, 58, and 21, respectively, resulting in a cumulative bank overdraft of 237 at the end of four months. This is calculated as follows:

	Jan.	Feb.	Mar.	Apr.	Total
Beginning bank balance	5	(68)	(159)	(217)	5
Cash receipts from collections	0	0	50	100	150
Expenditures	76	94	146	202	518
Less: Principal payment	0	0	34	77	111
Interest expense	3	3	4	4	14
Net operating expenditures	73	91	108	121	393
Total cash available (shortfall) without loans	(73)	(91)	(58)	(21)	(243)
Ending bank balance	(68)	(159)	(217)	(238)	(238)

This example illustrates one of the drawbacks in borrowing working capital funds on a revolving loan. Not only did the company need to borrow 280 on a term loan to keep it going until sales were sufficient to support a revolver (probably in the third quarter if sales growth continued as in the first four months), it also needed cash advances from a revolving credit line.

Compare this to the actual shortfall over the four months without any borrowings and it's easy to see the impact of debt service on cash balances. It would have been far cheaper to operate with equity capital if it had been available. Unfortunately, most small businesses don't enjoy the luxury of sufficient equity and are forced to turn to bank loans.

A CASH PLAN FOR RETAIL COMPANIES

Cash sales, fewer employees, less expenses, and faster inventory turns make a cash plan for a retail operation much less complex than for manufacturing companies. On the reverse side, small retail operations normally do not enjoy as high product margins as manufacturing companies. Furthermore, without receivables as loan collateral, bank borrowing becomes more difficult.

Figures 6-3 and 6-4 use the same format as the XYZ Manufacturing Corp. modified for a retail business.

Figure 6–3

ABC RETAIL CORP.
CASH FLOW FORECAST

For the four months ended April 30, 19XX

	Jan.	Feb.	Mar.	Apr.	Total
Sales	0	50	100	125	275
Beginning trade payables	0	40	90	100	0
Purchases	40	80	110	130	360
Less: Payments	0	30	100	120	250
Ending trade payables	40	90	100	110	110
CASH RECEIPTS					
Collections from sales (15%)	0	50	100	125	275
Bank loans	175	0	0	0	175
Total receipts	175	50	100	125	450
CASH EXPENDITURES					
Interest on bank loans	0	1	1	1	3
Payment of trade payables	0	30	100	120	250
Payroll and payroll taxes	5	5	5	5	20
Employee health insurance and worker's compensation	1	1	1	1	4
Building rent	3	3	3	3	12
Electricity	1	1	1	1	4
Fuel	2	2	2	2	8
Water	0	1	0	1	2
Telephone	3	3	3	3	12
Business insurance	6	6	6	6	24
Operating supplies	3	3	3	3	12
Office supplies	3	3	3	3	12
Lease payments	2	2	2	2	8
Transportation and freight	3	3	3	3	12
Advertising and sales promotion	10	10	10	10	40
Market research	1	0	1	0	2
Other operating expenses	2	2	2	2	8
Total expenditures	45	76	146	166	433
CASH SURPLUS (SHORTFALL)	130	(26)	(46)	(41)	17
Less: Owner's salary/draw	4	4	4	4	16
NET CASH SURPLUS (SHORTFALL)	126	(30)	(50)	(45)	1

Beginning bank balance	5	131	101	51	5
Net cash surplus (shortfall)	126	(30)	(50)	(45)	1
Ending bank balance	131	101	51	6	6
BANK LOANS					
Term loan balance	175	175	175	175	175

Figure 6–4

ABC RETAIL CORP.
INVENTORY FLOW SCHEDULE

For the four months ended April 30, 19XX

	Jan.	Feb.	Mar.	Apr.	Total
Beginning inventory	0	40	80	110	0
Add: Purchases	40	80	110	130	360
Less: Cost of sales	0	40	80	100	220
Ending inventory	40	80	110	140	140

Note that without credit sales and with an inventory of material only, the company can get by with a term loan of only 175. If sales don't pick up in the next two or three months, however, it may have to return to the well for an additional term loan.

Terms loans for retail establishments are frequently easier to arrange than for a manufacturing company. Resale inventory can be used as collateral and banks know that it can be liquidated for at least its cost. In a manufacturing operation, raw material liquidating values are far more uncertain. Personal guarantees will probably be required here as well.

A CASH PLAN FOR SERVICE BUSINESSES

The major variations between a cash flow plan for service businesses and retail companies relate to inventory and payables calculations. Although most service businesses purchase supplies and other items on credit and thus incur trade payables, because the amounts are generally small, they can be treated as cash purchases for purposes of the cash plan. In addition, since service businesses rarely maintain inventory levels of anything other than miscellaneous supplies, this asset cannot be used as loan collateral. On the other hand, as Figure 6-5 illustrates, the amount of outside capital required to start a service business runs significantly less than either manufacturing or retail businesses.

Figure 6-5

LMN SERVICE CORP.
CASH FLOW FORECAST

For the four months ended April 30, 19XX

	Jan.	Feb.	Mar.	Apr.	Total
Sales	0	25	30	60	115
CASH RECEIPTS					
Collections from sales	0	25	30	60	115
Bank loans	100	0	0	0	100
Total receipts	100	25	30	60	215
CASH EXPENDITURES					
Interest on bank loans	1	1	1	1	4
Payroll and payroll taxes	8	8	8	8	32
Employee health insurance and worker's compensation	2	2	2	2	8
Building rent	1	1	1	1	4
Electricity	1	0	1	0	2
Fuel	0	1	0	1	2
Telephone	6	6	6	6	24
Business insurance	3	3	3	3	12
Office supplies	8	8	8	8	32
Lease payments	2	2	2	2	8
Transportation (automobile)	3	3	3	3	12
Advertising and sales promotion	10	10	10	10	40
Market research	3	3	3	3	12
Other operating expenses	2	2	2	2	8
Total expenditures	50	50	50	50	200
CASH SURPLUS (SHORTFALL)	50	(25)	(20)	10	15
Less: Owner's salary/draw	4	4	4	4	16
NET CASH SURPLUS (SHORTFALL)	46	(29)	(24)	6	(1)
Beginning bank balance	5	51	22	(2)	5
Net cash surplus (shortfall)	46	(9)	(24)	6	1
Ending bank balance	51	22	(2)	4	4
BANK LOANS					
Term loan balance	100	100	100	100	100

In most cases, borrowing from a bank is nearly impossible without personal assets as loan collateral. With the exception of furniture, office equipment, and perhaps an automobile, all of which will probably be financed with an installment loan or other long-term debt, service businesses don't have any assets of interest to banks.

Most people find that starting a service business requires more equity capital, simply because of the lack of business assets to support debt. On the other hand, it normally doesn't take a service business nearly as long to get up and running as a retail or manufacturing company; and operating expenses can be more easily controlled.Once the business begins to generate sales, banks become more eager to participate in working capital loans. But in the beginning, their conservatism gets in the way.

PRIMARY SOURCES OF SHORT-TERM CREDIT

Regardless of the type of business start-up, short-term credit remains a serious problem. Creativity becomes the name of the game. The trick is to locate a financing source willing to gamble on your ability to grow the business and at the same time not charge exorbitant interest or fees.

Five primary sources of short-term working capital can be used for first-stage financing:

- Commercial banks
- Venture funds
- Small investment banks
- Foreign banks
- Small Business Administration

As previously explained, conservative commercial banks demand substantial collateral for any type of loan. They also shy away from start-up working capital loans, regardless of collateral. Other financing sources often look at first-stage funding differently. Given the right situation many jump at the opportunity to participate. For ease of discussion, four broad groupings can be used to match various types of businesses with the most likely funding sources:

1. Businesses offering products or services in industries experiencing rapid growth.
2. Businesses operating in stable industries with opportunistic local markets.
3. Businesses that are now or expect to be selling internationally.

4. Businesses engaged in selling products or services in highly fragmented, local markets that force a market "cap" on the growth of the individual company.

RAPID GROWTH MARKETS

Health care diagnosis and treatment, housing and transport for the elderly, top of the line travel and leisure activities, advanced telecommunications, and alternate fuel sources represent rapid growth markets. First-stage short-term financing for companies selling into these markets is more competitive and easier to arrange than for companies in less glamorous markets.

All risk-oriented, high-return financial sources—venture funds, small investment banks, foreign merchant banks, high net worth individuals—support companies in rapid growth markets. The advent of microcomputer markets brought thousands of small business start-ups to Silicon Valley and several other locations. Many of these companies obtained first-stage capital exclusively from venture capital firms. As these companies grew and eventually went public, venture capitalists netted huge appreciations on their investments.

Their success from investing in computer technology businesses encouraged venture funds to examine other industries as equally high potential targets. Throughout the 1970s and 1980s, small venture capital firms became large investment complexes. Higher levels of funds became available. The euphoric explosion on Wall Street encouraged even greater risk-taking in first-stage, rapid growth businesses.

Today high risk investment fervor has cooled somewhat. Even though enormous funds continue to be available, many venture firms have become more conservative in their assessment of first-stage risk. This cooling off period has seen venture firms and traditionally more conservative small investment banks merge activities to the point where today the two are practically indistinguishable. Small businesses in high-growth markets needing first-stage working capital funds still find the most ready source in small venture funds, however.

Venture capital is not cheap. These risk-takers typically demand annual investment returns of 25 to 40 percent, on average, over a five-year-period, *plus* substantial investment appreciation either by refinancing at the end of five years or through a public issue. Obviously, this is why venture funds seek out high-growth markets; no other company could afford to pay such high returns.

Complete listings of venture capital firms may be found in most libraries. The best two are "Pratt's Guide to Venture Capital Sources," published by Venture Economics, and the "Directory of Venture Capital Clubs," which lists private investment clubs formed specifically to invest in first-stage ventures. The latter publication is available for $9.95 directly from the International Venture Capital Institute, Inc, P.O.Box 1333, Stamford, Conn. 06904. Finally, a directory of members may be obtained from the National Venture Capital Association, 1655 North Fort Myer Drive, Suite 700, Arlington, Va. 22209; (703)528-4370.

STABLE INDUSTRY, GROWING LOCAL MARKET

Growing local markets are usually small, niche markets. An entrepreneur properly determines a local market need and starts a business to service it. The financial services industries offered such opportunities in several areas of the country during the latter half of the 1980s.

As regulations governing intrastate and interstate bank expansion loosened, a wave of bank mergers eliminated small local banks from neighborhoods and small towns. Evaluating this vacuum as a potentially high-growth niche market, investors formed new, small banks to service small businesses and individuals in the local area.

Waste management is another example of a growing local niche market. Evironmental pressures forced the development of technologies to convert liquid and solid waste to socially beneficial products. In several regions of the country companies grabbed the opportunity to develop technologies and facilities to convert trash to alternate energy sources.

Small, local investment banks were formed to provide first-stage working capital funding for companies involved in these opportunistic local markets. Many began as limited partnerships, soliciting investment funds from high net worth individuals and local corporations. Others branched out from original venture funds in an effort to diversify their holdings.

Today, small investment banks remain the best source of capital for stable, local market businesses. Just as with venture capital funds, however, expect to give up an ownership share, perhaps controlling interest, and plan to take your company public in five to seven years.

INTERNATIONAL MARKETS

Companies selling internationally or expecting to take this step in the near future, attract capital from both foreign and government sources. Selling internationally may mean exporting products. It may entail selling services overseas, as with global construction companies. Or it may mean actually establishing a presence on foreign soil. First-stage working capital financing takes three forms: trade credit, guarantees, and short-term debt. Most cash ultimately comes from commercial banks, but loan collateral must be raised from third parties.

Collateral to secure short-term bank debt comes from two primary sources: guarantees from the federally sponsored Export-Import Bank (Eximbank); and letters of credit (L/Cs) from foreign banks. An array of options exist in Eximbank programs. Some go through the SBA, others come direct from Eximbank. Trade credit may be extended to the foreign buyer who, in turn, issues an L/C for the exporter to draw against for working capital.

Eximbank also issues guarantees enabling an exporter's commercial bank to extend short-term working capital loans. This federal agency also lends short-term funds direct to the exporter. A quick phone call to Eximbank triggers a flood of information about how to apply for financial assistance.

Foreign banks play a vital role in financing exports from the United States. They also engage in financing the development of overseas facilities for manufacturing, distribution, or sales activities. Large British merchant banks such as Warburg or Morgan Grenfell have little interest in funding first-stage capital but divisions of clearing banks, such as Barclays de Zoete Weld, Lloyd's, and County NatWest, continue to support new business development. Although direct contact with these merchant banks can be made, working through a professional advisor brings better results. Commercial banks also help with reference letters.

Chapters 12 and 13 detail specific government programs and other sources of capital for global trade, and explore the pros and cons of these sources compared to merchant banks.

FRAGMENTED AND MATURE LOCAL MARKETS

Without question, raising first-stage working capital for businesses in fragmented, mature local markets is the most difficult of the four possibilities examined here. Businesses servicing these markets include machine shops, general and subcontractors in the building trades, auto repair shops, specialty food stores, professional practices, and so on. No obvious source stands ready to provide working capital loans. Most first-stage working capital must be raised through commercial banks or friends. Depending on the location and the current status of federal funding allocations, additional loans might be obtained directly from the SBA, although they have become increasingly difficult to arrange.

External capital for this type of start-up usually comes from small commercial banks. As previously pointed out, however, banks of any size shy away from first-stage financing without non-business collateral. The SBA remains a primary source of such collateral.

Rather than funding a small business directly, the SBA prefers to issue guarantees to secure commercial bank loans. Although criteria frequently changes, as of this writing, the SBA guarantees 90 percent of small business loans up to $155,000 and 85 percent for an additonal $500,000. Interest rates are limited to 2.25 to 2.75 percentage points over prime. In addition, the SBA charges a placement fee of 2 percent of the amount of the loan.

The SBA guarantees term loans, with repayment extending to 25 years in some cases. Typically, however, to placate recalcitrant banks, the SBA limits terms for pure working capital funding to five to seven years. (Chapters 9 and 10 describe SBA financing assistance for the acquisition of equipment and facilities.)

SBA offices are located in most cities and have application forms available. As previously mentioned, an appointment with a SCORE representative is part of the application process. Also, to qualify, the applicant must be turned down by at least two banks.

Unfortunately, not all commercial banks lend against SBA guarantees. For best results, first search out a bank willing to participate. Then contact the SBA. The application process generally moves quickly and smoothly with a participating bank already on board. Of course, a company must meet the definition of a small business to qualify, but this shouldn't be a problem at the first stage.

A relatively new program has been established under the Women's Business Ownership Act that encourages SBA-guaranteed loans up to $50,000. To avoid charges of sexual discrimination both men and women may apply. Pragmatically, women have a much better chance.

FINANCING START-UP RESEARCH AND DEVELOPMENT PROJECTS

If part of your need for working capital financing relates to the development of a new product, you might qualify for two special sources—the Small Business Innovation Research (SBIR) program or private foundation grants. Neither of these sources applies universally. Each requires that an applicant meet specific criteria as to size, definition of research project, and application of final product. For those companies qualifying, however, both the SBIR and private grants are an inexpensive way to raise working funds without pledging non-business assets for security.

SMALL BUSINESS INNOVATIVE RESEARCH PROGRAM

The Small Business Innovation Research (SBIR) program is a set-aside allocation of funds by 11 federal departments. These allocations are to be used for grants and initial contracts with entrepreneurs to develop new products and services, and then to bring these innovations to market. Small businesses fitting the SBA definition qualify. The application process involves the submission of competitive bids to one or more of these 11 departments and agencies (*see* Appendix D for listing).

The SBIR program consists of three phases. Phase I provides funding up to $50,000 to study the feasibility of or to perform theoretical research for projects with significant interest to the U.S. government. These studies may last up to six months. After completing the feasibility study, the applicant may submit a bid for funding under Phase II.

Both Phase I and Phase II require competitive bidding. Funding may be outright grants or it might involve actual contracts to develop a specific product. Small businesses applying for this assistance must be over 50 percent U.S. owned and operated. Furthermore, the project must provide the primary employment for the individual making application. (Primary employment is defined as over 50 percent of a person's time and income.)

Phase II provides financing of up to $500,000 for the further development of the most promising projects from Phase I. Generally, this involves developing a prototype of the product and satisfactorily testing its feasibility. Successful completion of Phase II leads to the opportunity to enter Phase III.

Phase III covers the commercialization of the product. This may involve the acquisition of a production facility and equipment, implementing a marketing organization, and advertising or sales promotion programs. Phase III is not funded by the government. However, companies successfully completing Phase II can expect to receive significant assistance from the applicable federal agency for sourcing private funding from either a bank or other financial institution.

Each of the departments and agencies involved in the SBIR program publishes annual listings of proposed topics. These topics cover very real needs of the department or agency. They reflect requirements for products or services that cannot be developed internally.

A great deal of departmental independence exists in determining what topics to solicit. Congress allocates R & D funds to each of the departments and agencies and the appropriate officials then decide how to spend these funds and when to grant the awards. It doesn't take long to determine that some agencies are easier to work with than others. The applicant has the right to choose which department or agency to submit a bid to. Several may list the same topic, in which case simultaneous bids may be submitted.

The SBA can tell you which SBIR projects will be included in forthcoming bid lists. They are published in "pre-solicitation" lists, available on request from the Office of Innovation, Research and Technology, U.S. Small Business Administration, 1441 L Street NW—Room 500, Washington, DC 20416; (202) 653-6458

After choosing the topic, or topics, contact the appropriate department or agency directly to receive solicitations as soon as they get released.

The content of bid packages follows the same format as financing plans used for private financial institutions, with slight modifications. One exception requires a narrative describing how you visualize the importance of the product you are developing. Be sure to include persuasive material explaining why and how the particular department or agency needs your product. This "vision" of your product's application frequently provides the edge in competitive evaluation.

Successfully meeting all the terms and conditions of the development contract enables the developer to retain ownership of the technology. A product with commercial value may be marketed in the private sector rather than to the government. There is no obligation to enter into extended government contracts.

As with raising capital from any source, relationships can be extremely important in any government bid. With hundreds of companies submitting bid proposals, yours can easily drift to the bottom of the pile. Two relationships prevent this from happening. First, get your congressional representative or senator to go to bat for you. We all know Washington is run on favors. Others employ this approach and you might as well, too, just to stay in the game. Second, employ a professional advisor to help with the preparation of the bid package. Be sure the advisor is well known in the specific department or agency to which you apply. Obviously, to be of assistance, the advisor must have concrete experience submitting SBIR bids. Don't use a novice under any circumstances. That can be worse than not getting any help.

Employees of state organizations that work with the SBIR provide excellent advisory assistance. They usually help you select the most favorable departments and agencies as well as the most desirable topics. Their contacts in the Washington bureaucracy provide a means for arranging confidential evaluations of your project before submitting the bid. They can also point the way toward professors in local universities whose stamp of approval on your bid will give it an air of legitimacy.

In addition to providing assistance in the preparation of bid packages, many states and some cities provide direct financial assistance for small business research and development projects. These local agencies do not compete with the SBIR but are complementary to the program. They finance companies not otherwise qualified to receive federal funds. Your state small business development agency can identify what is available in your locale. If you can't locate the phone number, ask your local chamber of commerce for it. Appendix C lists several of these state organizations.

PRIVATE FOUNDATIONS

In addition to providing financing for the start-up of socially beneficial businesses, many private foundations also get involved in funding development projects. Nearly all of these foundations insist that the project results in social benefits to the community or society in general, the same as when funding start-up companies.

To be socially beneficial, the new product, process, or technology must relate to one of the following: ecological conservation, human health, renewal of blighted areas, improving the living standards of the poor, historic restoration, religious understanding, transportation improvement, agricultural development, or community service. If your project qualifies, several foundations stand ready to assist in providing working capital funds, either as outright grants or in the form of very low-interest loans.

Foundation grants and loans are very small; most range between $1,000 and $25,000, occasionally as high as $50,000. After a research project has been started and market testing indicates both a demand and a high probability of commercial/social success some foundations increase their grants up to $70,000.

Grants for feasibility studies are hard to get. Most foundations insist that you bring the project through an initial market feasibility study before applying for assistance. They do fund the construction of a prototype model, however, and many help with initial marketing efforts.

Programs that further the charitable objectives of the foundation and those that flow through existing non-profit organizations under Section 501(c)(3) of the Internal Revenue Code qualify for aid. Private foundation loans and grants are most effective when used in conjunction with funding from other sources such as the SBA, the SBIR program, or private venture capital funds. It becomes easier to attract the interest of these parties if partial funding can be raised through private grants and awards.

SUMMARY

Raising short-term working capital during a company's first-stage development can be a difficult exercise. At this stage few, if any, business assets are available for use as loan collateral. An earnings history has not yet been established. Management expertise remains an unproven commodity. Market acceptability has not been solidified.

Lenders and investors put first-stage financing in the high-risk category. Conservative commercial banks are particularly hesitant to fund working capital prior to developing a solid base of receivables and inventory. Yet, life goes on. New businesses are started every day and the needs for first stage working capital are met.

THE CASH PLAN

Prior to approaching any financing source, cash requirement forecasts must be prepared as part of the financing plan. Manufacturing companies have the best shot at interesting a bank in a working capital revolver, providing receivables can be generated relatively quickly. A short-term loan secured by non-business assets should also be available from commercial banks, assuming market testing has been completed and the product introduction period will be short.

Retail businesses without a receivables base usually resort to bank term loans. Banks seem less hesitant to grant short-term loans to retail establishments because readily salable inventory can be pledged as collateral. Personal guarantees add to the collateral base.

Service businesses require less working capital to get started than either retail or manufacturing companies. Few hard assets or receivables make bank financing hard to arrange. Loans from friends and family members or equity contributions by the owner normally tide the business over until sales begin generating a profitable history.

Market Served

A company's market or industry influences where to look for operating capital. Rapid growth markets attract venture capital funds. Stable industries in growing local markets appeal to small investment banks. Financing from venture capital or small investment banks nearly always involves additional equity from these sources, necessitating sharing company ownership.

Foreign merchant banks play a major role in financing first-stage working capital for overseas branches and divisions. Working capital to support export programs can be obtained through various programs of the Eximbank. It takes the form of trade credit to the foreign buyer and direct loans to the exporter. Guarantees that enable commercial banks to provide short-term loans are the most common form of Eximbank assistance .

Companies in fragmented, local markets find the SBA the most likely source of capital. Although the SBA makes some direct loans, guarantees continue to be the most common form of assistance.

Research and Development

Unusual financing sources for small business research and development funding consist of the SBIR program and private foundation grants. Although requiring competitive bids, SBIR financing provides short-term loans and grants up to $50,000 under Phase I and up to $500,000 under Phase II. A variety of private foundations also make grants and low-cost loans, providing the project will have socially beneficial results. Funding is limited to $50,000, but more commonly in the $1,000 to $25,000 range.

CHAPTER 7

Funding A Franchise Start-up Business

Many people choose franchising over starting a business from scratch. Although more expensive to start and to operate, and certainly more restrictive, a combination of proven markets, franchiser training, and ease of entry make starting a franchise a popular alternative. Its popularity has made franchising practically a way of life in small business America.

Not counting the hundreds of very small, home-based franchises, the Department of Commerce lists well over one thousand franchisers eager to help a person start a business—for a fee. Franchising is especially prominent in small retail and service businesses. Fast food restaurants, laundries, budget hotels, employment agencies, and real estate firms owe their growth primarily to franchising. In addition to the Department of Commerce, several current books list the names, addresses, and criteria for hundreds of smaller franchises.

Franchising has been so successful over the past two decades because it offers a vehicle for the inexperienced entrepreneur to own a business. If you are willing and able to pay the franchise fee and possess the required personal net worth, you can become a business owner in nearly any industry you choose, regardless of prior experience. Reputable franchisers take the guesswork out of starting a business. They provide market research, advertising, personnel training, site selection, and a variety of other services to get a business up and running.

There are also two distinct disadvantages to owning a franchise:

1. It costs more to start and operate a franchise.
   a. You must buy all the equipment, furniture, and fixtures as specified by the franchiser. This eliminates the possibility of shopping for the best deal.
   b. The up-front franchise fee for the privilege of using the franchise name can be very expensive. Typical amounts range from $5,000 to $500,000; even much more in larger franchises.
   c. Once in operation, the franchiser takes a percentage of gross receipts as

royalties. Although the rate varies widely, royalties run 3 to 7 percent of gross revenues in most franchises.

2. You are not your own boss.

   a. It's your business, yet it isn't. You have the responsibility for the company's success or failure. You are solely liable for its debts. Yet, a franchiser dictates what location to choose, what and how much advertising to do, what systems and procedures to follow, and in general specifies precisely how the business will be run. You have the responsibility; but the franchiser has the authority.

In many respects, financing a franchise start-up involves the same steps as starting a business from scratch. The same elements must be included in a financing plan: market analyses, production and sales projections, estimated personnel requirements, and forecasted cash flow and earnings statements. Many of the same financing sources also participate: commercial banks, asset-based lenders, venture capital firms, SBICs, and the SBA. But here the similarity ends.

On the negative side, franchisees incur costs that a start-up business avoids: franchise fees, royalties, advertising allotments, and many others. From a positive perspective, however, a franchise business has many things going for it that a new start-up company doesn't. Much of the work and assimilation of financial performance data from other franchises has already been done by the franchiser. Lenders place high reliance on such financial performance.

Franchisers do a good job of documenting the key ingredients for reducing risk: market research to determine the level of sales to expect in the first and second years; equity cash requirements to support the early stages; operating cost structures and cash flow projections during the start-up period; and a variety of other information necessary to start the business from a sound base.

From a lender's perspective, starting a franchise is very similar to buying a going business. The product or service has already gained market acceptance. Production methods and equipment configurations have been defined. Personnel requirements, proven advertising campaigns, and favorable site parameters have been market-tested. In addition, many franchisers require new franchisees to attend intensive training classes conducted by the franchiser. Upon completion, this training gives a new entrepreneur the technical capability and presumably the supervisory talent to manage the business. With all this information and management training provided by the franchiser, financial institutions view their risk as substantially lessened. Although not as low as financing the acquisition of a going business, franchise risk is certainly less than with a non-franchise start-up.

Thousands of franchise businesses proliferate the marketplace. Many offer nothing more than a company name and perhaps a computer program, such as many of the so-called "home-based" businesses that have become so popular. Being so small, these businesses seldom need any external financing.

At the other end of the spectrum, franchises like McDonald's, General Motors and Ford dealerships, and 300-room Holiday Inn and Hilton hotels offer the franchisee a "blue chip" opportunity to walk into a profitable, well-known, quality business. The acquisition of blue chip franchises requires millions of dollars, a solid industry reputation, and a substantial amount of equity.

This chapter does not address financing the start-up of either simple, home-based franchises or large, blue chip businesses. The first is too simple, the latter too complex for a book of this scope. The remarks and analyses that follow address businesses that characterize the majority of reputable, well-established, mid-size franchise companies such as AlphaGraphics print shops, Midas auto repair shops, Baskin-Robbins ice cream stores, Days Inn roadside motor inns, West Coast video stores, and so on.

Because of the enormous number of manufacturing, distribution, retail, and service businesses that fit the franchise mold, it proves helpful to limit financing alternatives to some broad categories. The balance of this chapter focuses on franchises with the following characteristics:

1. Hard assets consisting of equipment, fixtures, or vehicles, either singly or combined
2. Soft assets consisting of inventory and a modest level of receivables, although many try to operate on a cash basis as much as possible
3. Owner-managed with not more than 10 employees
4. Annual sales ranging between $100,000 and $1 million
5. Equity capital of between $25,000 and $200,000
6. Franchiser-guaranteed exclusive sales territories

Although financial requirements vary with different businesses, certain minimum standards exist for most franchises. Initial funding to get the business up and running typically falls between $100,000 and $1 million. Six types of start-up expenditures must be covered during this initial phase:

- Franchising fee
- Space rental
- Equipment purchases
- Inventory purchases
- Organization and pre-opening expenses
- Operating capital

In addition, you will need money for personal living expenses while the business incubates.

SEED MONEY OR START-UP EXPENSES

Significant differences exist between the initial funding for a franchise and a non-franchise business. Chapter 6 discussed the need for seed money when starting a business from scratch compared to first-stage working capital to produce and market products or services.

Seed money was defined as capital needed to incubate an idea, to bring a potential new product or service through the initial stages of market research and product design. It was pointed out that except in those rare instances when a high-tech product might attract the attention of venture capital, seed money must be contributed by friends, family members, and the entrepreneur. Little possibility exists for raising seed money through financial institutions.

The amount of seed money required to launch a new business idea is generally quite small: most ideas can be incubated for less than $15,000. Once market demand has been identified and initial design and development work completed, first-stage financing brings the product to production capability. Equipment, inventory, facilities, and other first-stage operating needs can be handled with bank loans, venture capital, and SBA assistance.

Businesses starting from scratch develop slowly. Financing can be arranged gradually over a period of time. As the business begins to take hold, external capital becomes increasingly easier to attract until eventually a business achieves second stage status and expands to new heights.

COSTS OF FRANCHISING

A new franchise business takes a different road. Because the product or service is already established in the marketplace, product design and initial market research expenses do not come into play. Franchisers normally take care of any market investigation for choosing an appropriate site and establishing sales territories or market boundaries. Therefore, the need for seed money goes away. The franchisee immediately steps into the first stage of development, financed with external funds in much the same way as any other business.

Seed capital doesn't enter the franchising picture, but new expenses arise that are not present when starting a business from scratch. Although up-front expenses vary in magnitude and importance for different franchises, the following represent those typically included in small and mid-size franchise agreements:

- Franchising fee ($5,000 to $50,000)
- Quality control system ($2,000 to $5,000)
- Franchiser advertising (0.5 to 3 percent of gross revenues)
- Royalties (3 to 7 percent of gross revenues)

- Complete configuration of standardized equipment ($35,000 to $250,000)
- Specific location and facilities requirements (various)
- Standard signs ($5,000 to $15,000)
- Franchiser designated decor and appointments (various)
- Bookkeeping system ($1,000)
- Specified types and amount of inventory and/or operating supplies ($10,000 to $60,000)
- Personnel uniforms/dress code ($500 to $2,500)
- Personnel training charges ($900/day per person)
- Travel costs to and from the training site ($1,500 to $2,000 per person)

It cannot be categorically stated that it takes more money to start and operate a franchise than a non-franchise business, but it probably will. In addition to fees, royalties, training costs, group advertising, and standardized decor and signs, franchises require a complete configuration of production equipment and basic inventory levels before opening the doors. Seldom does starting a business from scratch require such large expenditures in the beginning.

Following is a typical example of a franchiser's estimate of the cost of starting a printing business requiring equipment and an inventory of supplies.

SIR SPEEDY, INC.

This fast-print franchiser boasts more than 1,000 individual franchises worldwide. The following information came from material furnished by the company to anyone interested in exploring the possibility of joining their network. This example also appeared in my book, *The Battle-Weary Executive.* Further information can be obtained directly from the corporate office of the franchiser at 23131 Verdugo Drive, Laguna Hills, CA 92653-1342.

The cost to own a Sir Speedy franchise printing center breaks down as follows:

Franchise fee—For the use of their name, logos, and trademarks $5,000 is payable with application for the franchise and the balance payable prior to attendance at the required training program. — $17,500

Start-up Costs—Covers the cost of the training program, travel and lodging while in training, market research, site-location study, lease negotiation assistance, applied window and wall graphics, initial fixtures, furniture, and inventory. Total is payable prior to attendance at required training program. — 22,500

Equipment—Includes equipment, cabinets, counters, shelving, and furniture. Though not required to buy this equipment from Sir Speedy, a franchisee must use this specific equipment. (How can you use it if you don't get it from them?) — 71,000

Signs—Must meet the specifications set forth by Sir Speedy. Cost will vary with local ordinances.	1,750
Working Capital—	
Pre-opening expenses	8,000
Operating capital for first few months	37,000
<u>TOTAL</u> Cash Required to Start	$157,750

In addition, Sir Speedy recommends that new owners have additional funds available to cover their personal living expenses for a minimum of eight months. In other words, the franchiser estimates that no cash will be available from the business for an owner's salary for at least eight months.

And, of course, royalties must be paid:

For the first year	4% of gross sales
Each subsequent year	6% of gross sales

An incentive program offers a descending sliding scale of royalties based on attaining specific levels of sales volume.

In addition to the name, logos, and trademarks, Sir Speedy provides the following support at the franchisee's expense:

- *Training*—Two weeks at Sir Speedy's National Training School in Laguna Hills, CA.
- *Equipment*—Offset printing, laser graphic, computer and fax equipment, fixtures and furniture.
- *Supplies*—Optional centralized national purchasing agreements.
- *Market survey and site selection*—Assistance in determining appropriate site location and in negotiating lease arrangements.
- *Opening promotion*—Opening marketing program and advertising.
- *National advertising*—Nationwide advertising campaign to promote Sir Speedy as "The Business Printers."
- *Continuing field support*—Qualified representatives to assist with the growth and development of the printing center.

The franchiser will, at the option of the new owner, provide an equipment lease arrangement totaling $71,000 through its affiliated leasing company. Monthly lease payments run approximately $1,400 plus sales tax for seven years. Additionally, the franchiser will assist in arranging SBA-guaranteed financing for up to $40,000 on a 10 year amortization schedule through Allied Credit, providing the owner has adequate personal collateral to secure the loan.

The Sir Speedy example represents the cost and franchiser support for one type of franchise. It is not intended as either an endorsement or repudiation of Sir

Speedy. It represents an example of how one franchise is structured, and it is by no means inclusive. Every franchiser dictates slightly different conditions.

In nearly all cases, however, the franchise agreement calls for a cash down payment, working capital, pre-opening and living expense requirements, and strict compliance with the facilities layout, advertising, and operating systems as defined by the franchiser.

The sources of funds for financing a franchise start-up are practically the same as for the first stage financing of any small business, with one exception. Some franchisers provide financing assistance, either through the parent company itself or through a finance subsidiary or affiliated company. Others have the capability of helping a franchisee source independent bank financing.

The major difference between financing franchise and non-franchise start-ups relates to the level of difficulty in obtaining appropriate funding. As previously described, franchises are far more attractive to banks and other lending institutions than non-franchise businesses because of the reduced risk of failure. In addition, loan packages that combine short-term working capital financing with equipment term loans can be arranged.

FRANCHISER ASSISTANCE

Most franchisers do not provide direct financing for new franchisees. And with good reason. The whole purpose behind franchising businesses is to create a capital fund from franchise fees and royalties to expand the chain of franchises. To lend to or otherwise reinvest these funds in a new franchise deprives the franchiser of capital to meet its expansion objectives. Some franchisers don't share this view and offer either sourcing assistance or direct financial aid.

Franchisers seem to view financial aid from two opposing positions:

1. Lending money or otherwise being in the finance business is not the primary mission of the franchiser and it should therefore stay away from any financial aid.

2. Financial assistance enables the start-up of new franchises that would not have the resources to do it on their own.

Those who share the second opinion structure financial assistance in a number of different ways. Nearly all car rental franchisers require the franchisee to provide all initial start-up funding. However, they do help arrange lines of credit with the major automobile manufacturers or third-party financial institutions for inventory purchases.

State-of-the-art AlphaGraphics printing franchisees can lease equipment through an affiliate of the parent company. For years the 7-ELEVEN convenience store division of Southland Corporation constructed store buildings and leased them to franchisees. A few service franchises such as Molly Maid housekeeping provide direct financing for a substantial part of the initial franchise fee just to get the franchisee up and running.

As a new franchisee, you should be able to arrange some type of financial assistance from the parent. It may not take the form of direct loans or in-house leasing facilities, but as a minimum the franchiser should be in a position to help arrange commercial bank loans. If a franchiser won't go this far, it is probably the wrong one to hook up with.

COMMERCIAL BANK LOANS

As indicated in Chapter 6, commercial banks shy away from first stage working capital loans, unless a borrower has sufficient receivables or other collateral to use as security. In early stage companies, the risk of failure escalates. Even with receivables as collateral working capital loans can be hard to arrange.

Chapter 9 offers the same warning relating to term loans for equipment purchases. The longer the term, the less interest from commercial banks. Even a three to five year equipment loan is hard to sell. Banks know that equipment depreciates in value, sometimes very rapidly. If the value goes down faster than the loan balance, the bank has a loan outstanding without sufficient collateral. Commercial banks view both first-stage working capital loans and term financing as risks that in many cases preclude participation without a pledge of significant non-business collateral.

Commercial banks are more lenient when financing franchise start-ups. Franchiser support eliminates much of the business risk. The only significant unattended risk is the ability of the new owner to manage the business. Franchiser training programs mitigate this risk, somewhat.

Banks also regard term loans against franchise equipment as less risky. The equipment is new. Its life span is clearly established by other franchise operations. And the franchiser makes sure that the new operator acquires only that equipment needed for an efficient operation.

A third facet of franchises also piques bank interest. Compared to a non-franchise business, franchises enjoy a very short-term start-up period. Bankers know that the shorter the interval between opening the doors and generating sales, the faster cash begins to flow. And the faster cash flows, the easier it will be to begin repaying debt obligations. Although banks direct more attention to underlying loan security, they also recognize the value of cash flow early in a company's life.

Applying for a bank loan—either for working capital or for the acquisition of capital equipment—involves the same process as doing so for non-franchise first-stage financing. Bank relationships must be nurtured. Professional advisory assistance should be used to prepare pro forma cash flow and financial statements. A carefully conceived financing plan must be prepared. And, a professional presentation made to bank loan officers.

Franchisees have a real advantage over non-franchise businessowners when it comes to preparing a financing plan. Franchisers are enormously helpful in providing operating cost structures, personnel requirements, and sales projections from a data base of other, operating franchises. For example, most franchisers know the average time span to reach a cash flow break-even sales level—a sales volume which generates enough cash to cover all operating expenses. A simple extension of the sales curve permits a fairly reliable estimate of when the business will support full debt service payments.

Franchisers also know the minimum configuration of operating equipment necessary to produce the product or service commercially; that is, how much and what type of equipment must be purchased initially to generate projected sales. Since many franchisers require that the franchisee either purchase equipment through the parent company or purchase identically configured equipment elsewhere, estimating how much capital is needed, and its cost, becomes a simple task.

Finally, since most franchisers stipulate the minimum equity contribution required from the new entrant, banks have a hard time arguing whether or not such an amount is sufficient to support short- or long-term debt. In other words, the franchiser has already established an acceptable debt to equity ratio. This relieves a borrower of the necessity to justify the level of debt that the business can support.

Assistance from franchisers in each of these areas increases your chances of successfully negotiating commercial bank financing. It isn't a sure bet, but at least you have a head start. Personal relationships remain a crucial element in the success of any loan application. So does personal credit history and the availability of personal assets to support a guarantee. All things considered, commercial bank loans remain a viable option for financing franchise start-ups.

ASSET-BASED LENDERS

Asset-based lenders (ABLs) approach franchise equipment financing with the same criteria as they do for non-franchise businesses. With an effective means of liquidating equipment collateral in the event of default, ABLs pay less attention to assurances and support from franchisers than do commercial banks. Chapter 9 examines the use of ABLs for financing second-stage expansion. The same high cost and interference risks described there apply to ABL financing for franchises.

Franchisees with a poor credit history might look to ABLs as a source of working capital financing also. Although application fees and interest rates range substantially higher than with a commercial bank, ABLs pay less attention to previous credit problems. In nearly all cases, however, their insistence on a first position against all business assets—hard and soft—plus personal guarantees to cover the entire loan balance, makes funding through ABLs a less desirable alternative.

SALE/LEASEBACK COMPANIES

New companies are now being formed specifically to handle sale/leaseback financing for the acquisition of land, buildings, and equipment by franchisees. This recent innovation in franchise financing is not readily available for all franchises.

One example of a leasing company specializing in restaurant franchises is the Franchise Finance Corporation of America (FFCA). It provides 100 percent of the financing needs for restaurant franchises to acquire the land, building, and equipment necessary to start the business. FFCA actually purchases the assets and then leases them back to the franchisee at rates and terms consistent with the development needs of the franchise.

Many other leasing companies provide similar sale/leaseback financing but do not specialize in franchises. Businesses requiring their own building from which to operate, such as hotels and restaurants, find sale/leasebacks especially attractive. Those requiring large amounts of equipment, such as dry cleaning and car washes, also use this technique effectively.

Reputable franchisers keep track of what leasing companies are interested in taking on new sale/leaseback transactions in their industry. Contact your franchiser directly to learn about this possibility. Chapter 11 explores the advantages and risks of leasing original equipment and real estate without getting involved in sale/leaseback transactions.

SMALL BUSINESS ADMINISTRATION

The Small Business Administration (SBA) provides financing assistance to franchise as well as non-franchise start-ups, with no distinction between the two. The same size criteria must be met. The same application process applies. The same collateral requirements exist. Identical interest rates and bank participation rules are in effect.

Chapter 6 describes the types of SBA assistance available for getting working capital funding. Chapter 9 covers SBA participation for equipment financing. Chapter 10 explains SBA assistance for financing the acquisition of land and buildings.

It should be noted that even though the SBA does not officially distinguish between financing assistance for franchise and non-franchise businesses, pragmatically most SBA offices do. Franchiser support influences SBA decisions as readily as commercial banks. In fact, since banks must participate with the SBA, the reduced risk factors weigh equally on both parties.

RAISING EQUITY CAPITAL FOR FRANCHISES

All reputable franchisers require equity capital as part of the financing package. The initial equity contribution usually covers the franchising fee and must be paid up-front, when executing the franchise agreement and before beginning training.

Since the success of individual franchises weighs heavily on the reputation of the franchiser, most parent corporations demand a fairly high amount of equity contribution: significantly more than seed money for starting a non-franchise business. Equity capital of 20 to 30 percent of the franchiser's estimate of total cost is not unusual.

Raising this much equity can be a difficult task. For many, it eliminates franchises as a viable alternative, regardless of their ability to arrange debt financing for the balance of the start-up costs. Other, more creative entrepreneurs find a way around this hurdle by raising equity through partnerships or venture capital firms. At the same time, they raise additional capital beyond that needed for start-up costs. This reduces the need for debt financing as the business grows.

LIMITED PARTNERSHIPS FOR FRANCHISES

Limited partnerships (LPs) are gaining in popularity as a means of financing larger franchise start-ups. Hotels, car dealerships, equipment and vehicle rental companies, restaurants, resort complexes, and movie theaters have been financed through limited partnerships for years, both before the 1986 tax changes and since. Recently, limited partnerships are springing up in such diverse industries as booksellers, specialty farms, beer distributors, boat chartering companies, travel agencies, and technical schools.

Franchise start-ups offer the same reduced risk advantages to equity players as to lenders. Projected estimates of start-up capital, operating expenses, and sales growth add a level of credibility and certainty to cash flow projections that non-franchise businesses cannot muster.

The partnership provisions in LPs are as varied as the businesses being financed. Pre-1986 agreements stressed tax-shelter advantages. Now, LPs stress investment gain. To cover the extra tax burdens of the limited partners, agreements set minimum annual cash distributions to be used by partners to pay their taxes on partnership profits. This keeps them even as far as taxes are concerned and allows their investments to grow with the business.

It's easy enough to form a limited partnership. Any contract lawyer can draw up the agreement. You should be the general partner, responsible for running the franchise. The following example shows how the start-up of a small hotel franchise could be handled.

Cost of franchise:

A.	Equity down payment required for franchise fee	$200,000
B.	Start-up expenses, including supplies	150,000
C.	Land purchase and building construction cost	250,000
D.	Equipment and furnishings	175,000
E.	Working capital reserve	50,000
	TOTAL cost of franchise	825,000

Financing to be provided by:

A.	Equity from limited partnership—	
	1. General partner's equity	$100,000
	2. Limited partners' equity	
	(30 shares at $10,000 each)	300,000
	TOTAL equity	$400,000
B.	Mortgage loan secured by land and building	250,000
C.	Commercial bank term loan secured by equipment and furnishings	175,000
	TOTAL cost of franchise	$825,000

Terms of the partnership agreement call for operating profits and losses to be allocated equally to limited and general partners. The agreement also calls for an annual cash distribution to limited partners for the first three years of $2,000 per partnership share, beginning nine months after start-up. Under this scheme the limited partners get their investment back in five years, they can use the annual distribution to pay the tax on allocated profits, if any, and they still own 50 percent of the company. The general partner has financed the entire deal with only $100,000 personal equity and $425,000 debt.

VENTURE CAPITAL FUNDING

Small investment banks and some of the newer small venture capital firms like franchise start-ups. When high-flying ventures from the 1980s dried up or collapsed, these smaller investment companies increasingly turned to investments in more mundane industries with a lower risk of failure.

Some of these smaller venture companies call themselves investment banks, others still prefer the venture capital label. They are all structured the same, however, and the types and terms of investment remain similar. For purposes of this discussion, the term "venture fund" designates companies concentrating on equity and long-term debt investments in stable small businesses with long-term growth prospects.

Venture funds may be self-perpetuating or they may be liquidating. Self-perpetuating funds plow the earnings from investments back into additional investment opportunities. These funds continue to expand by investing in as many companies as cash allows. Financial professionals normally start and manage these funds.

Liquidating funds distribute most of their earnings to shareholders currently, keeping a modest amount on hand for the next investment. These funds handle only one or two investments concurrently. Their objective is to return as much cash as possible to their shareholders in as short a time frame as possible. Non-financial investors, such as lawyers, physicians, consultants, and business executives typically originate liquidating funds and get a professional accountant to manage them.

Franchises are ideal investment vehicles for venture funds. Short start-up intervals and assured product marketability keep the initial risk low. A franchise in a growing industry, which many of them are, provides the opportunity for eventual, long-term investment gain.

These venture funds normally prefer to finance the entire start-up on their own, with the exception of short-term working capital credit, which they pawn off on a commercial bank. Although financing structures vary all over the lot, the following shows how one might look, using the data from the earlier hotel franchise example.

Cost of franchise:

A.	Equity down payment required for franchise fee	$200,000
B.	Start-up expenses, including supplies	150,000
C.	Land purchase and building construction cost	250,000
D.	Equipment and furnishings	175,000
E.	Working capital reserve	50,000
	TOTAL cost of franchise	$825,000

Financing to be provided by:

A.	Equity from franchisee	$100,000
B.	From venture fund—	
	Equity contribution for 40 percent ownership	500,000
	Term loan for 7 years, secured by all land, building, and equipment	175,000
C.	From commercial bank—	
	Line of credit secured by second position on hard assets and franchisee's personal guarantee	50,000
	TOTAL cost of franchise	$825,000

Some venture funds prefer to finance the entire start-up with equity. Others like to use all equity in the beginning and then refinance with long-term debt when the business gets up and running. Still others prefer to keep their equity investment to a minimum and utilize their sources in the financial markets to bring in debt financing right away.

Regardless of the exact combination, managers of the venture fund make the contacts and arrange the entire financing package. In return, of course, venture funds expect a handsome return on investment. Many expect to recover at least 25 to 30 percent on average annually over a five- to seven-year period.

SUMMARY OF FINANCING SOURCES

Each financing source carries advantages and disadvantages. As with non-franchise, first-stage financing, the best choice depends on how much equity you put in, the magnitude of start-up costs, the amount of hard and soft assets, the industry and market characteristics, general economic conditions, financial market trends, anticipated market demand, and projected cash flow. Parameters applicable to a wide variety of franchises are meaningless. Each situation has so many variables that the efficacy of financing arrangements changes with each deal.

However, some commonality does exist. All franchises require a sizable amount of initial equity—at least enough to cover the franchise fee. High leveraging is usually not acceptable to franchisers. Also, as in any business, the more equity put in, the less debt service must be provided for. Common sense dictates keeping both long- and short-term debt as low as possible, at least during start-up stages.

The following broad comparisons apply to the more common franchise start-ups.

   1. **Franchiser assistance:**
      Form of financing—direct working capital and equipment loans
                            —equipment and building leases
                            —third party sourcing assistance
      Cost   —direct loans, application fee and interest at prime plus 3 to 5
      Availability   —most franchisers offer only third party assistance
      Risk   —high, because franchiser can easily reclaim business on default

   2. **Commercial bank loans:**
      Form of financing—short-term revolving line of credit
                            —three- to five-year term loans
                            —small mortgage loans
      Cost   —interest at prime plus 2 to 3
      Availability   —high, with franchiser support
      Risk   —low, because banks don't like to foreclose

3. **Asset-based lenders:**

Form of financing	—revolver against receivables/inventory
	—five- to seven-year term loan on equipment
	—some offer mortgage loans
Cost	—high application fee; interest at prime plus 5 to 7
Availability	—high, if sufficient hard assets
Risk	—very high, will foreclose faster than franchiser in the event of default

4. **Sale/leaseback companies:**

Form of financing	—sale and leaseback of land, buildings, and equipment
Cost	—reasonable, terms conform to business needs
Availability	—scarce, service only certain industries, but more are on the horizon
Risk	—low, because of individually structured terms

5. **Small Business Administration:**

Form of financing	—mostly bank guarantees, some direct loans
Cost	—prime plus 2.25 to 2.75
Availability	—varies, if bank is eager to participate, so is SBA
Risk	—very low

6. **External equity:**

Form of financing	—equity contributions from limited partnerships
	—venture funds combine equity and term loans
Cost	—limited partnerships expect to recover investment in five years through cash distributions
	—venture funds want 25 to 30 percent return in addition to recouping investment over five to seven years
Availability	—usually easy to arrange for larger franchises
	—difficult for small ones
Risk	—very low, equity is risk capital for the investor

Although franchises offer a faster and many times an easier way to start-up a new business, initial and ongoing costs run high. Payments for franchise fees, royalties, advertising allocations, equipment reserves, and other expenditures demanded by the franchiser don't exist in a non-franchise business.

In addition, franchises rob an entrepreneur of operating independence. Franchisers insist on uniform signs, advertising, decor, dress code, reporting systems, and a variety of other operating standards. Franchisees have the responsibility for success or failure and for all financial obligations; franchisers retain the authority to direct how the business will be operated.

Other than being able to get into a franchise without any experience, the main reason entrepreneurs choose franchising is the ease with which the start-up can be financed. Lenders and investors regard franchises as safer havens than non-franchise start-ups. They also realize a faster return on their money and higher collateral values. Although definite drawbacks exist, franchising continues to grow in popularity.

Chapter 8

Financing the Purchase of an Operating Business

Buying a going business frequently brings more income, quicker, and with less risk than either starting a business from scratch or starting a franchise. Wall Street has popularized LBOs (leveraged buyouts) for more than a decade. Learning that financial institutions also jumped at smaller LBOs, individual entrepreneurs opted to go the same route and acquired going businesses with a minimal equity investment.

Many excellent reference books detail the various steps in buying a business. If you are seriously thinking about going this route, the book *Buying In: A Complete Guide To Acquiring A Business Or Professional Practice* provides a detailed, step-by-step roadmap for achieving your goal in the shortest period at the least cost.

Financing the acquisition of a going business requires a different approach than raising first stage funds, either for working capital or for the purchase of hard assets. Financial institutions like to participate in acquisition financing because the target company already has an established product line and management or technical talent. The historical cash flow of the business gives a good indication of how soon and with what certainty the debt or equity will be repaid. In other words, financing the acquisition of an existing business lessens the risk for both lenders and investors of earning their required return and eventually getting their principal back.

Before getting into the details of acquisition financing I should mention that significant variations exist between the financing available to an existing company buying another business, and that which is available to an individual entrepreneur buying his or her first business.

When an operating company makes an acquisition a lending or investing institution's risk is reduced even further. Existing management and marketing organizations, market-accepted product lines, and perhaps production facilities of the buying company can be integrated with, or at least support, the acquired company. This substantially enhances the probability of a newly acquired business being successful and profitable. Therefore, financial institutions are significantly more eager to finance the acquisition of a going business by an existing company than they are a purchase by an individual or individuals.

Similar financing sources exist for both categories of buyers, but the ease of arranging the deal increases when an operating company makes the purchase.

The balance of this chapter addresses financing techniques applicable to the acquisition of a going business by an individual or partnership. It specifically excludes any analysis of techniques available for acquisitions by existing companies.

Several criteria affect the structure of an acquisition financing package:

1. Size of the company being acquired and, hence, the amount of the purchase price.
2. Character of the target company—manufacturing, retail, or service.
3. Location of both the target company and the acquiring party.
4. Profitability and growth record of the target.
5. Conditions in the economy as a whole and in the target company's market specifically.
6. Amount of equity capital contributed by the buyer in relation to the purchase price.
7. Amount of assets a buyer can pledge as additional, non-business security.

There are three distinct types of financing for acquisitions—debt, equity, and seller financing. Most smaller deals priced less than $100,000 are financed exclusively by the seller. Deals between $100,000 and $500,000 can be accomplished through a combination of seller financing and commercial bank term loans, augmented by mortgages or term loans from finance companies when necessary. In most cases, when the purchase price exceeds $500,000, both debt and equity capital should be used.

Seller financing may take one or a combination of four forms—buyer promissory notes, profit sharing arrangements called "earn outs", contingency payments, or seller consulting contracts.

The debt portion may consist of commercial bank short-term working capital debt, finance company long-term loans, investment bank mezzanine debt, and mortgage debt if real estate is involved. In more complex acquisitions, industrial revenue bonds and public bond issues may supplement this debt.

Equity funds may be evidenced by common stock shares, preferred shares with or without warrants, or in larger deals, convertible debentures. Funds may be derived from small investment banks, venture capital funds, private investors, or working or passive partners.

ESTABLISHING A REASONABLE PURCHASE PRICE

The amount of acquisition capital that can be raised depends on three primary factors—the cash flow generated by the business, the hard assets in the business, and the purchase price. Since the purchase price determines whether or not cash flow will be sufficient to meet debt or investment return obligations it pays to negotiate this first, before beginning the search for capital.

The number of methods for valuing a going business are limited only by one's imagination. Investors value publicly-traded companies by the current per share price measured by the published price/earnings ratio. Such ratios do not exist for privately-held businesses, however, so other means must be employed.

Hundreds of books, articles and pamphlets have been written setting forth what the writer deems to be the most equitable valuation method. Corporate leaders insist that the price/earnings ratio of publicly-traded companies in the same industry is the best measure. Investment bankers and other financial gurus prefer methods that discount future cash flow with assumed present value factors. Consultants advocate a multiple of annual cash flow, either historical or future, depending on whether they are on the buying or selling side. Conservative bankers place the value at what the company's hard assets would bring at a liquidation auction. And on and on it goes.

Everyone has a "best" method based on personal criteria. Unfortunately for the entrepreneurial buyer, no one way is the right way. Different calculations are used by each financing source. Still, some standards do exist.

Pragmatically, any arithmetic calculation using the present value of discounting assumptions can be easily misunderstood by sellers unaccustomed to dealing with financial matters. Therefore, it makes sense to stay away from these methods for negotiating purposes.

The valuation of most small and mid-size privately-held companies can best be accomplished through one or a combination of four methods:—asset liquidation method, historical cash flow method, future cash flow method, and/or profitability method. For detailed descriptions and examples of each method see my book *Buying In* referred to earlier.

The following summarizes these methods:

1. *Asset liquidation method.* This method is used by finance companies and other financial institutions making long term loans with hard assets as collateral. Appraisals identify the value each asset might bring at an auction. The bank then lends 80 percent of the total liquidation value. No weight is given to the performance of the company, the growth potential, or the management acumen for generating increased profits and cash.

2. *Historical cash flow method.* This method is used by many buyers as the starting point in negotiations. They assume that without any additional investment in production assets, advertising, new products, or management techniques, a company should be able to generate at least as much cash in the future as it has in the past. Normally a multiplier is attached to the average annual cash flow from the previous three years. This multiplier ranges from two to five, depending on the growth potential of the business.

3. *Future cash flow.* Just as buyers start with historical results, sellers start with future prospects. They assume that the buyer purchases future potential, not past performance, and therefore should pay for the investments made by the seller that will generate higher cash flows in future years. The average annual cash flow projected for the succeeding three years is multiplied by a negotiated factor—once again ranging from two to five.

4. *Profitability method.* This method relates to the price/earnings (P/E) concept of publicly-traded companies. It assumes, for example, that if the average industry P/E ratio is 10, the purchase price should be 10 times the prior year's profit. This method seldom brings concrete results in negotiations, although large corporate sellers usually start here.

Regardless of the method used, if the purchase price does not accurately reflect both the assets and the cash flow of the business raising outside capital will be difficult. For a leveraged buyout the maximum price should be recoverable within three to five years. Deals financed exclusively by the seller can be valued differently, as described later in this chapter.

Because of the wide variation in financing arrangements for different types and sizes of acquisitions, a list of general rules governing capital sources and forms universally applicable is not practical. However, standard financing schemes currently in vogue can be viewed from the perspective of typical acquisition transactions. In each case, one or more individuals represent a buyer making the first acquisition.

The first example shows the purchase of a local retail florist shop turning sales of $75,000 per year.

FINANCING THE PURCHASE OF A SMALL RETAIL BUSINESS

Case assumptions for Flowers R Us, Inc.:

- Product—cut flowers and potted plants
- Annual sales—$75,000
- Average profit prior three years (before owner's draw)—$35,000
- Purchase price—$50,000
- Facilities—store front leased for five years
- Hard assets—furniture, fixtures, and delivery truck: total book value of $5,000
- Local economic conditions—stable

Using the financing "rule of four," that the purchase price should be no more than four times the equity contribution of the buyer, the Flowers R Us deal calls for an equity contribution of $12,500 and other financing for the balance of $37,500. A buyer must raise capital not only for the acquisition price but for working capital as well. In this case, assuming an average margin of 40 percent and an inventory turn of six, a working capital line of approximately $5,000 should be established. A commercial bank is the best source for a revolving line of credit using resale inventory as collateral. That brings us back to the problem of financing the balance of the purchase price of $37,500.

The low value of hard assets probably precludes a finance company from participating. The deal is too small for an investment bank. The local, fragmented market eliminates participation by a venture capital firm. By process of elimination, the seller must carry the balance of the purchase price.

A consulting contract won't work in this case because the seller of a flower business is probably not willing to stay around for two or three years assisting the buyer. Also, a stable business without any contingent transaction on the horizon that might mitigate the deal, or conversely, point to a higher purchase price, precludes the use of a contingent payout. That leaves two possibilities: either a promissory note from the buyer, or an "earn out" arrangement based on the future profits of the business.

A promissory note from the buyer, commonly referred to as "buyer paper" in acquisition financing parlance, calls for quarterly or annual payments over some period of time, normally three years. The interest rate typically stays at prime or close to it. The seller may or may not insist on personal collateral as security. As a minimum, a buyer should expect to pledge the stock in the acquired company, however.

A seller also may want a personal guarantee from the buyer. In the case of Flowers R Us, the business should remain fairly stable with a minimal risk of failure. Still, as a general rule, personal guarantees can be dangerous, psychologically if nothing else. For Flowers R Us a buyer may not be willing to risk the entire $37,500 with a promissory note. Perhaps $25,000 could be carried as a note and the balance as an "earn out" contract.

An earn out contract is an agreement to share the profits of the business with the seller over a period of years. It can be written with any number of variations: a straight percentage of profit split; a flat amount if the annual profit dips below a specified level; or cumulative annual guarantees with interest penalties attached for failure to make the specified profits. Clearly, the fewer restrictions the better for a buyer.

This is a typical way to finance the acquisition of a very small company. As long as the company has inventory or receivables, a bank should be willing to pick up the working capital line. In most cases, however, neither a bank nor any other financial institution will finance the purchase price, unless the buyer pledges sufficient personal collateral from outside the business—real estate, stock and bond investments, certificates of deposits, and so on. Short of pledging non-business collateral the only feasible way to finance the acquisition of a company like Flowers R Us is through seller financing.

FINANCING THE PURCHASE OF A BASIC MANUFACTURING COMPANY

Case assumptions, American Turned Products, Inc.:

- Product—turned metal components made to customer specification
- Annual sales—$5 million
- Average profit from prior three years (before owner's draw)—$700,000
- Purchase price—$3 million
- Facilities—company owned manufacturing plant: market value of $2 million
- Hard assets—machinery, equipment, office equipment, furniture and fixtures, truck, automobiles: total book value of $2 million
- Local economic conditions—stable

This small machine shop employs 50 people and manufactures components for the Navy and Air Force under government contract as well as small, turned parts used in office equipment and mainframe computers. These latter products are manufactured to customer specification and sold to IBM, DEC, and UNISYS. The negotiated price of $3 million amounts to 4.3 times the annual income and is therefore at the top end of a financable price. The "rule of four" criteria calls for an equity contribution of $750,000. The buyer, however, can only raise $300,000 and expects to leverage the balance of the purchase price.

If the buyer could come up with equity of $750,000, the financing of this deal would be very straightforward:

1. Equity from buyer $750,000

2. Term loan from asset-based lender, amortized over seven years with a balloon payment at the end of five years, interest at prime plus 3, secured by all production machinery and equipment   850,000

3. Mortgage loan (70 percent of market value), amortized over 15 years, interest at prime plus 2 1/2, secured by manufacturing plant   1,400,000
   TOTAL purchase price $3,000,000

4. Working capital line of credit from asset-based lender, payable on demand, interest at prime plus 2, secured by all hard assets other than real estate and production machinery and equipment $300,000

This is a classic leveraged buyout of a company with substantial hard assets. Book value of $2 million for non-real estate hard assets indicates a liquidation loan value of approximately $1.6 million. The building with a market value of $2 million should carry a mortgage loan of 75 percent, or $1.5 million. Receivables for this type of company probably run about $350,000, supporting a revolving line of credit of 85 percent of $350,000, or $300,000.

Using these maximum loan values a buyer could purchase American Turned Products with 100 percent leveraged funds and no equity contribution. Doing so would create a substantial debt service load, however, which the cash flow of the business probably wouldn't support. Therefore it is far more prudent to make the $750,000 equity contribution and use less debt.

Another financing scenario for the acquisition of American Turned Products, using the same data but with a smaller equity contribution, might be as follows:

1. Equity from buyer $300,000

2. Mortgage loan (75 percent of market value), amortized over
    15 years, interest at prime plus 2 1/2, secured by manufactur-
    ing plant   1,500,000

3. Sales/leaseback of production machinery and equipment with
    a book value of $1.5 million   1,200,000
        TOTAL purchase price $3,000,000

4. Working capital revolver from commercial bank, interest at
    prime plus 1, secured by 85 percent of qualified receivables $300,000

With this package the buyer stays away from high-cost asset-based lenders, limiting debt to a mortgage loan and a revolver. It should be relatively easy to find a leasing company for the sale/leaseback. With a book value of $1.5 million, a sale to the leasing company for $1.2 million seems very reasonable. Although receivables are now pledged to the working capital loan, miscellaneous equipment, such as trucks, automobiles, furniture and fixtures, and office equipment, remain free of liens and available for additional collateral if needed in the future.

Both of these scenarios assume an asset purchase, not a stock deal. The difference should be obvious. To pay $3 million for the common stock of American Turned Products means that all liabilities of the company remain after the purchase. This reduces the amount of cash flow for debt service. If trade payables and accrued expenses totaled $150,000, the purchase price is really $3,150,000, not $3 million, and immediate cash flow after closing would be needed to liquidate the trade payables.

As a general rule, financing the purchase of a company such as American Turned Products, owning substantial hard assets, and serving a restricted, stable market can and should be accomplished with straight debt. Asset-based lenders are the best source of capital, using machinery and equipment as collateral. Mortgage banks look favorably on financing the real estate portion of the deal. Commercial banks, though usually not interested in long-term debt—regardless of the security offered —remain a logical source for short-term working capital funds. Manufacturing companies with a solid base of receivables as collateral can easily interest a commercial bank in a revolver or other operating credit.

The one exception to this rule occurs when the make-up of the assets are attractive to leasing companies. In that case a sale/leaseback—either of the machinery and equipment alone, or these assets plus the real estate—could result in a lower monthly payment than long-term debt. Sale/leasebacks are very common when acquiring hotels, heavy equipment construction companies, or any other type of business with a fairly rapid turnover of production assets. Chapter 9 examines leasing opportunities in detail.

FINANCING THE PURCHASE OF A HIGH TECH MANUFACTURING/ASSEMBLY COMPANY

Financing the acquisition of companies selling proprietary, technically complex products in rapid growth markets requires a different approach than that used for companies in stable, fragmented markets. These companies characteristically do not employ a large volume of expensive equipment and machinery. Many are pure assembly operations relying on suppliers to actually manufacture components. Others get heavily involved in research and development rather than production. Still others accent application engineering expertise modifying existing products to customer specifications.

Examples of high technology, rapid growth markets include health care diagnosis and treatment equipment, alternate energy development products, oceanic and atmospheric exploration equipment, and products designed to aid in the transportation and care of the elderly.

ACME Laser Sensors, Inc. serves to illustrate the financing of this type of acquisition. Case assumptions for the acquisition of ACME Laser Sensors, Inc.:

- Product—laser sensor equipment for medical diagnosis and treatment
- Annual sales—$8 million
- Average profit before owner's draw—$1.6 million
- Purchase price—$8 million
- Facilities—assembly plant leased for five years with options
- Hard assets—testing equipment, office equipment, furniture and fixtures, and automobiles: total book value of $500,000
- Industry economic conditions—bullish

Sticking with the "rule of four" a buyer should have equity of about $2 million to make the financing of this deal reasonable. However, few beginning entrepreneurs can come up with this amount of capital solely out of savings and personal investments. Many find a limited partnership an excellent vehicle to raise initial equity capital. As described in Chapter 7, the tax-shelter advantages of limited partnerships have long since been negated by changes in tax laws. However, this vehicle continues to be an attractive way to encourage passive investors to gamble on rapid appreciation in growth companies.

In the case of ACME Laser Sensors, the entrepreneurial buyer contributes personal equity of $200,000 and forms a limited partnership to raise the balance of the $2 million requirement. The partnership agreement designates that the limited partners will receive annual cash distributions of not less than $2,000 nor more than $5,000 per partnership unit.

It also stipulates that limited partners have the right to convert to common shares in a ratio of one partnership unit to 10 common shares when, and if, ACME goes public. The capital account of the buyer, who is the general partner, will be credited with 70 percent of the annual income (or loss) with the limited partners receiving 30 percent.

Once the $2 million equity contribution has been raised, an acquisition financing package can be put together. Following is one such scenario:

	($ million)
1. Equity contribution	$2.0
2. Mezzanine, or bridge loan from investment bank, payable in two years, interest at prime plus 3	1.0
3. Long-term loan from British merchant bank, amortized over 10 years, interest at prime plus 2.5, secured by general partner's units with option to acquire 15 percent of ACME common shares at the end of five years for a total price of $500,000	3.0
4. Long-term loan from asset-based lender, amortized over five years, interest at prime plus 3, secured by all tangible personal property	.4
5. Equity from small investment bank, secured by 5 percent preferred shares with warrants convertible to 51 percent of outstanding common shares in the event of default on any of the above loans or to $8 million worth of common shares when the company goes public at the end of five years, whichever comes first	1.6
TOTAL purchase price	$8.0
6. Working capital line of credit from commercial bank, interest at prime plus 1.5, secured by 85 percent of qualified receivables	$1.0

An investment bank has the ability to arrange this type of complex package, whereas an individual would have trouble. When an investment bank takes a lead position, other lenders and investors are more willing to gamble on the outcome. Presumably, the safeguards built into the investment bank's contribution provide a high comfort level to lenders.

To entice an investment bank to invest in ACME, the buyer was required to execute a contractual document guaranteeing a 30 percent average annual return to the investment bank and the right to allow the bank to determine when, and if, the company should be taken public. The investment bank also demanded a contractual agreement specifying one of its officers as the official ACME board of directors' advisor. A default in any of the loan agreements or the 30 percent annual return automatically triggered the convertibility of the warrants to ensure the investment bank controlling interest.

Many different sources of both debt and equity funds for this type of acquisition can be managed by a competent investment bank. Pension funds, insurance companies, wealthy private investors, foreign companies and banks, and a variety of other funding sources remain immensely interested in getting a piece of the action as long as an investment bank takes the lead.

Investment banks have contacts in the financial community to ferret out the most advantageous combination of financing sources. Although the cost of using an investment bank as a lead packager is high and the penalty for nonperformance is normally the loss of controlling interest, this remains one of the best ways to finance a high growth, low asset base acquisition.

FINANCING THE PURCHASE OF A SERVICE BUSINESS

Financing the purchase of a service business presents a unique set of problems. Characteristically, service businesses have virtually no hard assets, so asset-based lenders have no interest. Many service businesses are not in high-growth markets or remain entirely dependent on the relationships and sales contacts of the owner. This negates the possibility of using an investment bank. Commercial banks have no interest except in those companies sporting solid receivables, and then only for a short-term revolving credit line. Foreign banks tend to shy away from service businesses, unless a clear direction can be established for expanding overseas.

The difficulty in financing the acquisition of service companies is one reason for the popularity of franchises. As described in Chapter 7, several franchisers assist new franchisees source enough capital to get the business started. Buying an operating franchise is a different story, however. Now the buyer is in the same boat as if the company was not franchised. Financing must be arranged independent of the franchiser.

Methods for financing the acquisition of service businesses do exist, however. Since so many different types of companies fall into this category no universal financing guidelines make sense. However, the following example for the acquisition of Authorized Repair Experts, Inc. should stimulate a few creative ideas to transpose to other situations.

Case assumptions for the acquisition of Authorized Repair Experts, Inc:

- Service—on-site repair and maintenance of office equipment and computers
- Annual sales—$2 million
- Average profit before owner's draw—$300,000
- Purchase price—$1.2 million
- Facilities—leased office and small repair space for five years
- Hard assets—testing equipment, office equipment, furniture and fixtures, and automobiles: total book value of $100,000
- Local economic conditions—depressed, thereby causing the repair business to boom

As with small retail operations, it's almost impossible to arrange outside financing for the entire purchase price of most service businesses, even when a buyer can put up one-fourth of the capital. Exceptions exist, however. A service business that relies on employees rather than the businessowner for technical ability and sales contacts can be just as attractive to small investment banks as manufacturing companies. As a rule, the larger the service business, and the greater the number of technically qualified employees, the easier it is to interest lenders and investors— even without asset collateral. The market served also exerts a strong influence. An engineering consulting company selling environmental compliance services is a far more attractive investment than a small stock brokerage or an investment advisory business.

In the case of Authorized Repair Experts, the following financing package illustrates one way to handle the funding, again using the "rule of four" as a guideline.

1. Equity from buyer $300,000

2. Term loan from commercial bank used by Authorized Repair, payments due monthly over four years, interest at prime plus 2.5, secured by common shares of Authorized, all hard assets, and personal guarantee of buyer $600,000$

3. Promissory note from buyer, payable quarterly over three years, interest at prime plus 1.5, secured by buyer's personal guarantee $150,000$

4. Consulting contract to seller for three years, payable monthly
in equal installments   150,000
    TOTAL purchase price $1,200,000

5. Line of credit from Authorized Repair commercial bank,
interest at prime plus 2.5, secured by all inventory of supplies,
receivables, and personal guarantee of buyer $200,000

As with most small service businesses, the seller must be willing to carry part of the purchase price. In this example buyer paper was used. In other cases an earn out contract might be more appropriate. A consulting contract for the seller frequently makes up the balance of the purchase price that cannot be financed. Many sellers prefer such an arrangement because it provides a stream of income. Buyers enjoy tax advantages because payments are treated as ordinary expenses and written off as incurred.

In the Authorized Repair case, the commercial bank used by the target company was willing to extend a term loan in deference to their knowledge of the history of the business. Banks unfamiliar with this history would probably not be interested. The fact that the seller was willing to carry a buyer's note and also take part of the purchase price as a consulting contract, indicated the level of confidence their old customer had in the ability of the new owner to be successful. This more than anything else influences a bank's participation.

Personal guarantees were also required. Although neither the bank nor the seller are likely to enforce collection against such a guarantee, it adds comfort to the transaction. From a buyer's perspective, however, personal guarantees present real and constant danger.

PERSONAL GUARANTEES USED WITH ACQUISITION FINANCING

Nearly all institutions involved in acquisition debt financing require the individual buyer, or buyers, to execute personal guarantees for the payment of all debt obligations. From a lender's perspective, this is a perfectly reasonable request. Banks and other lenders surmise that without a significant personal financial commitment, a buyer isn't truly committed to making the post-acquisition business a success. Right or wrong, any individual or group of individuals choosing to buy a going business encounters this demand.

For some people, a personal guarantee isn't worth the paper it's written on. If you don't own any assets that a lender could foreclose against, why not execute the guarantee? For others, however, executing a personal guarantee constitutes a real dilemma, especially when it endangers a nest egg tucked away for future needs—a college education for the kids, retirement, medical emergencies, or estate provisions.

Personal guarantees can cover the entire acquisition debt obligation, or a portion of it, or can be structured to decrease in coverage as the outstanding debt balance drops. Many lenders try to get a spouse or other third party to co-sign the guarantee, especially if the buyer has few assets in his or her name. With a co-guarantor, a lender has two parties, or in some cases more, to go after in the event of default.

In addition, a spouse's co-signing allows the lender to lay claim to jointly-held assets as well as those owned separately by each of the spouses. This can be most helpful when assets, such as real estate, stock and bond investments, certificates of deposit, bank accounts, and so on, are held jointly. Without a spouse's co-guarantee, jointly-held assets remain exempt from a creditor's claim against the individual buyer.

State laws govern the right of a creditor to lay claim to personal assets. This is especially relevant when an individual declares personal bankruptcy rather than lose assets to a creditor. Corporate bankruptcies fall under federal jurisdiction; state laws apply to personal bankruptcies. Since each state has slightly different laws affecting creditor/debtor rights, if a buyer wishes to exercise a defense all the way to the bankruptcy courts, it can become extremely difficult to actually collect against a personal guarantee.

On the other hand, no one consciously wants to engage in lengthy legal battles regardless of the probable outcome. In the case of personal guarantees, the best offense is often a strong defense. This means developing a protective strategy before coming under the gun from a lender. Three steps should be taken to protect personal assets if it looks like a personal guarantee must be executed.

1. Well in advance of a potential default, transfer title of all personal assets that have significant value to a safe third party. In the case of cash or cash equivalent assets, such a third party might be a spouse, an adult child, or other close relative. Obviously, care must be taken to ensure that this third party permits you to continue to enjoy the benefit of your assets and does not abscond with them.

   If a spouse, child, or relative won't work, a trust can be established to hold your assets with your spouse, children, or relatives as beneficiaries. The trustee may be a trusted family attorney, a banker, a friend, or anyone else who will follow your direction for investing or otherwise administering the trust. Two conditions must exist to protect assets with a trust: you cannot be a beneficiary or executor of the trust, and the trust must be irrevocable. Some people go so far as to set up the trust through a bank in an off-shore location to afford further protection. A separate corporation in which you are not a shareholder can also safely hold title to your assets.

2. Execute a detailed estate plan, including a will, providing for the distribution of your assets to nominated beneficiaries in the event of your death. This is extremely critical because the obligation to satisfy a personal guarantee passes to your estate upon your death. This means that your spouse, children, or other heirs become liable. Now the same asset protection plans necessary for your assets becomes imperative for your heirs. Structuring a protective estate plan early in the game relieves your heirs of potential disaster at a later time.

3. Transfer any assets held jointly solely to your spouse's name. This should include your homestead, even though most states exclude a homestead from creditor's liens. Better to be safe than sorry. More than one entrepreneur has been told by competent attorneys that homesteads and other jointly-held assets were safe from creditors only to learn too late that a loophole existed. If you are worried about a future divorce, execute a side agreement with your spouse excluding these transferred assets from any divorce settlement.

These steps won't always guarantee protection from creditors. Lawyers have a way of finding loopholes in nearly any contractual agreement we choose to execute. But taking these steps is better protection than doing nothing.

In addition to executing an asset protection plan, and regardless of the pressure from banks or other lenders, your spouse, friend, or other third party should never co-sign your personal guarantee. Better to find a new financing source, or not make the acquisition at all, than to succumb to pressures for a co-guarantor.

SUMMARY

As a prerequisite to arranging acquisition financing, a reasonable purchase price must be negotiated with the seller. Methods for valuing a company proliferate on the business scene. The most reasonable and easiest to understand for a privately-held company is a combination of projected future annual cash flow *multiplied* by a negotiated factor—generally two to five—*plus* the value of significant company hard assets. At times the asset value will be subjugated to the cash flow and payment incorporated in the cash flow multiplier. The "rule of four" is a good yardstick for determining how much you can afford to pay based on available equity.

Because of the wide variety of situations involved in business acquisitions and unlimited creative financing techniques, it is impractical to establish definitive sources that fit every deal. However, certain broad guidelines remain operable. The following encapsulates the types and forms of financing generally applicable to broad categories of acquisition targets.

1. Small retail businesses with purchase price of $50,000.
   a. Financing source for acquisition capital—seller

    b. Form of financing—promissory note, earn out contract, contingency payments

    c. Normal interest rate—prime plus 2

    d. Collateral—target company common stock, personal guarantee

    e. Financing source for working capital—commercial bank

    f. Collateral—resale inventory

2. *Basic manufacturing company* with a purchase price of $3 million

    a. Financing source for acquisition capital—asset-based lender, mortgage bank, equipment leasing company

    b. Form of financing—long-term debt, mortgage, sale/leaseback

    c. Normal interest rate:

        long-term debt—prime plus 3 to 5

        mortgage—prime plus 2 1/2

        lease—N/A

    d. Collateral:

        long-term debt—target company tangible property excluding building

        mortgage—building and other real estate

        lease—equipment leased

    e. Financing source for working capital—commercial bank

    f. Collateral—receivables, inventory

3. *High tech manufacturing or assembly company* with a purchase price of $8 million

    a. Financing source for initial equity—limited partnership

    b. Financing source for acquisition capital—small investment bank, foreign merchant bank, asset-based lender

    c. Form of financing—mezzanine debt, long-term debt, preferred stock

    d. Normal interest rate:

        mezzanine debt—prime plus 3

        long-term debt, merchant bank—prime plus 2 to 3

        long-term debt, asset-based lender—prime plus 3 to 5

        preferred stock—5 percent dividend

    e. Collateral:

        mezzanine debt—unsecured

        long-term debt, merchant bank—general partner's units, common share options

        long-term debt, asset-based lender—all tangible personal property

        preferred stock—convertible warrants, board advisor seat

    f. Financing source for working capital—commercial bank

    g. Collateral—receivables

4. *Service business* with a purchase price of $1.2 million

    a. Financing source for acquisition capital—seller's commercial bank, seller

b. Form of financing—term loan, buyer note, seller consulting contract
c. Normal interest rate:
   term loan—prime plus 2 1/2 to 3
   buyer note—prime plus 1 1/2 to 2
   consulting contract—N/A
d. Collateral:
   term loan—target common shares, all hard assets, personal guarantee
   buyer note—personal guarantee
e. Financing source for working capital—seller's commercial bank
f. Collateral—receivables, supplies inventory, personal guarantee

Financial institutions granting short- or long-term acquisition debt usually ask for personal guarantees. Prudent buyers take steps to protect their personal assets early in the game. Although many lenders insist a spouse or other third party co-sign the guarantee, this should be avoided at all costs, even if it means starting all over again with a new source.

Even if it is difficult to collect against a personal guarantee, the psychological pressure of knowing you could lose everything, including your contingency nest egg, should be sufficient motivation to put an asset protection plan in place immediately.

Chapter 9

Funding The Purchase Of Equipment, Machinery, And Vehicles For Start-ups And Second-Stage Expansion

Most retail, service, and distribution companies, as well as manufacturing businesses, require land and/or building space from which to operate the business. Most also require some type of equipment to produce the product or service or to carry on sales and administrative activities.

The financial community calls land, buildings, and equipment of all types "hard assets." Parking lots, outdoor storage space, open testing areas, recreation parks, and open grounds typify land assets included in the definition. Examples of building space include offices, factories, warehouses, and laboratories. Production machinery, forklift trucks, delivery and other transport vehicles, office machines, computers, automobiles, furniture and fixtures, and testing equipment fall under the broad heading of equipment.

An operating company acquires hard assets by leasing them or by purchasing them. Leased assets do not appear on a company's balance sheet except under certain circumstances. Since the company does not have title to leased assets, they cannot be used as loan collateral.

According to generally accepted accounting principles (GAAP) purchased assets must be stated on the company's balance sheet at the actual amount paid for them. Qualified assets are then depreciated. The term "book value" refers to the original cost of the asset less the depreciation taken to date. In nearly all cases, neither the amount originally paid for an asset nor its book value reflect its actual market value at any given time.

A grasp of asset terminology becomes useful when developing appropriate financing strategies for both business start-ups and expansions. Since financial institutions insist on loan collateral at least equal in value to the amount of the debt, an understanding of how to determine asset value helps to decide how much financing to go after and which direction to go for the funds.

Hard assets can be purchased in three ways:

- With borrowed funds
- By exchanging company stock for assets
- With internal cash generated by the company

In some instances, hard assets may be donated to a company by a charitable or other organization, or an individual. A company either records free assets on its books at their fair market value at the contribution date or not at all. Discussions of the tax consequences and accounting conventions relating to donated assets are beyond the scope of this book.

Furthermore, the procedure for purchasing hard assets with internally generated cash is self-explanatory and deserves no further comment. The same holds true for assets acquired in exchange for company shares. This chapter covers only methods for financing the acquisition of hard assets with debt capital. Lease financing is dealt with in Chapter 11. Chapter 10 covers sources of capital for expanding land and building assets.

Several lending sources and types of debt exist for the purchase of hard assets. Some work most effectively for a business start-up or during the first stage of business development. Others lend themselves more appropriately to acquiring assets for second-stage expansion after a company has been operating for a few years.

The major sources of equipment loans are:

- Commercial banks
- Asset-based lenders
- Equipment dealers
- Government agencies/programs

EQUIPMENT FINANCING THROUGH COMMERCIAL BANKS

As repeatedly stated in previous chapters, most commercial banks do not like to make long-term loans. There are exceptions, however. Generally, the larger the bank the more latitude it has in structuring different types of loans. Regional banks and money center banks view requests for hard asset term loans more favorably than smaller banks.

In addition, the larger the amount of capital required, the higher the probability of interesting a bank, regardless of the type of collateral. Borrowing $500,000 on a term loan to purchase a complex, computer-controlled milling machine is much easier than getting a term loan for the purchase of a $5,000 personal computer.

The location of the bank relative to the borrower and the type of equipment to be purchased also make a difference. An upper midwest regional bank such as FirstBank or Norwest, both out of the Twin Cities, looks more favorably on financing grain processing equipment for a company in Minnesota than would a New York money center bank.

Although banks prefer short-term loans secured by readily convertible collateral, given the right situation, at times they can be convinced to grant term loans to purchase equipment. Commercial bank term loans generally take one of three possible forms:

- Installment loans for up to five years
- Straightforward term loans with principal reducing monthly payments for periods up to five years
- Short-term line of credit secured by receivables, inventory, and demand notes

The use of short-term funds to purchase hard assets violates the matching principle of short-term money for short-term assets and long-term money for long-term assets. Nevertheless, many companies already burdened by oppressive debt service take this route. Surprisingly, in their zeal to increase loan portfolios, many banks go along with them. Smart financial managers, however, realize that borrowing mismatched funds nearly always leads to operating cash shortfalls later on.

INSTALLMENT LOANS

Nearly everyone who has financed a car has used installment loans. Of all bank debt instruments, installment loans continue to be the most expensive. The reason rests in the calculation of interest. Assume a bank grants you an installment loan of $10,000 to purchase an automobile. Terms call for equal monthly payments over 48 months. The bank charges 12 percent interest. Monthly payments are calculated as follows:

Amount of loan	$10,000
Annual interest @12 percent	$1,200
Loan period of four years	× 4
TOTAL interest due	$4,800
Add: Original loan	10,000
TOTAL amount to be paid	$14,800
Divided by number of months	48
Monthly payment	$308.33

Compare this to borrowing $10,000 for four years at 12 percent interest calculated on a declining principle balance. In the latter case, equal monthly payments would be $263.50 compared to $308.33. Total interest paid over four years would be $2,638 compared to $4,800 using the installment method.

Although installment loans are very costly, without a strong working relationship with the borrower and compensating balances on deposit, most commercial banks won't go any further for financing smaller equipment purchases. A computer, automobile, small testing equipment, and a few pieces of furniture are all normally financed with installment loans.

One advantage of using installment loans is that nearly every commercial bank jumps at the opportunity to make them. The amounts are not high, but if you need small purchases, the corner bank should be able to help. Larger purchases present a different picture. The maximum installment loan tends to range between $25,000 and $50,000 for very good customers. Beyond that, term loans do the trick.

Term Loans

As earlier chapters pointed out, a strong working relationship with a commercial bank opens doors that otherwise remain locked. Nowhere is this phenomenon more visible than when trying to borrow large sums on a five year or longer term loan. One reason commercial banks do not specialize in long-term, hard asset collateral loans is that collateral values keep changing over time, occasionally rising from the initial purchase, but more often declining. If the underlying asset value declines faster than the loan balance, obviously the lender eventually becomes undercollateralized. And commercial banks don't like this at all.

Banks also stay away from equipment term loans because the underlying asset—the equipment—is too difficult to liquidate for cash in the event of default. A piece of heavy production machinery, firmly bolted or otherwise fastened to concrete floors and attached to a variety of oiling, cleaning, electrical, or plumbing fixtures can not readily be moved to a buyer's plant. The cost of disassembling and then reassembling often exceeds the cost of buying the used machine.

To liquidate the collateral asset, a bank must either hold a time-consuming and costly auction or advertise it for sale in trade and other journals, which might take several years to bring results. And then when the asset is finally sold, very often the loan balance exceeds the selling price.

Most commercial banks cannot manage equipment liquidation sales. Some of the very large regional or money center banks with separate finance company divisions do have the personnel and skill to dispose of foreclosure equipment. Others have recently added so-called "work out" departments responsible for keeping a company operating while gradually disposing of its assets. Unfortunately for banks, these work out specialists seldom have either the experience or the skills to make this happen. Most banks going this route learn very quickly that they are better off pouring new money into the company to try to keep it alive than liquidating its assets.

Commercial banks that make equipment loans insist that, in addition to pledging the equipment, borrowers provide:

- A compensating balance equal to at least 25 to 35 percent of the loan balance
- Liquid assets, such as receivables or easily salable inventory, as additional collateral
- A personal guarantee

Also, many banks require non-business collateral, such as liquid investments, real estate investments, pension entitlements, and so on, to compensate for the potential declining value of the underlying equipment.

Typically, commercial bank equipment loans do not extend beyond five years. Terms call for monthly principal and interest payments with an interest rate of a point or two higher than that demanded for working capital loans. Current bank rates run prime plus two to four points. On the plus side, commercial banks seldom charge exorbitant placement fees.

Banks frequently merge a company's collateral pledged to working capital debt with equipment securing the term loan. Although loan balances remain separate, cross-collateralization provides easier administration. Also, since banks don't like to foreclose, you can usually renegotiate deferred payment terms or other concessions from the bank if you get into a cash bind and can't keep up with debt service payments.

Customarily, banks execute voluminous loan agreements for term loans. Quite often these agreements include, in addition to the terms and conditions of the loan itself, a set of covenants that the company must abide by to avoid default. These covenants range from maintaining a defined working capital ratio, to restricting compensation to officers of the company, to abiding by an established equity to asset ratio (or many other ratios), to requiring bank approval before hiring additional personnel.

Some of these covenants can be extremely bothersome. Some are meaningless. Each bank has its own pet control mechanisms, and each loan agreement specifies different covenants. These examples are only a few that can be expected to appear.

ASSET-BASED LENDERS (ABLs)

Financial institutions specializing in long-term equipment loans go by a variety of names. Forty years ago they called themselves finance companies or industrial finance companies. Since the late 1970s, the terms "asset-based lender" and "industrial credit company" have been used to describe these firms. Recently such terms as "capital" companies and "secured lenders" have become popular. To be consistent, the terms "asset-based lender" and "finance companies" are used interchangeably throughout this book to describe a financial institution whose primary business is to make business loans against hard assets, and occasionally soft assets.

The role of asset-based lenders has also changed over the years. After World War II industrial finance companies were quite small compared to today's counterparts. They concentrated on loaning money to companies whose credit rating or lack of collateral made it impossible to borrow from commercial banks. Sister organizations called "factors" specialized in loaning funds against receivables, or actually buying receivables, always at significant discounts. Businesses that could not borrow from commercial banks used these firms.

As entrepreneurs discovered the techniques of leveraged buyouts, asset-based lenders gained new respectability in financial circles. These lenders, steeped in techniques for dealing with poor credit risks and sporting hard-nosed management accustomed to expediting foreclosures, found a new market niche. The mystique of LBOs led ambitious entrepreneurs with hardly any equity capital to their doors.

As described in Chapter 8, asset-based lenders, familiar with used equipment markets and maintaining close working relationships with most of the auction houses in the country, eagerly loaned 80, 90, even 100 percent of the funds necessary to complete an LBO—as long as target companies had substantial hard assets. This new role in entrepreneurial acquisitions, especially of manufacturing companies, brought asset-based lenders to the next rung.

As acquisition prices soared with the stock market in the 1980s, asset-based lenders found themselves unable to justify full leverage financing without also picking up receivables and inventory collateral. Today, they lend against every type of business asset, not just equipment and real estate.

Partial deregulation opened the doors for commercial banks to enter this lucrative term loan market. Most were ill-equipped to administer such loans, however. Instead of developing their own expertise, they merely gobbled up most of the major asset-based lenders, making them separate divisions of the bank. Two examples of shifting ownership of major ABLs were the acquisition of Armco Capital (an ABL subsidiary of Armco Steel) by Glendale Federal S & L, and the purchase of Trefoil Capital by Fidelity Bank of Philadelphia. After acquisition, these ABLs were renamed Glenfed Financial Corp. and Fidelcor Business Credit Corp., respectively.

Recently the trend reversed and divestitures have become popular. For example, in early 1991, First Fidelity Bancorp, parent of Fidelity Bank, sold Fidelcor to CIT Group, Inc. CIT is a finance company, of which 60 percent is owned by a large Japanese bank, Dai-Ichi Kangyo, and 40 percent by Manufacturers Hanover Corp., New York. Many commercial banks still own asset-based lenders, although ABL divisions maintain independent staffs and loan authority.

Companies undergoing second-stage expansion find asset-based lenders a ready source of capital. They prefer to make larger rather than smaller loans. Large, expensive pieces of equipment can be easily financed through this source. Equipping a branch plant or adding equipment for major new product lines, frequently necessary during third-stage expansion, also attract asset-based lenders. Occasionally, a small ABL makes a term loan on one, two, or three pieces of equipment for first-stage development, although first stage-financing is not their choice. Either commercial banks or leasing companies offer better possibilities for business start-ups.

A manufacturing company in business for at least three to four years represents the ideal profile of a second-stage situation most appealing to ABLs. Its products are well accepted in a stable but growing market. The manufacturing process utilizes large—albeit standard—off-the-shelf equipment, not specialized, made-to-order tooling. The cost of the planned equipment expansion ranges between $500,000 and $3 million. The company shows pre-tax profits of at least 10 percent. The owner, or owners, will execute personal guarantees for the full amount of the loan, and have personal assets to back up the guarantees.

Under these conditions, a long-term loan for $1.2 million might have the following characteristics:

Amount of loan	$1.2 million
Interest rate	Prime plus 5
Amortization	7 years
Collateral	1. All new equipment to be purchased.
	2. A first position on all unencumbered hard and soft assets.
	3. A second position on any assets already pledged to another secured creditor.
	4. Personal guarantees from the owners for $1.2 million.
Payments	Monthly principal and interest
Interest calculation	Declining loan balance

In addition to a very high interest rate, asset-based lenders charge "placement fees." A placement fee must be paid when applying for the loan. It is non-refundable once the loan application has been approved. If the customer decides to go elsewhere, it forfeits the fee. The amount of placement fees varies, but for a $1.2 million commitment, $15,000 to $25,000 would not be unusual.

In addition to a placement fee, most ABLs charge a monthly "service" or "maintenance" fee. This theoretically covers their cost of administering and monitoring the loan. Also, expect to submit a monthly financial statement to the ABL and be subjected to regular—monthly or quarterly—audits by their staff. Customers usually pay the travel and living expenses for these auditors.

Finally, although asset-based lenders stand ready, willing, and able to finance large equipment expansions and, therefore, serve a real market need, most are very difficult to work with after the loan has been placed. When a company doesn't meet its sales or profit forecasts, loses a key management employee, or runs into a cash bind and can't meet a monthly debt service payment, be assured that auditors and loan officers will descend like a plague of locusts.

Because of their experience with poor credit risks, ABL officers are fully capable of closing a company down and liquidating its assets to satisfy the outstanding loan. And they have little hesitancy taking this route if you don't follow their recommendations for improving your operations. It has happened more than once; it will happen again.

EQUIPMENT MANUFACTURER OR DEALER FINANCING

Manufacturers and dealers that sell production equipment and larger pieces of office equipment (large copying machines or mainframe computers) generally offer financing arrangements along with the sale of the equipment. In the past, many manufacturers believed that they could increase sales by maintaining a division or subsidiary that specialized in lending long-term installment or other loans to assist buyers finance equipment purchases. Lately, however, more and more industrial giants have divested themselves of finance subsidiaries and replaced in-house financing with working arrangements with large, national finance companies, such as GE Capital Corp.

General Motors automobiles and some trucks remain financable through the General Motors Acceptance Corporation (GMAC), a subsidiary of the parent corporation. Ford and Chrysler have similar arrangements. Financing for most non-vehicular equipment, however, is now referred to independent finance companies, or in some cases money center banks such as Citicorp.

Manufacturer or dealer financing has definite advantages. Used as a selling tool, the creditworthiness of the buyer is a secondary consideration. Although credit checks will be made, unless a buyer happens to be at the bottom of the list, a loan can be expected to be approved. The equipment being purchased serves as the only collateral with personal guarantees occasionally required.

On the flip side, expect to pay a premium for the convenience of financing through manufacturers or dealers. Using a finance company as the source of funding, interest and monthly payments run significantly higher than those required by commercial banks. Terms are also more stringent than those negotiated direct with asset-based lenders for larger purchases. Interest rates run as high as prime plus 6 or 7. Monthly payments get calculated on an installment basis.

Companies purchasing single pieces of equipment usually get a better deal through a commercial bank, even with an installment loan. On the other hand, with a poor credit history or if other reasons preclude borrowing from a bank, manufacturer or dealer financing may be the only way. Even with a superior credit rating, a company may find that the number of pieces being purchased or the amount of the purchase price rules out commercial bank participation.

In the spectrum of financing sources, manufacturer and dealer financing falls between commercial banks and asset-based lenders. Single purchases of relatively inexpensive equipment can best be handled through a commercial bank. Large, expensive pieces, or groups of equipment with a purchase price over $1 million, attract asset-based lenders. Manufacturer and dealer financing falls between these two extremes. With a purchase price between $50,000 and $500,000, financing arranged through a manufacturer or dealer seems to be the quickest and easiest, albeit the most expensive, way to go.

VENTURE CAPITAL TERM LOANS

Chapter 6 explored the use of venture capital firms for meeting start-up and first-stage working capital needs. Along with providing early stage funds to meet payroll, buy material, and pay operating expenses, venture capital firms also get involved in financing equipment purchases. They do so through two channels. They use their own funds to make long-term equipment loans, and they assist in sourcing loans from commercial banks, finance companies, and other institutions. Although a few small venture capital firms have allocated internal funds to make term loans, most act as loan brokers.

Banks and asset-based lenders look more favorably on loans solicited by venture capital firms. They believe that lending to a company with an astute venture capital partner substantially reduces their risk. Whether risk is in fact lessened is immaterial. They believe it to be so and, therefore, are more anxious to make the loan.

Small Business Investment Companies (SBICs) are venture capital firms that specialize in first stage financing for businesses in fragmented, local markets that cannot attract private venture funds. Although many SBICs remain under private ownership, an even larger number operate as divisions or subsidiaries of large commercial banks.

SBICs have been around for more than three decades. Partially funded by the Small Business Administration, SBICs must follow federal regulations governing the types of financing they can and can't engage in. SBICs concentrate on first-stage financing, although they also participate in smaller, second-stage loans. The dollar amounts vary, but generally anything under $100,000 interests them. Commercial bank SBIC divisions also have the ability to package their financing with bank participation.

Equipment term loans from SBICs normally extend three to five years, occasionally longer. Interest runs higher than bank loans but less than that charged by asset-based lenders—currently ranging between 3 and 5 percentage points over prime. Some SBICs also charge placement fees similar to asset-based lenders but normally much lower—$2,000 to $5,000 for the typical loan.

SBICs do not require outside collateral against the loan, other than the equipment being purchased. On the other hand, personal guarantees are nearly always required. The outstanding exception relates to companies already doing business with the parent commercial bank.

As additional security, many SBICs insist on restrictive covenants embedded in the loan agreement. These covenants, just like those demanded by commercial banks, enable the SBIC to monitor the borrower's business and provide another set of criteria to control the company. In addition, for larger amounts, loan provisions giving the SBIC equity interest in the company either upon default or after a period of years if the loan is not fully liquidated are prevalent. However, they normally don't go beyond 15 percent ownership.

Just like private venture capital firms, SBICs participate in working capital financing as well as equipment term loans. In fact, many prefer to operate in both spheres. Obviously, this makes it easier to get the financing you need when it comes time to expand operations. However, it also reduces competition between financial institutions, making it more difficult to get new financing at the lowest cost and best terms, when and if you need it in the second or third stage. A listing of SBICs in your area may be obtained from the National Association of Small Business Investment Companies, 1156 15th Street, NW, Suite 1101, Washington, DC 20005; (202)833-8230.

FINANCING THE PURCHASE OF USED EQUIPMENT

A large market exists in used equipment of all types and sizes. Used machinery dealers buy and sell production equipment at a fraction of the cost of new pieces. Advertisements in used equipment trade journals and city newspapers are a good source for locating these dealers.

Used office furniture and equipment dealers furnish entire offices at one-tenth, or less, of the cost of new assets. These dealers frequently advertise their wares in newspapers and the telephone yellow pages directory of any large or mid-size city.

Recently, a national market for used personal computers and peripheral equipment has developed. Regional used computer companies have sprung up throughout the country. The Boston Computer Exchange (617-572-4414), and the National Computer Exchange (212-614-0700) are two of the largest.

Manufacturers' warranties don't normally apply to used equipment. Notwithstanding this drawback, many companies look at this market first because of significantly lower prices and very often better availability and selection. The risk is obviously there, but so is the gain.

The same sources that handle the financing of new equipment purchases lend against used equipment, with one fundamental difference. Whereas the price, and therefore the loan value of new equipment comes directly from the manufacturer or dealer, similar pricing standards do not exist for used equipment. Asset-based lenders and many banks who make equipment term loans maintain a computer data base of recent sales of used equipment. From this they have a good idea whether the price you negotiate represents market value and can therefore be used to determine the amount of the loan.

EQUIPMENT APPRAISALS

When purchasing groups of equipment, loan values must be established with a formal appraisal. Many companies specialize in performing appraisals for used equipment. Some are charlatans and appraise equipment at values designated by the company hiring them, regardless of the true market value. Others try to get in on the used equipment boom by taking appraisal assignments that they are ill-equipped to handle.

Financial institutions know which appraisal firms perform questionable work. Appraisals from an unacceptable one immediately kills any interest there may have been to make the loan. For this reason, it makes sense to ask financial institutions, especially asset-based lenders, for references of reputable appraisal firms. It also pays to verify an appraisal firm's performance with other customers before engaging one.

Asset-based lenders work closely with equipment auctioneers who also perform equipment appraisals. If an ABL seems like a logical choice for financing, it certainly pays to use one of its recommended appraisers to establish loan values. A note of caution when using appraisers referred by financial institutions: Because appraisers know that most of their future business will be generated by financial institutions, they tend to place very conservative values on used assets, hoping such a tact will ingratiate them with the lender. Very often such appraised values are so far below asking prices that the purchase dies.

A second way to locate equipment appraisers is by watching the auction ads in city newspapers. All equipment auctioneers also perform appraisals. It doesn't take long to establish which firms handle the most business in your area. The ones that have the most business are also probably the most reputable.

Once you select an appraiser, it's always a good idea to check with your lender to be sure the appraiser's results will be acceptable before executing a contract. Otherwise the appraisal could be worthless. One national appraisal firm acceptable to most lenders is American Appraisal Company. It has branch offices in most cities with phone numbers listed in local telephone directories.

Equipment appraisals do not come cheap. The fee is always negotiable, however. Theoretically, appraisers base their fee on the amount of time it takes to do the appraisal and write a report. A typical price charged by American Appraisal in a midwest location for a group of standard production equipment sufficient to furnish a small facility would be between $5,000 and $10,000. If you want more than one value assigned to each piece of equipment, the price goes up.

When contracting for an appraisal, it's important to designate what type of appraised value you want included in the final report. Four different values can be assigned to any piece of equipment: replacement cost, fair market value, orderly liquidation value, and forced liquidation or auction value.

REPLACEMENT COST

Replacement cost represents the amount that would have to be paid to replace the piece of equipment in the event it was completely destroyed, as in a fire. Insurance companies use replacement cost to set fire and casualty insurance coverage and premiums. Of the four values, replacement cost runs the highest and often substantially exceeds the asking price for the equipment. It has no value at all to lending institutions.

FAIR MARKET VALUE

Fair market value stipulates the theoretical price that a willing buyer would pay a willing seller for equipment that's in place and operating. This is frequently used to value assets in a going business for purposes of negotiating a purchase/sell price for the business. Purely theoretical, fair market value does not reflect prices paid for stand-alone pieces in the used equipment market. Although useful for negotiating the acquisition price of a going business, it has no value to financial institutions for lending purposes. Fair market value may or may not reflect the price asked by the seller. This appraised value runs about 60 to 70 percent of the replacement cost.

ORDERLY LIQUIDATION VALUE

Orderly liquidation value is the amount a seller could theoretically get by selling the equipment piece by piece in an orderly manner over a period of twelve months. It does reflect recent sales in the used equipment market. Orderly liquidation values frequently approximate the advertised asking price. These values range between 75 and 80 percent of fair market value, although in some cases the percentage can be higher.

Lending institutions consider orderly liquidation values as reasonable loan values for certain types of equipment—relatively new, easy to move to a new location, close to state-of-the-art design, off-the-shelf and not specifically designed for a single product line or plant. If the equipment does not meet this criteria, lending institutions discount these values to forced liquidation or auction values.

FORCED LIQUIDATION OR AUCTION VALUE

Forced liquidation value typifies the theoretical amount a seller could raise if the group of equipment offered for sale was auctioned off at one time to the highest bidders. Anyone who has been to a commercial or industrial auction knows that bid prices fluctuate wildly. To predict with any certainty what a specific piece of equipment, or even a group of pieces, will bring at an auction is at best rudimentary guesswork.

Nevertheless, lenders use appraised forced liquidation value more than any other standard to determine loan value for certain types of equipment. If the equipment is old; if it is large, set in concrete, supported by a variety of fixtures, and therefore difficult to pick up and move; if it is designed for a specific application, product line, or facility and has limited utility other than in its existing location, forced liquidation values apply. Forced liquidation values are predicated on recent auction sale prices of similar equipment. This value approximates 80 percent of the appraised orderly liquidation value.

Using these definitions, the maximum negotiating price is fairly easy to establish. Whether a financial institution lends funds or a company uses internal cash, these guidelines establish minimum standards.

FINANCING THROUGH GOVERNMENT AGENCIES

Previous chapters identified several federal and state agencies that stand ready to assist small businesses fund first-stage working capital and early stage research and development efforts. Assistance from these same agencies is available for buying equipment. Two major criteria determine which agency to approach for a long-term loan: the amount of capital needed, and the use to which the purchased equipment will be put.

Standards for judging the first criteria are the same as used for banks, asset-based lenders, or venture capital firms. A clear and present need for the equipment must be shown in the accompanying financing plan. No one, including government agencies, will be interested in loaning funds for equipment that might be needed in the future. The amount requested must fit the maximum guidelines of the particular agency and obviously must be used only for the acquisition of the stated equipment.

Criteria governing the use of the equipment can be just as important. Separate agencies and funding programs finance equipment purchases for different uses. For example, equipment for the production of newly developed products might be financed through the SBIR. Equipment specifically designated to manufacture products under government defense contracts can frequently be financed directly from the Army, Navy, Air Force, or other Department of Defense agency awarding the contract. Departments of Transportation, Agriculture, and Interior fund projects relating to their specific field of interest. Chapter 12 describes financing programs from Eximbank for equipment to manufacture export products. The SBA considers equipment loans for nearly any commercial use.

Far too many federal and state agencies provide equipment financing assistance to present an inclusive listing here. However, two federal agencies that engage in funding broad categories of projects are worthy of note: the SBA and the SBIR program.

EQUIPMENT FINANCING FROM THE SMALL BUSINESS ADMINISTRATION

Don't expect to raise large amounts of long-term capital through the SBA. With the exception of a few joint programs with state agencies, the maximum amount the SBA can loan to any one business is currently $750,000. This includes working capital funds and long-term loans.

The SBA offers assistance under several programs, some designated by the numbered section of the Small Business Act to which they apply:

- 7(a) loans
- 502 program
- 504 program
- Handicapped Assistance Loans
- Energy Loans
- Disaster Assistance Loans
- Pollution Control Financing
- Minority-Owned Business Loans

Section 7(A)

The largest program carries the label "7(a) loans and guarantees." This program is specifically designed to help small businesses with credit problems. The same criteria described in previous chapters that related to granting or guaranteeing working capital loans applies to equipment loans. The applicant must be turned down by at least two banks.

Guarantees require a commercial bank to actually supply the funds. The bank must participate for 10 percent for loans up to $155,000 and 15 percent for loans between $155,000 and $750,000. Interest rates cannot be more than 2.25 to 2.75 over prime. The equipment to be purchased serves as collateral, although personal guarantees might be required.

The 502 Program

The 502 program is specifically designed to help small businesses acquire hard assets—equipment and facilities. Financing through the 502 program requires a combination of the SBA, a commercial bank, and a local development company (LDC). Local development companies are business development organizations formed by municipal governments and private businesses to improve the local economy in a specific area. The 502 program restricts assistance to those companies located in an area served by a LDC.

The LDC actually borrows the funds from a local bank under a guarantee from the SBA. A small business doesn't take title to the equipment it acquires under this program. The LDC lays out the funds and then leases the equipment to the small business under a lease-purchase plan. The SBA guarantees 90 percent of loans up to a maximum of $500,000. The loan period goes to 25 years, with the standard SBA interest caps—2.25 to 2.75 percentage points over prime. Since a bank must participate, the borrower must locate one that is willing to amortize its share of the loan over the same period.

The 504 Program

The 504 program was updated and finalized in 1989. Although similar to the 502 program, the 504 program provides assistance for much larger projects. Most of these large projects are for the acquisition or construction of facilities. Chapter 10 examines how the program works for this application.

With the radical changes currently transpiring in the banking industry and the continuing emphasis on bank liquidity, locating a bank willing to participate in SBA guaranteed funding can be a chore. If one can be found, however, SBA guaranteed long-term debt is an excellent way to keep debt service payments to a minimum.

EQUIPMENT FINANCING THROUGH THE SMALL BUSINESS INNOVATIVE RESEARCH PROGRAM

Formed to assist small businesses fund the development of new products with applications to the government, the Small Business Innovative Research program consists of three Phases. As described in Chapter 5, Phase I consists entirely of small amounts of funding for the first-stage development of product design and modeling, and Phase II assists companies in developing product prototypes reaching to eventual production status. Most companies engaging in Phase II eventually need to acquire small quantities of production and testing equipment. Funding in the form of grants, awards, and low-cost loans during this period can be used for the acquisition of this equipment as well as to supply working capital needs.

SBIR funding is not available to every company. To gain entrance to the program, companies must submit bids to government agencies for products the agency, or government department, has listed as needed. There is no assurance of winning the bidding competition. To participate in Phase II funding, a company must first enter, and win, the competition for an award under Phase I. A second roadblock stipulates that the products resulting from research efforts must have a practical, and needed, use in the specific government department or agency sponsoring it. This eliminates a great many products developed every year with commercial value.

Continued annual funding by Congress ensures that money is available to successful bidders. Whereas the top award under Phase I is only $50,000, grants or low-cost loans of up to $500,000 are available under Phase II. Clearly, if a company is in the prototype development stage of products and if these products fit government applications, SBIR money can be a cheap, effective way to acquire first stage financing for at least some production and testing equipment.

Phase III does not provide direct funding from the government. However, once a company achieves success through Phases I and II, the appropriate agency stands ready to lend a hand in sourcing private capital for production uses.

From the perspective of a bank or other financial institution, such backing goes a long way toward assuring immediate and serious attention to a company's loan application. Quite often, knowing a government agency backs an applicant, a financial institution offers lower interest rates, demands less outside collateral, and grants longer payment terms than a small business could muster by itself.

Phase III is the commercialization of the product. There is no obligation to sell the finished products to the government. They can be, and most are, sold in the private sector. Identification of the ultimate customer of production run products has no bearing on getting assistance from the government for equipment financing.

STATE AND MUNICIPAL FINANCING ASSISTANCE

Several local government bodies maintain small business development agencies that assist in the financing of start-up and first-stage small businesses. Previous chapters identified small business development companies as sources of advisory services as well as direct working capital funding. Many of these development agencies also provide either direct financing for small quantities of production equipment for first-stage companies or offer assistance in arranging equipment loans through commercial lending institutions.

Several states have committed funds to statewide development organizations with the specific mission to lend money to established, healthy private businesses in an effort to stimulate business in depressed areas. Several other states, especially those with large segments of urban decay, utilize Community Development Block Grant (CDBG) funds allocated by the federal Department of Housing and Urban Development. The amount and types of funding through this channel varies with current federal funding levels and the degree of participation by state government. You can learn about the current status of this program by calling your state department of economic development.

Each state and municipality have different criteria and levels of assistance. Before going through the hassle of applying for a term loan from a bank or asset-based lender, researching the availability of funds and qualification criteria through local development agencies could save a lot of time and money.

SUMMARY

A vast range of financing sources exists for the acquisition of business hard assets, exclusive of real estate. Within commercial banking circles alone, wide variances in loan amounts, terms, interest rates, and outside collateral exist. Privately-owned asset-based lenders apply criteria different from secured lending divisions of commercial banks, insurance companies, or industrial corporations. Venture capital firms also become interested in equipment financing under the right circumstances. SBICs practice more lenient term loan policies than private funds. The SBA and SBIR also get their oars in the lending waters, expanding alternatives even further.

Although the range of alternatives seems limitless, the following summarizes the most likely choices.

    A. *Commercial banks*—up to $50,000
        Installment loan
        Prime plus 2
        Personal guarantee
        The smaller the amount the easier to obtain

B. *Asset-based lenders*—$500,000 to $8 million
   Term loan up to 7 years
   Prime plus 5
   Placement fee to $25,000
   The larger the amount the easier to obtain
C. *Equipment manufacturers/dealers*—purchase price
   Installment loan to 5 years
   Prime plus 4 to 5
   Usually placed through asset-based lender
   Easy to obtain
D. *Private venture capital funds*—up to $250,000
   Term loan to 5 years either direct or through other institutions
   Prime plus 2 to 5
   Venture capital firm already investing in the company
E. *SBIC*—up to $100,000 (higher with bank participation)
   Term loan to 5 years
   Prime plus 3 to 5
   Small placement fee
   Option for equity participation
F. *SBA*—guarantees up to $750,000 (including working capital)
   Term—up to 25 years
   Prime plus 2.25 to 2.75
   Requires bank participation for 10 to 15 percent
G. *SBIR*—up to $500,000 for Phase II
        —search assistance only for Phase III
   Grants and awards for Phase II
H. *State and municipal agencies*—various

Chapter 10

Financing Second-Stage Real Estate Expansion

As a new company grows, the time eventually arrives when it makes sense to consider owning its own facility rather than to continue collecting rent receipts. Improving cash flow, reducing taxes, and increasing operating freedom are a few of the advantages companies gain when owning rather than leasing office, warehouse, and production space. Even in depressed real estate markets forward-thinking businessowners take steps to acquire their own facility. Actually, financing the acquisition of commercial and industrial real estate during tough economic times can be easier than during boom times.

Several avenues exist to raise capital for facilities expansion. Debt and equity capital are both available, either separately or combined. On the debt side, simple mortgage loans suffice for smaller deals. As transactions increase in size, state and municipal financing programs—such as Private Activity Bonds (formerly Industrial Development or Revenue Bonds)—offer interesting financing possibilities. Still larger property deals can be handled through multi-owner investment companies such as Real Estate Investment Trusts (REITs) and Real Estate Mortgage Investment Conduits (REMICs). Larger operating companies that have a substantial earnings record use public stock and bond issues to raise capital for major property acquisitions.

Equity capital flows freely into real property. Prior to the Revenue Act of 1986, real estate limited partnerships provided significant tax savings to investors while enabling property managers to acquire vast complexes without resorting to debt. Even today, real estate limited partnerships remain attractive investment vehicles for wealthy private investors, pension funds, corporate treasurers, and small investors (through special real estate investment funds).

Raising capital for the purchase of real property has been and will continue to be in the foreseeable future, one of the least troublesome financing tasks for small and large businesses. This chapter examines the major avenues open to small businesses to achieve this end. Many of the more sophisticated approaches for raising capital through public offerings and other more complex and costly avenues open to larger transactions are not applicable to second-stage expansion and, therefore, will be ignored.

Mortgage loans remain the most prevalent form of debt financing for real property acquisitions. All commercial mortgage loans (as opposed to residential) have similar characteristics. They are long-term, amortized over 15 to 30 years. Interest rates are controlled by the commercial mortgage market with little variance between lenders. The performance of 30-year Treasury bonds is the major influencing factor, although perceived conditions in national or regional mortgage markets also impact rates.

Interest rates change from time to time, but the range stays relatively minor. Shifts of 2 to 3 percentage points over several years are the norm. Nearly all commercial mortgages require monthly payments (although some are quarterly) with interest calculated on a declining principal balance.

PRELIMINARY CONSIDERATIONS

Before beginning the search for capital, several administrative matters need to be resolved. As previous chapters have described, approaching financing sources without adequate preparation substantially reduces the likelihood of getting the funds. To prepare a meaningful financing plan, you must first assimilate how, when, and why a new property is needed and what its price will be.

ESTABLISHING A PRICE

The loan value of commercial real estate runs between 60 and 80 percent of the true market value—that price which real estate agents can sell the property for in the open market or the price that you negotiate for the property. Financiers do not employ fictitious orderly liquidation or forced liquidation values to real estate. Market value, and corresponding equity requirements vary with location, age, and condition of the property. The current state of local commercial real estate markets also severely impacts upon market value.

In addition, new construction in the area influences market price. To the extent that new construction results in excess capacity and rental occupancy rates get depressed, selling prices will be depressed also. The reverse situation exists in high demand markets. Old yardsticks of $10, $15, or $20 per square foot hardly apply any more. Property in Manhattan may sell for $100 per square foot, or much more, while property in Pierre, South Dakota brings $8 per square foot.

The specific location within a given community also influences market price. A manufacturing facility in a desirable industrial park brings top dollar. The same square footage in a depressed, run-down neighborhood can be purchased for half the price.

To determine whether the asking price for a specific property is within the bounds of reasonable market values, get appraisals from qualified commercial appraisers. An average of at least three separate appraisals provides a reasonable range. Any competent mortgage company uses the same approach, so it's better to know ahead of time whether the property is priced in your ballpark or not.

Qualified commercial appraisers commonly work for, or closely with, major commercial real estate agencies. These large firms usually oblige with two or three appraiser names. Large regional banks know of qualified appraisers, as do commercial mortgage brokers. If all else fails, many list their services in the yellow pages of city telephone directories.

Once a realistic market price has been established and negotiations result in a mutually agreeable price, it's time to look for money. Several sources of mortgage loans exist. Some restrict their loan limits to small transactions, while other, larger institutions prefer the bigger deals. The size of the purchase determines to a large extent which source to select. Equity capital may also be available and the latter part of this chapter examines some of the major sources of these funds.

The primary sources of mortgage loans for smaller businesses are:

- Commercial banks
- Large asset-based lenders
- Mortgage banks
- Foreign banks

The availability of funds and the advantages and risks of selecting a specific source varies with several factors: the size of the deal, the type of property, the location of the property, the current state of the financial markets, the creditworthiness of the applicant, professionalism of the financing plan, and last—but certainly not least—current tax laws.

Asset-based lenders, mortgage divisions of commercial banks, and savings and loan associations (or thrifts) service smaller transactions under $500,000. For deals of this size, a 20 to 25 percent down payment continues to be common. Amortization periods range between 15 and 25 years (30 years for some new property). Interest rates are comparable to the going rates for residential properties in the area. These institutions can be contacted directly, or you can get to them through a mortgage broker.

Financing larger deals gets far more complicated. Changes from the Tax Reform Act of 1986 increase the burden. Typically, three funding sources do the bulk of the business in this market:

- Commercial mortgage banks
- Foreign banks
- Real estate syndications

FIXED OR VARIABLE RATES

The interest rate roller coaster ride of the early 1980s renewed interest in so-called variable-rate mortgages. When rates were in the mid- to high-double digits, companies were unwilling to commit to exorbitant fixed rates for the next 20 years. Knowing that eventually rates would fall, the market forced lenders to flex interest rates on existing mortgages downward as conditions improved.

Lenders were just as worried about getting stuck with low-interest rates over long periods when they had to pay double digit rates for their money. The solution for both sides was the variable-rate mortgage charging interest that swings automatically with changes in prime.

Trial and error by several of the leading mortgage banks finally resulted in fairly wide acceptance of the standard variable-rate arrangement in evidence today. Rather low, stable rates that have prevailed for several years now have caused variable-rate mortgages to lose their popularity. Nevertheless, some customers and lenders still use them.

Modern-day variable rate mortgages typically allow the interest rate to move within a fairly narrow band of prime—normally up to 3 percentage points. Pragmatically, no bank will allow its interest earnings to fall below prime, so this becomes the floor. As long as prime remains relatively stable it's hard to tell the difference between a variable-rate mortgage and one with a fixed rate. If we ever get into another inflation spiral, such as that experienced in the late 1970s and the early 1980s, however, companies stuck with variable-rate mortgages and lenders caught with fixed rates will once again cry the blues.

Obviously, similar risks prevail with fixed-rate mortgages, but this time the borrower suffers when the prime drops. Many businesses that expanded in the 1978 to 1982 period signed up to fixed-rate mortgages in an attempt to beat the prime roller coaster. Now, 12 years later, with commercial rates running in the 10 to 12 percent range, these companies are stuck with mortgages at 12 to 14 percent. Of course, you can always refinance a property and take out a new mortgage at lower fixed rates. If the original mortgage doesn't carry prepayment penalties this works fine; otherwise, it can be a very costly exercise.

In the end, individual businessowners must use their own judgment about the future of interest rates. Everyone has a different perspective of future economic events, and no hard and fast rules exist to judge the efficacy of using fixed- versus variable-rate mortgages.

BROKERS IN THE MORTGAGE MONEY MARKET

Before getting into specific comparisons of financing sources, it's probably a good idea to explore the role of mortgage brokers in commercial property financial markets. Chapter 5 described the role that loan or money brokers play in assisting companies locate appropriate sources of operating debt. Mortgage brokers play the same role, except they specialize exclusively in mortgages.

Mortgage brokers operate more formally than loan brokers. Many list their services in city telephone directories. Mortgage companies and commercial banks rely on mortgage brokers for a good part of their business. Although fee structures vary, 1 to 1.5 percent of the mortgage amount is not uncommon. Commercial real estate agents also employ the services of mortgage brokers. Contact with private and public funds not readily known to agents places mortgage brokers in a position to source the best deal for any given transaction. Also, with close contacts to large, overseas funds, both private and public, mortgage brokers broaden the money base beyond the horizons of either an agent or a bank.

Although mortgage brokers typically prefer to work through commercial real estate agents, many will work directly with a borrower for special deals. Usually, the larger the deal, the more anxious brokers are to work directly with you. Fees for direct placements often exceed amounts charged agents or banks, however. They can easily run 3 to 5 percent of the mortgage balance.

Mortgage brokers also assist in sourcing REITs and REMICs currently open for new placements. They work both sides of the street, helping investors locate appropriate REITs and REMICs and assisting commercial real estate agents, developers, and corporate borrowers identify available funding.

A special form of real estate ownership, REITs (real estate investment trusts) permit a widely held entity to own real estate and pass the income through to its owners without the entity incurring a tax. A REIT is to real estate investments what a mutual fund is to stocks, *and* what a REMIC is to real estate mortgages.

A REMIC (real estate mortgage investment conduit) is a special type of mortgage investment company created by Congress with the Tax Reform Act of 1986 in mind. It consists of a pooling of real estate mortgages used as collateral to publicly-traded security interests in the pool. REMICs create a larger investment base for investing in additional mortgages by selling these security interests on the open market. Both REITs and REMICs function very much like limited partnerships, giving multiple investors the opportunity to share in the profits of larger transactions than individuals could customarily afford on their own.

SELECTING THE RIGHT AGENT

Without a strong background in buying and selling commercial real estate and enough spare time to devote weeks—maybe months—to sourcing properties and mortgage money, it makes sense to use the services of a commercial real estate agent, or a commercial real estate broker as some prefer to be called. Not only will a qualified agent present a choice of available properties, but a good one also will help negotiate an equitable purchase price. Even more important, competent commercial agents have their fingers on rapidly changing sources of mortgage funds.

Even if you end up with a mortgage broker to do the actual sourcing of funds, the services of a competent commercial agent can be invaluable. Many charlatans call themselves mortgage brokers and a good agent weeds out the bad from the good.

A wide array of mortgage funds exist. A qualified agent helps choose the best source for the specific deal. If the agent knows your company well enough, you can get assistance in structuring a loan to fit your company's capabilities. This can be a priceless service.

The secret to success in mortgage financing is to choose the right agent, one that fits not only the needs and capabilities of your company but is also honest and easy to get along with. Several years ago I prepared the following questionnaire to help clients make the right choice. As a minimum, it identifies key topics that must be resolved. This questionnaire won't ensure the best choice, but clients using it have been ahead of those who didn't.

Questionnaire For Selecting A Commercial Real Estate Agent

A. Prior closings
1. How many deals have you closed in the last year?
2. What were the prices?
3. What were the approximate sizes of the purchasers?
4. What type of properties were they?
5. Where were the properties located?
6. What was the source and the form of the financing?

B. Financing contacts
7. Do you work through mortgage brokers? Who?
8. What contacts do you have in commercial bank mortgage departments?
9. What contacts do you have in mortgage banks?
10. Do you ever work with foreign banks? Which ones?

C. Syndications
11. What syndicated deals have you closed?
12. Have you sourced funds through REMICs? Which ones?
13. Can you structure and manage a REIT to get it off the ground?
14. What other syndications have you worked with?

D. Services
15. What can you do to help negotiate a deal?
16. What correspondent firms do you work with?
17. Will your firm carry a portion of the mortgage paper?
18. Will you arrange for a property appraisal?
19. Will you set up appointments and accompany our representative to view the properties?
20. Can you arrange for legal assistance for writing the contract?

21. Will you arrange the title search?
22. What other services do you provide?
E. **References**
23. Bank references—at least three.
24. Prior customer references—at least two.
25. Legal reference.

RAISING MORTGAGE CAPITAL

With preparations completed and a financing plan in hand, it's time to begin the search for capital. Most second-stage property financing is accomplished through long-term mortgage loans. Many sources of mortgage funds exist throughout the United States as well as in foreign ports. Characteristics of each transaction determine how, when, and where to do the sourcing.

Smaller deals can be handled locally. Larger purchases require a financial institution with connections in national, and perhaps international, financial markets. Constructing a property normally necessitates an affiliation with a competent commercial developer who may or may not have separate access to financing.

A good starting point, however, is with the same commercial bank that handles your company's other financial matters. The search may not end here, but it's as good a place as any to begin.

MORTGAGES FROM COMMERCIAL BANKS

Contrary to the general reluctance in the commercial banking industry to make long-term loans, most banks encourage loan officers to go after real estate mortgages. Until the recent collapse of commercial real estate markets in some sections of the country, a lender was assured of continued appreciation in real estate values and, therefore, steadily increasing collateral values. During the past decade especially, banks of every size invested heavily in real estate lending—both commercial and residential. Now with the severe collapse of real estate values in the Northeast and other sections of the country these same banks scrutinize mortgage activity much closer; however, they still actively participate in the market.

Whereas money center or regional banks are capable of handling mortgages of practically any amount, local banks restrict themselves. Also, since mortgages represent only one segment of a bank's loan portfolio, local and regional banks may from time to time be fully loaned in this segment and, therefore, they may stop making mortgage loans for a while. It pays to shop around. This can be done most effectively by engaging either a competent commercial real estate agent or a mortgage broker.

Interest rates charged by commercial banks stay fairly competitive both within the banking industry and with non-bank mortgage lenders. Although some variation exists, it usually doesn't spread much more than .5 to 1 percentage point between banks in a given region.

True to their conservative colors, commercial banks currently prefer to cap mortgage loans at no more than 60 to 65 percent of the appraised property value, although this percentage goes up for smaller transactions. This high down payment, commensurate with other conservative bank policies, provides them with an extra cushion in the event of default. Customarily, collateral beyond the subject property will not be required. Occasionally, with a poor credit history, a personal guarantee may be required, but this is the exception rather than the rule. With appreciating property and a declining loan balance, a bank should not insist on this extra coverage.

Ideally, the same bank that holds a company's working capital line, and perhaps a term loan against equipment, could take the mortgage loan. On the other hand, many bankers shy away from holding this much paper from a smaller business. In that case, a reference letter to another bank should bring a warm reception. As previously mentioned, most banks will invest in mortgages providing the balance is not too large. For larger commercial mortgages, you may have to use a specialized mortgage bank.

MORTGAGES FROM MORTGAGE BANKS

As their name implies, mortgage banks specialize in mortgage loans. For decades mortgage banks restricted their lending activity exclusively to mortgages. They had little interest in other types of lending activity. Liberalized rules in the banking industry have now permitted mortgage specialists to become active in a variety of other lending and periphery services: installment loans, depository services, investment certificates and funds, asset-based lending, and many other financial services cutting into the domain of traditional commercial banks and finance companies. However, several of the larger mortgage banks, especially those serving national markets, continue to specialize in mortgage lending.

Mortgage banks go by a variety of names in different parts of the country. A few of the more commonly used designations are "mortgage company," "financial corporation," "bond and mortgage," "mortgage investment company," "capital corporation," "financial services," "thrift," or "savings and loan." However, the term "mortgage bank" generically describes these lenders throughout the country.

Locating a mortgage bank gets confusing because many of those that have branched out into other services have chosen to be listed in the telephone directory under *everything but* "mortgage banks." They can be found under "business financing," "commercial finance," "commercial and industrial mortgages," and a variety of other less conspicuous headings, along with asset-based lenders and other financial institutions. Contacting larger mortgage banks through commercial real estate agents or brokerage houses is usually the fastest way to get moving.

Amounts required for most second-stage facility expansions tend to be toward the bottom of the spectrum of financing packages handled by the larger mortgage banks. Purchasing or constructing only one plant, warehouse, or office building tends to localize these transactions. Financing availability and terms depend to a large extent on immediate regional economic conditions. Therefore, it usually works best to locate a mortgage bank in, or near, the area you wish to locate, as opposed to going through one of the very large national or international houses.

Although smaller mortgage banks handle commercial mortgages as low as $100,000, most prefer larger deals—at least over $1 million. Many won't touch anything less than $50 million. The large nationals set their minimum even beyond that. All loan terms and conditions are negotiable with mortgage banks. The larger the transaction, the more latitude a borrower has to negotiate everything from interest rate to amortization schedule to loan covenants.

The Origination Of Mortgage Money

Developers of large commercial and industrial buildings also work through mortgage banks. If building a facility seems to make more sense than buying one, your developer can probably arrange the financing; or, the developer might finance the deal internally. Many larger developers, as well as mortgage banks, raise their own lending capital through a variety of sources: limited partnerships, REITs, foreign investors, merchant banks, REMICs, public stock and bond issues, and others.

First time buyers of commercial and industrial properties often become confused, and sometimes perturbed, when, six months after signing the mortgage papers, they receive a notice that monthly payments should be made to a strange company, not the bank they signed up with. Traditionally commercial mortgages were supported by iron-clad collateral appreciating up to 25 percent or more each year. This created a lively market for buying and selling mortgage paper.

It would not be surprising if national mortgage brokerage houses made higher profits trading mortgages than through interest income. As long as a secondary market exists in first and second mortgages, mortgage banks and other financial institutions find it difficult to justify holding the paper for the duration of the loan.

One vehicle that serves this market well is the real estate mortgage investment conduit.

Real Estate Mortgage Investment Conduit

Real Estate Mortgage Investment Conduits (REMICs) originated with the Tax Reform Act of 1986. Although a full discussion of the regulatory, tax, and accounting advantages to mortgage banks using REMICs goes beyond the needs of most businessowners, a brief exposure to this new investment vehicle can't hurt when deciding which way to go for financing help.

The emergence of REMICs was predictable by anyone in the commercial property financial market. The mortgage-backed securities industry which creates and sustains secondary markets in mortgage paper had been booming for years. By 1985, unmanageable, inconsistent tax laws caused the industry to begin to slow down. Tax problems hindered the ability of these dealers to structure a mortgage-backed vehicle that maximized economic, regulatory, and accounting benefits for both issuers and investors. In 1986, Congress attempted to rectify this problem by creating a new investment entity—the REMIC.

Aside from tax considerations, the main benefit of using a REMIC is that by issuing securities from the REMIC intermediary, multiple-class securities can be structured as to coupon rate, credit, risk, secured collateral, and so on, independent of the underlying mortgages. Direct ownership of the mortgage resides with the REMIC. Investors only buy and sell the REMIC securities.

This procedure makes a REMIC a true brokerage house and enables it to raise significant amounts of capital through public trading. Tax laws permit the pass-through of income directly to REMIC shareholders, bypassing any tax liability for the REMIC. Mortgage banks, developers, commercial real estate brokerage houses, and other investors raise substantial funds through REMICs which, in turn, are used to fund additional mortgage requirements.

LOCAL DEVELOPMENT COMPANIES

Large and mid-sized cities, as well as many small towns, have established quasi-public agencies to assist small companies finance business development in specific areas of the community. The town fathers designate these areas as being in need of commercial development to sustain or add to the local job base. Additional tax revenues also play a motivating role.

Some development companies concentrate on urban redevelopment sections. Others focus on high unemployment areas. Still others encourage business development in Foreign Trade Zones. Local development companies get funds from many sources: federal assistance, state allocations, corporate contributions, and local tax revenues.

The Philadelphia Industrial Development Corp. (PIDC) program represents one example of a local development agency's efforts to stimulate local business. The PIDC is a quasi-public agency that helps attract and expand business in Philadelphia through low-cost loans, grants, and tax credits. Its loan program offers working capital loans, term loans, and mortgage loans at interest rates approximating one-half of prime. PIDC loans traditionally represented 40 percent of the total financing package, the balance coming from local banks and mortgage companies. In the face of tightening credit, the percentage has recently been increased to 60 percent. Most companies have no difficulty interesting private financial institutions in picking up the balance.

Each municipality supports slightly different business development programs, but all require participation from local financial institutions. With the ridiculously low interest rate and long amortization period, small businesses find development financing hard to beat, providing the mandated location doesn't conflict with company strategy.

SMALL BUSINESS ADMINISTRATION ASSISTANCE

As mentioned in Chapter 9, in 1989 Congress updated and finalized the SBA's "504 loan program" to help finance large projects costing well above $1 million. Because of the high level of funding, this program is especially helpful for financing new facilities, although it can also be used for major equipment purchases. Several features make 504 funding significantly different from other SBA assistance.

1. The financing must be structured as follows:
   - The borrower must contribute 10 percent of the cost of the project
   - A private-sector lender (non-federal) must contribute 50 percent
   - The SBA loans 40 percent

2. To qualify for 504 assistance, the project must demonstrate a positive impact on the local economy. The normal standard necessary to meet this criteria is the creation of at least one new job for each $15,000 worth of debt secured by the SBA guarantee, which of course is 40 percent of the total project cost. The higher the job ratio, the greater the likelihood of getting the funding.

3. A Certified Development Corporation (CDC) must act as the agent for the loan. Many municipalities already have CDCs in existence. For those that don't, state CDCs meet this criteria. Local SBA offices know which condition exists in your area.

4. No 504 program funding may be used for working capital.

5. In order to enlist commercial banks, mortgage banks, and other private lenders, the program consists of two separate interest rates. One rate applies to the loan from a private lender and is set at the lender's discretion. A second rate applies to the SBA guaranteed portion. This rate fluctuates between .25 to .75 above U.S. Treasury bond rates of similar maturity.

6. The company's ability to generate cash flow to service the debt determines the primary criteria in placing this financing. Collateral consists of the building or other assets being acquired. In addition, personal guarantees are usually required, as well as an insurance policy on the owner's life payable to

the lending institutions. On the other hand, owners do not have to pledge all or even a major portion of their net worth if the project has significant economic impact on the community.

Mortgage banks like to participate in 504 programs because, even though they only lend 50 percent of the project cost, they get a first position on all the collateral. The SBA settles for a second.

Raising Mortgage Capital through Foreign Banks

A fourth source of debt capital for buying or constructing facilities comes from overseas. Corporate and wealthy private investors in Europe, the Middle East, Japan, Australia, Asia, South America, and other regions of the world continue to regard investments in American business and property as one of the most secure places to put their money. Even though interest rates in other countries remain significantly higher than in the United States, a measure of security in the American political and social systems continues to weigh heavily on investment decisions.

The recent rash of acquisitions of and significant investments in American companies by the Japanese, Germans, Dutch, French, and British bear witness to the perceived long-term strength of the American economy by foreign investors. Significant investment funds also have flowed practically non-stop into American commercial and industrial real estate. Although many of these investments have been made with the intention of owning and developing real property—such as the Japanese investment in Rockefeller Center—many other foreign investors remain content with investing in long-term mortgage loans.

These foreign mortgage funds flow through several different conduits. Merchant banks like Charterhouse (British) and Sumitomo (Japanese) play roles similar to investment banks when placing foreign equity and debt funds. Multi-national industrial corporations, such as the industrial equipment giant Siemens (Germany), the telecommunications conglomerate British Telecom, and the investment bank branch of Mitsui (Japanese), have extended mortgage loans to comparably large American firms. These investments exceed billions of dollars.

Most smaller companies are not in this league, however, and do much better soliciting funds from foreign banks. Many foreign banks are active in the American mortgage market—Standard Charter (British with a strong South African flavor), Credit Agricole and Banque Indosuez (French), Hong Kong & Shanghai Bank (Hong Kong), Barclays (British), Credit Suisse (Swiss), and Bank of Nova Scotia (Canadian), to mention only a few.

The lending policies of foreign banks tend to be less conservative than their American counterparts. More liberal accounting and regulatory controls undoubtedly contribute to their success in achieving global roles while American banks languish in domestic tranquility. Regardless of the reason, many smaller companies find dealing with foreign banks a breath of fresh air compared to their traditional American counterparts.

It's easy enough to make contact with a foreign bank. A telephone call will normally get you an appointment. A characteristic of foreign investors—be they banks or other institutions—is that most look at either a debt or equity investment as a long-term proposition. They seem to be more interested in earning a solid return over a long period of time rather than quick profits and rapid loan or investment turnover. This offers both an advantage and difficulty for many American businesses.

On the plus side, their long-term perspective makes foreign banks easier to work with structuring creative loan terms and conditions, as well as loan agreements. Foreign banks are less likely to push the panic button when a borrower runs into short-term cash shortfalls. Foreign banks represent not only investors from their own countries, but from other nations as well, providing a seemingly limitless source of funds. And finally, foreign banks are still trying to gain a foothold in many areas of the United States. This makes them more apt to look favorably on smaller mortgage loan applications.

On the flip side, don't expect to get any favors in reduced interest rates. Inflationary spirals in Europe, Australia, Canada, and Japan, open doors to cross-border funds that yield significantly higher returns than the American prime rate. Foreign banks may like the safety of U.S. investments but they are not going to throw their money away. Also, because many managers are still trying to learn the American business system, expect close monitoring of your company's performance. They generally don't interfere, but they do want to know what is happening in your business.

OTHER SOURCES OF CAPITAL

Mortgage funds are not the only way to finance real property acquisitions. Equity capital also plays an important role. Although smaller companies tend to shy away from these methods as being too complex, they at least bear scrutiny to determine if they might be applicable to your circumstances.

Equity capital is seldom used for smaller property transactions. The cost, effort, and time expended to raise equity funds outweighs the benefit. Except for unusual circumstances, transactions under $10 million should probably be financed with mortgage debt. On the other hand, larger purchases or major development projects can nearly always be financed at lesser cost through one of the following equity arrangements.

REAL ESTATE SYNDICATIONS

A building, or buildings, costing more than $10 million can be efficiently financed directly by an operating company—not by internally-generated cash, but by forming a real estate syndication. A real estate syndication is just a fancy name for a group of investors who invest exclusively in real property. Although other vehicles can certainly be used, limited partnerships have become extremely popular as a tool to raise investment funds for this purpose.

Long-term security and probable appreciation in value makes real property a natural investment for limited partnerships. Commercial and industrial property resale values tend to be affected by long-term trends in economic cycles, not short-term fluctuations. Managing a real estate limited partnership requires a relatively minor amount of administrative effort and time. These advantages make limited partnership syndications easy to organize and partnership units attractive to private investors.

Raising syndicated equity capital can be accomplished relatively quickly. The limited partners know that once purchased, or constructed, the property will have an immediate tenant—the general partner's operating company. Not only should the property itself appreciate in value over time, but a ready tenant assures a steady stream of income for distribution to partners or to use for investments in other properties.

Several clients have in fact used real estate syndications to actually start-up a second business independent of their operating company. As long as reasonably-priced, income-producing properties can be found to provide a positive cash flow to the limited partners, such diversification makes economic sense.

Another vehicle used in real estate syndications is the real estate investment trust, or REIT. A REIT may be structured as a corporation or as a trust. The mechanics of a REIT work in much the same way as a mutual fund for investing in traded stocks and bonds. Several small investors pool their money by buying shares in a REIT. The REIT then invests in commercial and industrial properties. Tax laws allow REIT income to be passed through to its owners without tax liability to the REIT. Although the mechanics of forming and operating a REIT have been simplified immeasurably by the 1986 tax changes, it remains a cumbersome vehicle compared to limited partnerships—and the benefits to shareholders are comparable.

OFF-SHORE SITES

An increasing number of companies choose to locate their new plant, warehouse, or office beyond U.S. borders. Off-shore locations offer unique opportunities to service new foreign markets and to save taxes from domestic business. Very often both reasons justify the decision.

To service this booming market, several commercial real estate agencies have developed skills for sourcing and selecting appropriate countries and sites for serious customers. Any of the more than one-hundred world trade business and news magazines carry advertisements of brokers and agents willing and able to handle the site selection job. Because of the increasing globalization of world markets, the advertisements of professional, international real estate agencies list foreign locations as their home base. London, Paris, Amsterdam, Hong Kong, and Costa Rica seem to be popular for agencies serving respectively broad markets.

U.S. branches of major foreign banks also have direct contacts with overseas property management firms. Most of these companies, in addition to managing rental properties for investors, provide site selection and mortgage financing services. Beginning the search for foreign sites through a foreign bank can be very advantageous. Establishing a banking relationship at this stage makes financing the acquisition that much easier once you select a site.

United States and host country governments have established several agencies to assist in arranging financing for investments in a variety of regions. Developing countries are eager for American production and technology investment. With a bank as the intermediary, sourcing financing from multi-national and host country development banks becomes a fairly straightforward exercise.

It's a good idea to choose a foreign bank noted for handling work in the country or region you are interested in expanding to. Not only do they have the most contacts with property sales and management companies in the area, but they also are most likely to handle the mortgage financing themselves. At least they can recommend excellent contacts for local financial sources. Chapter 13 describes a variety of sources in addition to banks for financing off-shore expansions.

FINANCING THROUGH JOINT VENTURES

Joint ventures with other domestic or foreign companies is fast becoming a way of life for financing major expansions in a company's third stage of development. Not infrequently, smaller operating companies offer new product or service lines that a larger corporation can utilize in its marketing strategy. In return, larger companies see an opportunity to make a secure investment in real property with an assured, long-term tenant. Combining forces makes economic sense to both parties.

It also alleviates the necessity for the smaller business to incur significant amounts of mortgage debt. Joint ventures can be a win-win situation outdistancing benefits of any financing scheme from lending institutions.

However, not all joint venture financing is done with internally-generated equity capital, especially for larger property transactions. A corporate partner might conclude that incurring new debt is more economical. Tax, regulatory, and accounting restrictions frequently dictate the use of external mortgage capital rather than either internal cash or public issues.

Foreign joint venture partners with immediate access to foreign exchanges frequently float Eurobond issues to raise development capital. These firms also have access to foreign-government funding, specifically designed to subsidize investment in American property. Last, but certainly not least, corporate partners from industrial nations—such as Britain, France, Germany, Taiwan, and Japan— accustomed to quasi-government investments for international expansion, have the ability to finance property acquisitions with a combination of equity and debt funds from global consortiums combining corporate, government, and private investor participation.

Joint venture financing has become a major source of funds for smaller American companies establishing off-shore facilities in the Caribbean, Mexico, and Central America. Joint venture partners in many of these countries consist of equally small local manufacturers or distributors. Federal agencies and private banks of both the United States and host countries eagerly solicit investments in production and distribution facilities from American firms.

Special programs have been established to finance these investments. Many times an American parent sets up a facility without incurring any debt on its books and without using any of its own funds. "Super" and host country development banks, Eximbank affiliated agencies, and other U.S and foreign government subsidy programs make investments in one of these areas extremely lucrative.

Although a joint venture partner may not provide direct funding, host government restrictions on foreign investments frequently require a partnership with a local company in order to get local financing. Once again, Chapter 13 explores the detailed steps to take advantage of this approach.

HOLDING REAL PROPERTY IN A SEPARATE COMPANY

Tax strategies and legal liability protection play important roles in any long-term financing program. Many fine reference works explain what to look for and how to structure business entities to minimize both concerns. Practicing attorneys and public accountants also offer sound advice for planning the most advantageous structuring. A detailed examination of various business structures designed to minimize both taxes and legal liability is beyond the scope of this book. However, one part of the puzzle is so important to many smaller businesses that it would be a travesty to ignore the issue completely—and that is, the use of a separate business entity to hold title to real property and the related mortgage loan.

Either a new corporation, partnership, or limited partnership can be established specifically to own buildings and land used by the operating company. The new entity then leases the property to the operating company on a long-term lease approximating the term of the mortgage. Lease payments should cover mortgage debt service, building depreciation, and a small margin for administrative costs. The lease should be *triple net* to fix responsibility for property taxes, insurance, and repairs on the operating company.

Several advantages accrue under this scheme. From the perspective of the operating company:

1. The operating company's balance sheet stays free of mortgage liability, thus improving the opportunity for future borrowings if needed.

2. Mortgage default claims fall on the new entity, thus freeing the operating company from this contingent liability.

3. The full rental payments are tax-deductible as business expenses.

For the entity holding the property:

1. An S corporation or partnership passes profits and losses, if any, directly to the shareholders, presumably taxed at rates lower than an operating company pays.

2. Cash distributions to the shareholders, approximating the building's depreciation, create a tax-free way to extract company cash.

3. Different ownership arrangements may be established to hold the property in trust or in an off-shore entity for estate purposes.

4. When, and if, the operating company is sold, the property can be retained as an investment.

Competent tax and legal counsel should be retained to be certain that all relevant considerations are incorporated in the structuring. Existing plant, warehouse, or office property owned by the operating company can also be transferred to the new entity, increasing the above benefits.

SUMMARY

Before beginning the search for long-term capital, several preliminary steps need to be taken. An agreement should be reached with a competent commercial real estate agency to actually perform the property search. Once a property or site has been selected, a company needs to match the purchase price with internal cash flow projections to make sure it is economically feasible. If considering debt financing, an analysis should be made to determine the advantages and risks of fixed versus variable interest rates. And finally, the possibility of using a mortgage broker to source the financing should be investigated.

Property transactions under $10 million are normally financed with long-term mortgage loans. Once the preliminary steps have been completed, the search for mortgage funds begins. The following compares the major pros and cons of five major sources of mortgage financing:

1. *Commercial banks*

Typical loan size	—regional and money center banks—unlimited
	—smaller local banks—up to $1 million
Interest rates	—same as residential rates
Down payment	—35 to 40 percent
Additional collateral	—occasionally personal guarantees
Availability	—varies with size of loan and section of the country
Special features	—best to first try the same bank used for other loans

2. *Mortgage banks*

Typical loan size	—small local banks—$100,000 to $1 million
	—mid-size regional banks—$1 to $50 million
	—large national banks—over $50 million
Interest rate	—negotiable
Down payment	—negotiable
Additional collateral	—N/A
Availability	—readily available in most sections of the country
Special features	—funded through REMICS

3. *Local development companies*

Typical loan size	—varies, but usually up to $500,000
Interest rate	—less than prime
Down payment	—various
Additional collateral	—N/A
Availability	—readily available to qualified applicants
Special features	—special site location, bank participation to 40 percent

4. *SBA 504 program*

Typical loan size	—varies, can exceeed $1 million
Interest rate	—competitive for private portion, .25 to .75 over Treasury bonds for SBA segment
Down payment	—10 percent
Additional collateral	—personal guarantee
Availability	—available for large projects with economic impact on community
Special features	—special site location, bank participation to 40 percent

5. *Foreign banks*

Typical loan size	—no limit
Interest rate	—comparable to American mortgage banks

Down payment   —typically 20 percent
Additional collateral—N/A
Availability   —the larger the loan the easier to get
Special features   —prefer solid value locations/properties

Equity and special financing for property acquisitions is also available. Syndicated limited partnerships and REITs work well as equity raising vehicles for development properties. Off-shore financing can be sourced for plant or other facilities located in foreign countries. Joint ventures enable a company to combine financing resources with other partnership advantages, both domestic and off-shore. The following summarizes major equity sources for purchasing and developing real property.

1. *Real estate syndications*
   Typical levels of capital—over $10 million
   Sources of investors   —individuals, other companies, the public
   Cost   —nominal to $250,000 initially
                           —administration of REIT, up to $100,000 per year
   Ease of achieving   —straightforward with qualified advisor
   Special features   —use limited partnerships or REITs as the investing vehicle

2. *Off-shore sites*
   Typical levels of capital—$1 million to $50 million
   Sources of investors   —local investors, foreign banks, development banks, government agencies
   Cost   —up to $100,000 plus various continuing administrative costs
   Ease of achieving   —straightforward with qualified advisor
   Special features   —foreign banks and local development banks supplemented by federal financial assistance

3. *Joint ventures*
   Typical levels of capital—no limit
   Sources of investors   —large American and foreign corporations, host country companies, host country government agencies
   Cost   —N/A
   Ease of achieving   —time-consuming to source partner
   Special features   —business advantages other than financing may encourage joint ventures

Regardless of the financing method, setting up a separate company to hold title to the property results in significant tax savings and liability protection.

Chapter 11

Leasing Equipment and Real Estate

Although the popularity of leasing fluctuates with changes in tax laws and accounting regulations, it still offers a viable alternative to either debt or equity financing of hard assets. Industry executives estimate that in 1990, leasing accounted for over $100 million per year as an annual source for financing first- and second-stage growth. According to figures released from the Department of Commerce, the total amount of outstanding equipment leases in the United States in 1990 approximated $130 billion. Public offerings account for the highest volume of third-stage financing, but leasing runs a close second.

The reasons seem obvious. Small and mid-size businesses can ill-afford to tie up large amounts of cash, either with or without bank loans. Equipment leases generally have longer repayment terms than bank loans. And, it is much easier to interest a leasing company in making a deal than a bank.

The form a lease takes varies all over the lot. Certain leases take on the characteristics of lease-purchase agreements. The equipment or property is recorded on your company's balance sheet as an asset and the lease obligation shows up as a liability. Others get treated as off-balance sheet leases with rental payments written off currently, just like any other operating expense. Negotiated terms and structure of a lease have major implications for tax purposes as well as for balance sheet purists.

Equipment and property leases are relatively simple to understand and to source. They require little or no down payment. With the proper lease structure, a company's balance sheet remains untarnished, making it easier to raise additional bank debt or equity infusions later on.

IRS provisions affecting the deductibility of rental payments, lease-related expenditures, and tax credits play a major role in a company's cash flow. These tax benefits may be greater or less than when purchasing an asset. Repayment terms, tax considerations, and asset recording conventions could make leasing a good choice, especially for financing second-stage expansions. However, its high cost remains a major deterrent for many companies.

Leasing has other negatives. The decision to lease or buy is not always straightforward. Complex tax laws that keep changing every year affect not only the availability of leases but their cost and structure. Rental payments usually exceed term-loan interest expense for comparable financing, and this detracts from a company's income statement. Complex lease agreements cause legal fees to soar. And finally, an asset that appreciates in value (such as real property) is lost to the company as a valuable addition to its balance sheet.

Before getting into comparisons and analyses of leasing options, it might be helpful to review lease terminology, fundamental leasing principles, and the lease structures currently in vogue.

LEASING TERMINOLOGY

Leases are categorized as either finance leases or operating leases. Finance leases normally extend over a long time frame with the total of monthly, quarterly, or annual payments approximating the purchase price of the asset plus finance charges. Large pieces of production equipment, heavy-duty trucks, store fixtures, and production facilities are examples of assets typically falling under a finance lease.

Finance leases represent long-term financial commitments by both lessor and lessee. These leases typically run for the entire normal useful life of the asset. From the lessor's perspective, rents must be sufficient to cover the original equity investment in the asset, any debt service payments for financing the asset purchase, administrative costs, and a profit.

The lessor also uses projected cash flow as a factor in setting monthly rentals. Cash flow to a lessor represents the actual rent charged, tax benefits of the lease, and the residual value of the asset after the lease expires. To the extent that actual tax savings are realized and the asset can be sold on the open market after the lease term, these two cash contributors reduce the amount of rent needed from the lessee.

Because a finance lease involves a long-term commitment and the lessor relies on the entire lease period to recover costs and earn a profit, severe prepayment provisions discourage lessees from breaking the lease. As a minimum, penalties include the lessor's investment recovery, costs, and profit to the date of cancellation.

Most finance leases are "net" leases, under which the lessee remains responsible for the maintenance of the asset, property and other taxes, and insurance premiums. The lessor's role is strictly that of a financier whose responsibility extends to financing the asset purchase but stops short of any liability arising from its use.

Equipment obsolescence under a finance lease must be dealt with by the lessee. Theoretically, and under the best of conditions, rental payments over the term of the lease yield zero residual value. Lessors don't care if the equipment becomes obsolete or not during the period because they recoup their entire investment and profit through rent payments. Pragmatically, however, to keep rents competitive, lessors do calculate a small residual value and, therefore, assume some responsibility for obsolescence.

The biggest risks to a lessor are default by the lessee, and the destruction of the asset through a casualty occurrence such as a fire, flood, or explosion. Most lease agreements include provisions to protect against both conditions.

Insurance coverage for the full price of the asset reduces casualty risk. The lessee pays the premium with the lessor nominated as first-party beneficiary. In leasing jargon, a "hell or high water" provision protects the lessor from default. This provision stipulates that the lessee must pay the lease in full, come "hell or high water." The lessee may not offset any claims against the lessor, regardless of the source of the claim. Without these two provisions, rent payments would inevitably be significantly higher.

OPERATING LEASE

Equipment and property leases that do not fall into the finance category must be operating leases. Operating leases involve shorter term financial commitments. The lease term may or may not approximate the life of the asset. The lease period may be measured in hours, days, or months. The sum of the rental payments is less than the purchase price of the asset. Automobiles, computer equipment, and office furniture represent assets usually leased under operating leases.

Rapid obsolescence can be a major problem for lessors. With the lease period so short, the lessor bears the brunt of product usage or design obsolescence. To compensate for this risk, rents run substantially higher than under finance leases. Also because of the short rental periods, lessors cannot expect to recover their investment and profit over the term of a lease, as with finance leases. Therefore, lessors place heavy reliance on selling or otherwise disposing of the asset at the end of the lease period to recover a large part of their investment. The costs and risks of this exercise also get added into rents.

Even though operating leases require higher rental payments, they serve an important market niche. If an operating company needs equipment with rapid technological obsolescence, such as computers, short-term leases can be a good tradeoff against keeping the equipment for 10 or more years, even with higher rental payments. Also, as with rental cars, if you only need the asset for a short period of time, the higher rent is still less expensive than buying the asset.

Both finance and operating leases can be structured as leveraged leases, non-leveraged leases, or service leases.

LEVERAGED LEASE

A leveraged lease is exactly what the term implies—a lease covering an asset that a lessor purchases with borrowed money; that is, the lessor "leverages" the acquisition. The distinction is important to lessees. Rental payments are always calculated to return investment, cover administrative expense, and make a profit for the lessor. With a leveraged deal, lessors earn 100 percent return on their money but invest only 20 to 40 percent of the price of the asset. Therefore, rental calculations under leveraged leases tend to be significantly lower than those for non-leveraged leases. Nearly all net finance leases are leveraged. Therefore, this form of long-term financing competes to some extent with term loans.

The long-term loan used to acquire assets for a lease is nearly always nonrecourse. This means that the lender, in this case a bank or other financial institution, has no recourse against the lessor in the event of default. The lender must look for recovery to the stream of rental income, the lessee, and the leased asset. However, recourse against a third party can be very difficult to collect. To compensate, lessors assign their rights in the lease to the lender, giving the lender direct recourse to the lessee. As an alternative, a lessor merely subordinates lease rights to the lender's first position.

NONLEVERAGED LEASE

A non-leveraged lease covers equipment or property whose purchase was financed entirely by the lessor, without resorting to borrowed funds. Lease agreements for non-leveraged leases are always much simpler than for leveraged leases. This saves a lot of time in negotiating the transaction and a significant amount of legal fees, for both the lessor and the lessee. Nothing is free, however. Legal fees may be less, but rents under non-leveraged leases run substantially higher.

SERVICE LEASES

Under a service lease, the lessor retains responsibility for the expenses associated with operating the equipment or building. The lessor maintains the asset, pays for insurance coverage, and remains liable for all property, sales, and use taxes. Service leases are all relatively short term. Rentals must be very high to compensate for the extra expenses incurred by the lessor.

ADVANTAGES OF DIFFERENT TYPES OF LEASES

Over the years, the simple idea of charging rent to use an asset under contract has undergone enormous changes. Although changes mean added complexity, a corollary benefit has been additional flexibility in structuring leases. This flexibility results in many benefits to both leasing parties.

TRADITIONAL LEASE STRUCTURE

Traditional lease structures have been around for generations. Typically used for real property (e.g. land, buildings, office space, farmland), traditionally structured leases can also be used for equipment with long useful lives. The major characteristics of traditional leases are:

1. The lessee has a legal obligation to pay for the use of the asset for a specific period of time for any purpose that does not violate the lease agreement. The lessor cannot deprive the lessee of such use; this is known as the *principle of quiet enjoyment.*

2. The lessor owns the property and retains responsibility for its upkeep. Such upkeep may involve repairs and maintenance, insurance coverage, and property taxes. With net leases, typically used as finance leases for equipment, the lessor charges the lessee for part or all of these expenses.

3. The lessor benefits by any appreciation of the asset over the course of the lease, and likewise suffers any depreciation in value.

4. Tax benefits associated with the asset flow to the lessor—deductions for depreciation, interest, and property tax, as well as any tax credits currently in vogue.

Traditional leases offer the lessee three primary advantages:

1. The risk of unusual loss of asset value rests with the lessor.

2. Leases are simple, straightforward agreements that can be executed without a lawyer in most cases. Lessors cannot vary the standard terms with peculiar restrictions or covenants.

3. Traditional leases are executory contracts. This means that you don't have to record either the asset or the lease liability on your balance sheet.

Although traditional leases are far and away the easiest to execute and understand, they seldom appear any more—except for certain long-term real property. Nowadays, lessors seem to want either special restrictions or covenants included in the lease document or unusual terms applied to rental payments. These complications turn a traditional lease into a more complicated document frequently referred to as a "capital lease."

CAPITAL LEASE STRUCTURE

Although it is impossible to list all the possible modifications that can be incorporated, the following represent some of the more common provisions in capital leases.

1. The life of the lease is indeterminate. You may rent the asset for a long as you wish.

2. The lessee pays for maintenance, insurance, and taxes on the asset.

3. Purchase options can be added allowing you to purchase the asset at the end of the lease or during the lease. Prices may be fair market value, stipulated value, or one dollar.

4. Terms may include a mandatory purchase of the asset at the end of the lease for a flat amount, fair market value, or other amount.

5. Rental payments can be variable. They can be based on a percentage of operating results—sales, profits, production levels—or they can be geared to interest rate fluctuations.

6. Leases may cover groups of assets without specifying specific assets. Rent is then based on a percentage of asset value. This allows addition or deletion of assets without re-writing lease agreements.

Capital leases may be called "leases" but they are really loans, collateralized by the equipment. The lessor finances the acquisition of equipment. The lessee pays the loan back through rental payments corresponding to principal and interest on a loan plus the lessor's profit. Currently, implicit interest in most capital leases reaches 6 to 9 percentage points over prime. The two major advantages of using capital leases rather than borrowing money directly to purchase assets are that the lessor retains the risk of ownership, and capital leases require little or no down payment.

Ownership risk of certain assets can be substantial. For example, computer equipment leased under a five-year operating lease may have a calculated residual value of 20 percent of its original cost; but, new technology makes it practically worthless after 3 years. The lessor suffers this loss, not the lessee.

Many operating leases give the lessee the option of rolling the lease over against new equipment. Trading in the old computer for a new variety in three years provides an operating company with state-of-the-art equipment without re-writing the lease or, alternately, buying a new computer.

Capital leases can be written to change the rules of ownership. Provisions can be included to treat the operating company as the owner of the assets rather than the lessor. Also, the residual value of the asset at the end of the lease may revert to the lessor, it may revert to the lessee, or the lessee may be required to purchase the asset for residual value or a portion thereof.

VENTURE LEASES

Venture leases are a recent innovation in the leasing industry. They have been invented to encourage lessors to participate in the growth of start-up or first-stage companies. A venture lease is nothing more than a capital lease with provisions giving a lessor the right to acquire an equity interest in the lessee company.

Venture leases come with very low rental payments in the first year or two to reduce the cash outflow for the new operating entity. In exchange for this concession, the agreement provides warrants or stock options for the lessor to acquire equity interest in the lessee's company within a specified time. In the same manner as venture capital funding, the venture lessor wins if the company grows rapidly and eventually goes public. Conversely, it loses along with equity investors if the company fails.

TAX CONSEQUENCES OF LEASING

Acceptable methods for recording leases and reporting rental payments frequently influence how to structure a lease for a given asset acquisition. The optimum agreement, of course, balances benefits between lessor and lessee, recognizing both accounting and tax regulations. Smaller companies find tax implications the most important of the two. Accounting niceties have virtually no impact on first-stage companies. If the recording of leases or rental payments for accounting or balance sheet purposes raises questions or seems to present a problem, review the current alternative treatments with a qualified accounting advisor.

The subject of the tax treatment of leases is complex enough to fill an entire book. Because of its overriding importance when making the decision to lease or buy, a brief review of its salient features might prove helpful, although the following is far from inclusive.

When is a Lease a Lease

Both the IRS and the accounting fraternity worry about whether a specific lease is really a lease or merely a camouflaged purchase. Although accounting definitions affect balance sheet ratios and hence, potential borrowing power in the future, IRS treatment affects immediate cash flow.

In the case of a purchase, the lessee must record both the cost of the asset and the full lease obligation on its books. Depreciation deductions can be taken over the useful life of the equipment. Rental payments must be separated into theoretical interest expense and principal retirement payments. Conversely, if the IRS rules that a lease is really a lease and not a purchase, no recording of asset or liability becomes necessary and the full rental payment can be deducted as a business expense.

The IRS has established four tests to reach this determination. If the transaction passes all four, it is a lease; otherwise, it will be classified as a purchase. These four tests are categorized to meet minimum investment standards; purchase and sale rights; lessee participation through equity investments, loans, or guarantees; and a profit requirement.

1. *Minimum Investment.* Throughout the period of the lease, the lessor must demonstrate at least a 20 percent equity interest in the asset. With a leveraged lease, the lessor can fulfill this requirement by establishing the reasonableness of estimating a residual value for the asset at the end of the lease period equal to 20 percent of its original useful life, or one remaining year of usefulness. Under a non-leveraged lease, the lessor retains a declining equity interest in the asset for the lease period at which time the 20 percent rule applies.

2. *Purchase and Sale Rights.* At the end of the lease period, or at any time during the period, an outright sale of the asset to the lessee cannot be made at less than the asset's fair market value at the time of transfer. Neither can the lease agreement stipulate that such a right exists, even though it may never be exercised.

3. *Lessee Investment, Loan, or Guarantee.* The lessee is prohibited from financing any part of the purchase of the asset or any improvements made to it. Such financing prohibition includes equity investments, loans, or guarantees to or on behalf of the lessor.

4. *Profit Requirement.* The lessor must present demonstrable proof that a profit will be made on the lease transaction. Such a profit may not include tax savings resulting from the transaction.

OTHER TAX CONSEQUENCES

The Tax Reform Act of 1986 eliminated several complex tax questions, one of which was the determination of which leasing party gets the investment tax credit. Most of the main tax questions involve deciding which party is entitled to specific deductions. The character of the lease and its special provisions, as discussed above, clarifies most of these questions. Two special situations are worthy of note, however.

The first involves leasehold improvements made by the lessee in addition to normal rent payments. Prior to 1986, such improvements were allowed to be amortized and deducted by the lessee over the remaining life of the lease. Now, the amortization period must be the same as the remaining useful life of the asset, as defined by depreciation guidelines. For real property, this creates a major negative impact on the lessee.

The second case involves leasing luxury automobiles. Prior to 1986, many companies leased Mercedes', BMWs, Cadillacs, and other luxury cars as an additional fringe benefit for executives. Now, the lessee of a luxury business car must include an additional amount in gross income to offset rental deductions taken each lease year. The amount to be included must be based on how much the original price of the car exceeds an inflation-adjusted amount, which was $12,800 in 1990. Each year's calculation of additional income consists of three steps:

- Match the line amount from the IRS supplied table of inclusion amounts at stepped fair market values with the fair market value of the leased car at the beginning of the lease term.

- Prorate the dollar amount specified in the table for the number of days of the lease term included in the current year.

- Multiply the prorated amount by the percentage of the year that the car was used for business purposes.

MAKING A LEASE OR BUY DECISION

Over the years, academicians, statisticians, lawyers, consultants, leasing executives, and a variety of other experts have written volumes detailing complex formulas and formats for making lease or buy decisions. Although many of these approaches serve as useful mathematical evidence to back up a calculation, the final decision must be based on business operating factors. Availability of capital, current interest rates, down payment requirements, asset obsolescence, the length of time the asset is needed, and a variety of other operating matters impact the final decision. Knowing how much a lease will cost you is a good starting point.

PRICING A LEASE

The cost of a lease to you, a lessee, derives directly from the cost of that lease to the lessor. Lessors view investing in a lease the same way that a lender or investor evaluates a loan or investment: How much cash must be paid to acquire the investment compared to how much cash will be received from the investment. To the extent that the actual cash received over the lease period covers a lessor's cash outlay for acquiring the asset and all associated costs and still yields a satisfactory profit, it has been a good investment.

Rent is a function of the lessor's costs (including the cost of capital which is usually a combination of borrowed and equity funds) and investment risk. A lessor's costs remain beyond the jurisdiction of a lessee, but risk assumptions do not. The level of risk in projected cash flow over the lease period represents the key variable that a lessee must attempt to negotiate.

A lessor views risks in two ways—credit risk and residual-value risk. Credit risk relates to leases exactly as it does to loans. If a lessee fails to meet lease payments the lessor must stand ready to reclaim the leased asset. The more evidence to prove a good credit history against loans and other obligations, the higher the chances of negotiating a lower credit risk factor. Such evidence is derived in the same way as when dealing with banks—with credit reports, bank reference letters, character verifications, and so on.

Residual-value risk is a different story. No step in evaluating lender risk compares to evaluating a lessor's residual-value risk.

RESIDUAL-VALUE RISK

A lessor mitigates residual-value risk in two ways. First, the lessor writes provisions in the lease agreement requiring the lessee to guarantee a specific residual value at the end of the lease. If the asset doesn't bring such a price, the lessee must make up the difference. Assessing this type of risk follows the same lines as determining credit risk. If a lessee has a good credit history and meets obligations when they are due, the probability of recovering any shortage in residual value escalates. A poor credit history results in the reverse, and rent payments increase.

The second method relates to shorter-term leases, or leases covering equipment with a limited technological or useful life. For short-term leases, a lessor relies heavily on cash flow generated from the sale of the asset after the lease ends to recover investment and make a profit. This means higher rental payments. The type of asset leased, its marketability as a used asset, alternative uses for the property, the cost of refurbishing or repairing the asset, costs involved in relocating the equipment, and the historical and current market price movements of similar assets all affect the residual-value decision.

Historically, lessors of real property estimated high residual-values because the market prices of commercial real estate continued to climb. This enables a lessor to settle for less rent. The residual value of automobiles is well documented in "blue book" catalogs and used car auctions. This makes rental payments for cars less negotiable.

Conversely, office equipment, specialized production equipment, and customized office facilities carry high residual-value risk. Rentals covering these assets nearly always go for a premium. Renting specialized equipment or high-tech equipment direct from a manufacturer or dealer usually results in lower payments than structuring a deal with an independent leasing company.

Lessor Tax Benefits

Granting tax concessions to the lessor can be a mighty tool for negotiating better lease terms. Deductions for depreciation, for example, might be more valuable to a lessor than to you. In that case, permitting the lessor to reap this benefit should result in reduced rental payments. Unfortunately, not all lessors need or want tax benefits and try to negotiate higher rents by letting you keep the deductions.

On the other hand, many lessors willingly reduce rental charges in exchange for tax benefits, and then turn around and sell the lease. A solid secondary market exists in the leasing industry, especially for leases covering large commercial or industrial property.

EXPLODING THE LEASING MYTHS

Once the elements affecting negotiating strategy have been assimilated and the rental price established, it's time to take a hard look at the true cost of leasing versus buying the asset. Misconceptions abound about the tax advantages of leasing. Time and again, clients tell me that they lease automobiles rather than buy them because they get more tax deductions. As described in the previous sections, this is a fallacy. The IRS applies the same deductibility definitions to lease payments as to depreciation and interest payments for purchased assets.

Another common misconception is that the sum of the payments over the life of a lease will be less than the original purchase price of the asset. Once again, the previous sections exploded this myth. The cost to the lessor *plus the lessor's profit* is the cost to the lessee. A lessor's cost is measured by the price paid for the asset, *plus* administrative costs, *less* the residual-value of the asset. If you were to sell the asset yourself, you should get the same recovery as the lessor.

Perhaps a lessor can borrow money at a lower interest rate than you could; and for a leveraged lease, this of course means lower cost. On the other hand, by paying a lessor for administrative costs and profit it seems unlikely that you couldn't do better buying the asset outright, even paying a higher interest rate.

A third misconception is that leasing conserves operating cash. This argument assumes that the sum of the lease payments will be less than the combined principal and interest payments on a term loan. If the residual value is very high relative to the original cost, this may have some merit. The lessor takes less rent but plans to sell the asset to recoup investment and profit.

Nothing prevents an operating company from doing the same thing. If you don't have a need for the asset anymore, why not sell it? If a lessor can get market price, so should you. Considering residual value on both sides, it is hard to see how lease payments that include a lessor's costs and profit can be less than principal and interest on a term loan.

It doesn't take an elaborate calculation to determine that leasing costs more and results in more cash outflow than buying an asset. The lease versus buy decision must be based on factors other than cost. In fact, there are several advantages to leasing other than a straight cost comparison; although, in some instances, cost and cash flow do enter the equation.

THE PROS AND CONS OF LEASING COMPARED TO BUYING

As with so many other business decisions, no pat answer can be given to the question, "Should I buy or lease?." If a definitive answer was forthcoming, either the leasing companies would be out of business or banks would no longer make hard asset loans. The facts obviously tell a different story.

As a financing tool, leasing makes sense for some companies but not for others. With all the variations of lease agreements, the number of factors influencing a decision to lease may very well be limitless. Nevertheless, certain circumstances seem to favor a lease decision while others quite clearly point in the other direction. Following are the main features that make companies choose leasing along with several circumstances that dictate buying.

The advantages in leasing rather than buying are:

1. When a company does not have the capital to make a down payment.
2. When the asset will probably become obsolete before the end of its useful life.
3. When a company has a poor credit rating and financial institutions insist on very high interest rates. This is not always a good reason, however, because a lessor takes this into consideration when evaluating credit risk for establishing rental payments.
4. If implicit lease rates are similar to borrowing rates but a loan results in other costs or restrictions, such as commitment or application fees, compensating balances, non-business collateral, or personal guarantees.
5. If the equipment has unusual service problems that would be costly, or even impossible, to handle internally.
6. If the equipment or building will probably be difficult to dispose of or has a very low resale value when no longer needed.
7. When assets are needed for only a short period of time.
8. When a company wants to use its collateral and borrowing power for other financing.
9. When a comparison of tax advantages clearly favors leasing.

The biggest disadvantages to leasing revolve around five situations:

1. When the sum of the lease payments exceeds the cost of buying. The purchase price, of course, must be reduced by the asset's resale value.

2. When a company gains an advantage in owning the asset free and clear after the loan gets repaid.

3. When tax benefits clearly point to buying.

4. When a possibility exists for selling the company before the expiration of a lease period. Many sellers find that their company brings a significantly lower sell price with leased assets. This frequently precludes an LBO purchase.

5. When the property will likely appreciate in value.

SALE/LEASEBACK AS A FINANCING TOOL

Selling currently-owned assets to a leasing company for cash and then leasing them back over a period of time—commonly referred to as a sale/leaseback transaction—is a popular mechanism used in third-stage financing. Sale/leasebacks are especially useful for raising immediate capital when two conditions exist:

- A company has poor bank relations and cannot arrange additional credit; and
- A company owns assets that are not secured, or at least not fully secured, to existing debt obligations.

Sale/leaseback arrangements allow a company to raise capital against its assets while still maintaining control over them. When bank loans are scarce and asset-based lenders want exorbitant interest rates and fees, this can be an excellent way to bring cash into the company.

Manufacturing businesses with equipment securely in place find sale/leasebacks calculated with zero residual value a bit expensive. On the other hand, with cash scarce, paying a high rental may be preferable to many other forms of survival financing. When a zero residual value results in rental payments that are too high to meet, a company can arrange a purchase option in the lease to buy back the equipment at the end of the lease period. Hopefully by that time, the company will be on its feet again and able to raise capital elsewhere.

Older hotels that need cash infusions for remodeling or for new appointments frequently employ the sale/leaseback technique. In this case, leases are structured to include all equipment, fixtures, furniture, and certain building fixtures—such as a central air conditioning system. These operating leases stay open-ended, allowing the lessee to add and delete assets at will, without re-writing the lease. When an asset needs replacing, the lessor merely buys the new asset and adds its rental payment to the existing lease.

The biggest disadvantage in equipment sale/leasebacks arrangements, other than losing the value of owned assets for future collateral, is the very high rental payments required by lessors. Since many companies going this route have poor bank credit ratings and a sale/leaseback presents their last chance to raise capital, lessors price the leases accordingly.

Sale/leasebacks are also popular for real property. Because real property tends to appreciate rather than depreciate over time, very often the lease value of a building far exceeds its existing mortgage (which, as Chapter 10 pointed out, is why financial institutions favor mortgage loans).

The sale/leaseback technique for commercial and industrial buildings is not restricted to companies with poor credit ratings or those who cannot raise capital elsewhere. For example, assume a company took out a 20-year mortgage for 80 percent of a building's value. It has made mortgage payments for 10 years, and the mortgage balance has decreased 30 percent.

If the property has risen in value 3 percent per year, its market value today is 38 percent higher than when the mortgage was placed. By combining a 30 percent decrease in the mortgage loan with a 38 percent increase in the asset's market value, an equity increase of over 40 percent results. For a property originally worth $100,000, a sales/leaseback would result in a cash infusion of $82,000!

Since leasing companies also recognize that real property values tend to appreciate, many welcome the opportunity to compete for a sale/leaseback arrangement. This competition keeps rental rates much lower than for equipment deals. In many cases, monthly rentals will be no more than with the old mortgage. If mortgage rates have been dropping, rents could even be less.

Sale/leasebacks are seldom used in first- or second-stage financing, however. During these stages a company expands and usually doesn't have sufficient equipment or real property on its books to make a sale/leaseback viable.

The tax and accounting issues involved with sale/leaseback transactions are enormously complicated and the laws keep changing. If a sale/leaseback seems like a viable alternative, it wouldn't hurt to consult a competent advisor about the current status of tax laws and accounting regulations.

WHO DOES THE LEASING

The leasing industry underwent many changes over the last 20 years. As in the banking industry, a wide assortment of business and financial institutions entered the leasing arena. They range from independent leasing companies to divisions of large corporations, departments of commercial banks, subsidiaries of asset-based lenders, affiliates of franchisers, branches of mortgage banks, and subsidiaries of commercial real estate agents. Even the investment banking and venture capital industries have representation in both equipment and real property leasing.

LeaseAmerica Corp., Cedar Rapids, Iowa, and GE Capital Corporation (with offices in all major cities) are two of the most active equipment leasing companies. All commercial real estate agents with national affiliations maintain direct contacts with lessors handling real property.

Specialized Leasing Companies

Independent and affiliated leasing companies have recently sprung up to service specialized industries (as seen in Chapter 7 for the restaurant industry). Automobiles, hotels, airplanes, boats, and machine tools are other industries that sport specialized leasing companies. Your trade association should know about leasing companies in your industry. Also, most leasing companies advertise in trade journals.

Venture Leasing Companies

Private limited partnerships are rapidly becoming a major factor in the leasing of specially-designed equipment and custom-built commercial property using so-called venture leases. Venture leases for equipment used in industries such as health care diagnostics, laser sensing and penetrating, advanced telecommunications, space technology, electronic guidance systems, and so on, are frequently placed through limited partnerships. Most of this high-tech equipment serves limited applications and experiences rapid technological obsolescence. It is extremely expensive and out-of-reach for most small companies to buy.

These highly-specialized limited partnerships raise capital by soliciting funds from wealthy U.S. and foreign private individuals, large corporations interested in technology development, venture capital funds specializing in these industries, and a few foreign securities houses. They do not advertise. If this source fits your criteria, your best source of contact is through one of the reputable brokerage houses that maintain large investment banking capabilities—e.g. Bear Sterns, Morgan Stanley, Goldman Sachs. They won't handle a deal directly but can put you in touch with someone who will.

One caution about going this route: As with every high-risk, high-reward venture deal, the cost is high. To get one of these venture partnerships to handle your leases, you will certainly have to give up a piece of equity in your business. In return, they offer deep-pocket funding.

INTERNATIONAL LEASING

Using leases to finance the export of large capital equipment is becoming increasingly popular for larger companies. Although export leasing involves complex agreements which very often stipulate secondary collateral guarantees from the supplier, the technique works well when transactions are between large buyers (frequently foreign governments) and large exporters. Export leasing tends to be too complex for smaller companies, however. Chapter 12 describes how export leasing works as a financing tool.

Expanding production or distribution facilities to foreign lands can also be financed through leasing channels. Cross-border leasing gets extremely complex, also. It involves a leasing company in one country leasing property—equipment or facilities—located in a second country. It gets more complicated when the lessee resides in a third country. Customs and contractual peculiarities, collateral rights, foreign tax structures, creditor/debtor rights, government expropriation risks, and a variety of other matters unique to each country add a level of administrative complexity that someone must pay for. Since the leasing company isn't going to absorb the extra costs, high rentals compensate.

If you plan to use leasing as a financing tool in the international arena, you are probably better off using a host country leasing company rather than one from the United States. Local lessors know the local rules. They are structured to take advantage of local tax regulations. And, by far the most important consideration, they can source their own funds locally to purchase the asset. This reduces both the risk and the cost of capital built into rental payments. Chapter 13 covers a more detailed description of international leasing as a financing tool for global expansion.

Commercial or merchant banks handle most international leasing. Multinational investment banks also have divisions to manage international leasing. The quickest way to start the ball rolling is to contact the major Japanese, French, British, Dutch, or German merchant banks with offices in the United States. Asking American money center and large investment banks for help also leads to appropriate contacts.

In addition, names and addresses of leasing companies active in the international sphere are listed with the following:

- American Association of Equipment Lessors (AAEL). This trade organization's membership roster lists most active equipment leasing companies based in the United States. The listing identifies domestic lessors as well as companies handling international leases.

- Foreign leasing companies can be identified through the World Leasing Yearbook, published by Hawkins Publishers, Ltd, London. Leasing industry descriptions from more than 40 countries are covered. Leasing companies operating in over 60 countries are listed by name and address.

SUMMARY

Although leasing equipment and facilities space remains a popular method for financing the expansion of operating companies, it also remains one of the more expensive ways to go. Grasping the differences between finance leases and operating leases and how leveraged, non-leveraged, and service leases work, business managers can intelligently negotiate the right lease structure for their companies. Distinct advantages exist in each of the three broad lease structures—traditional, capital, and venture leases—not the least of which are the tax consequences to both lessor and lessee.

One of the most important tax considerations is to structure a lease that clearly identifies which party has ownership rights to the property. Current tax laws affecting the deductibility of leasehold improvements bear heavily on leasing decisions for real property. New regulations also affect the leasing of luxury automobiles for business use.

Making a lease/buy decision requires the weighing of several factors in addition to pure cost. Capital available for a down payment, credit history, asset obsolescence, expected period of use, additions and deletions of grouped assets, technical maintenance difficulties, and residual-value risk all contribute to the decision. Generally, the total cost of leasing equipment or facilities is substantially more than buying the same asset with borrowed funds.

The sale and leaseback of equipment and real property remains a viable technique to raise third-stage capital for mature companies. Either the asset must be free of liens or it must have appreciated in value since original acquisition. If one of these conditions doesn't exist, sale/leasebacks won't work. Like other forms of leasing, sale/leaseback transactions carry a high cost as a trade-off for ready capital.

A multitude of leasing sources exist in the United States and overseas. Commercial banks, asset-based lenders, small investment banks, venture capital partnerships, and independent leasing companies all offer leases for equipment and real property. Equipment leasing is not as competitive as real estate and therefore the cost runs higher. Implicit interest of prime plus 6 points, or more, is not uncommon. The American Association of Equipment Lessors (AAEL) and the World Leasing Yearbook are excellent sources for the names and addresses of leasing companies handling both domestic and international leases.

CHAPTER 12

Financing an Export Program

As the globalization of trade escalates at an ever-increasing rate, more and more small and mid-size companies recognize that to hold their own in domestic markets, they must also learn to compete in the export sphere. Others see exporting as a viable expansion alternative, providing wider margins and stronger demand than domestic markets. Regardless of why companies choose to enter the export market, an increasing number are doing so. During 1990, the percentage of small and mid-size firms engaged in exporting doubled from the year before; 1989 and 1988 each witnessed a similar doubling of activity.

Exporting also has its downside. Aside from marketing and delivery roadblocks, financing exports appears to be too complex to make the effort worthwhile. During the past decade, leveraged buyouts and easy credit left many companies debt heavy and cash poor with little inclination or ability to incur further debt for developing export markets, regardless of the advantages. This chapter should take the mystery out of export financing and resolve that side of the equation at least.

In many respects financing an export program is easier to arrange than other expansions. Federal and state agencies give birth to new export assistance programs every year. Hesitant to loan funds for working capital and long-term term capital at home, commercial banks jump at the opportunity to participate in export financing with government guarantees that proliferate in the export landscape. Any company, large or small, in practically any industry that truly wants to begin exporting should never let the lack of capital stand in its way.

This chapter examines six sources for financing export trade:

1. Letters of credit and other trade credit instruments.
2. Lease financing.
3. Eximbank and other government agencies.
4. Private export funding sources.
5. City and state financial assistance programs.
6. Countertrade techniques.

Commercial banks participate in every aspect of export financing, either as a lender or as an intermediary for letters of credit, wire transfers, and currency conversions. Foreign customers, as well as Eximbank and the SBA, work through the banking system, not around it. This means that choosing the right bank becomes a critical first step. If your local bank doesn't measure up, now is the time to search out one that does.

A bank should have the following characteristics to efficiently handle export transactions:

1. It must have an experienced, diversified international department. Without this expertise, it will be nothing more than an intermediary with another larger bank. This only confuses the issue, adds significant time to clearing transfers, and makes transactions more costly.

2. Decision-making bank executives must be familiar with the role letters of credit (L/Cs) play in international trade. The use of letters of credit in exporting differs from domestic business.

3. It must accept Eximbank and SBA guarantees as collateral. This means that the bank must carry 10 to 20 percent of the loan balance itself. It should agree to do this without insisting on additional collateral or personal guarantees.

4. If your bank is not a money center bank or the home office of a regional bank, it at least must be large enough to be recognized in foreign banking circles. It should also have a list of correspondent banks in foreign countries. Acting as an intermediary with a money center bank costs more and confuses export transactions.

5. It must be organized to handle foreign currency translations, currency hedging (if necessary), and wire transfers directly to and from other banks around the world without going through a money center bank. The greater the variety of international services it offers the better.

Stay away from exporting until you locate a bank with these characteristics. Anything less invariably causes unnecessary problems.

Straightforward trade credit is the starting point for financing export transactions, albeit with slightly different twists than the normal 30-, 60-, or 90-day terms.

TRADE CREDIT TERMINOLOGY USED IN EXPORTING

Domestically, trade credit refers to buying or selling "on time." Payments against open account transactions are made in 30 days, 60 days, or some other mutually agreed upon time frame. However, the term "trade credit," as used in international transactions, has different connotations. Bankers, government agencies, trading companies, and customers who deal in global trade have their own terminology to reflect sources and uses of credit. Some of the more common terms are defined below.

1. *Supplier credit* refers to credit extended to the buyer from the seller (exporter). An exporter may extend credit independently, or it may obtain outside financing from banks, government agencies, or any other source. If an exporter records a receivable on its books, even temporarily, the credit extension is regarded as "supplier credit."

2. *Buyer credit* refers to credit extended to the buyer by someone other than the supplier. Credit may be extended by an American bank, a foreign bank, a U.S. government agency, a foreign government agency, or other third party. The credit can carry guarantees, or it may be stand-alone. Receivables do not get recorded on the exporter's books because cash, or cash equivalents, are received as the products ship.

3. Loans with *recourse* assign responsibility for paying off any indebtedness incurred by the buyer in an export transaction. *Full recourse* means that the seller remains fully liable for a buyer's performance against the transaction. Nonrecourse means that the seller has no responsibility for payment. *Limited recourse* makes the seller liable only if fraudulent representation occured in any of the export documentation. In this case the seller must make up any payment deficiency. Limited recourse documents are seldom used and should be avoided, except under very unusual circumstances.

LETTERS OF CREDIT

Letters of credit continue to be the heart and soul of global trade credit. A letter of credit (L/C) is a universally accepted form of payment for all international transactions. A L/C comes in many forms. It may carry a variety of provisions. It can be revocable or irrevocable, confirmed or advised, a straight or negotiated letter, payable at sight or over an extended period of time. A letter of credit may be transferable, assignable, or restricted.

Banks honor L/Cs upon presentation of bills of lading or other transport documents, proving that the goods have in fact been delivered as specified in the order. L/Cs can be written to include or exclude virtually any specific provisions. They may read "clean on board," "about," or "approximately" (referring to quantities shipped). They cover partial shipments, full shipments, or transshipments. The L/C can be for one shipment or revolving. L/Cs must be properly prepared and executed to be valid. A bank will not honor an L/C, unless all supporting documentation accompanies a payment request. Letters of credit are so crucial to export financing that instructions for handling the various options fill entire books.

Using Letters of Credit to Fund Working Capital

L/Cs enhance working capital in four ways—back-to-back L/Cs, off-balance sheet credit extension, assigned proceeds, or transferred L/Cs.

1. Back-to-Back L/Cs. Back-to-back L/Cs are used when vendors or subcontractors demand payment from the exporter before collections come in from the customer. For example, assume a manufacturing company gets an order to ship 100 generator sets to a buyer in France. Payment will be made against the buyer's L/C placed on a New York bank. The order calls for shipments in increments of 25 generator sets every three months. The L/C allows for payments against partial shipments.

The manufacturing company subcontracts the assembly of armatures to be used in the generator sets. The subcontractor wants payment for 100 armatures in 30 days, refusing to wait for payment until all four orders have been shipped to France.

The manufacturer merely presents the buyer's L/C to the bank and asks the bank to issue a new L/C to the subcontractor, payable in 30 days. The new L/C is from the manufacturer to the subcontractor but it uses the French L/C as collateral. The manufacturer's L/C and the buyer's L/C are called back-to-back L/Cs. Not all banks will issue back-to-back L/Cs because the manufacturer remains obligated to perform fully against the buyer's L/C. If default occurs, the bank is left holding worthless collateral. As long as you maintain sound relationships, a reasonably good credit rating, and your bank has solid internationsl experience, you shouldn't have a problem. Once again, solid banking relationships mean everything!

2. Off-Balance Sheet Credit Extension. Off-balance sheet credit is a variation on the back-to-back L/C theme. By extending off-balance sheet credit, a bank does not use the buyer's L/C as collateral. This eliminates the risk of the exporter not performing against its buyer's order.

Rather than collateralizing its L/Cs with letters of credit against a shipping order, the bank issues new L/Cs directly to an exporter's vendors. The general credit of the exporter secures these L/Cs and becomes an addition to the exporter's line of credit. This procedure is not as gratuitous as it appears at first glance. Once you draw down on the buyer's L/C, deposits of these funds pay down other outstanding loans with the bank, keeping everything in balance. Once again, banks extend extra credit only when customer relationships remain strong. The fact that credit is extended against a specific order and that the buyer's L/C assures payment—thus reducing the bank's exposure to practically zero—won't make any difference. If relationships aren't strong, the bank will say no!

A bank could very likely want additional security against the credit extension. If so, it always has the option of filing a lien against the goods to be exported under the Uniform Commercial Code (a UCC filing). This ensures that the proceeds will be deposited when the buyer's L/C is drawn down.

Both back-to-back L/Cs and off-balance sheet credit extensions cost money. Commercial banks rarely offer any free services. Issuing L/Cs is not an exception. Rates vary considerably, but normal fees range between .5 to 2 percent of the value of the L/C. Some banks charge as much as 5 percent. In addition, many banks extract an additional commitment fee that can range between .5 to 5 percent.

3. *Assigned Proceeds.* Exporters also use their buyer's credit to raise working capital. This is achieved by assigning the proceeds from the buyer's L/C. Any L/C can be assigned without permission from the buyer, a bank, or anyone else. Assigning an L/C is easy. It merely involves telling the bank holding the L/C that it should pay either the entire proceeds or a percentage of the proceeds drawn on the L/C to a specified third party.

If a vendor doesn't believe in the authenticity of a foreign buyer's letter of credit just send a copy of it. If you want to prevent a vendor from knowing the identity of the buyer, merely black out the buyer's name from the L/C and all supporting documentation. The only time a vendor or subcontractor really gets hurt by accepting an assignment is if the shipment is held up for reasons outside of anyone's control. Obviously, when that occurs payment against the L/C will also be withheld.

In rare cases, an imperfection in the customer's L/C prevents draw downs. If it carries nonrecourse terms, the assignee has no option but to try to collect directly from the exporter or the exporter's customer. Obviously, any assignee should scrutinize the L/C carefully before accepting assignment. Assigning an L/C involves no additional cost or additions to credit lines. Just complete a simple assignment form.

4. *Transferred L/C.* Transferred letters of credit come into play when an exporter requires certain materials or products be shipped directly from its supplier to the foreign customer rather than relayed to the exporter for inclusion in the complete order. The exporter acts as an intermediary in such a transaction. If these items have a high value, the supplier might demand that the exporter actually transfer the customer's L/C intact, avoiding reliance on the exporter's performance as a condition of getting paid.

A buyer must grant permission to transfer an L/C, either partially or in its entirety. Obviously, the foreign buyer then knows that a third party is the original supplier of these goods, not the exporter. This might cause the buyer to believe that the exporter is not financially viable and additional business could be lost.

A foreign buyer has the right to refuse permission to transfer the L/C. This seldom occurs, however, unless the relationship between buyer and exporter rests on shaky ground to begin with.

Terms of payment, shipping instructions, insurance provisions, product markings, draw down documentation, and all other terms and conditions stipulated in the letter of credit remain intact when transferring the L/C. If part of the order is manufactured and shipped by the exporter and part by the exporter's vendor or subcontractor, the exporter can still avoid negotiating an entirely new L/C for its share of the order. It accomplishes this by instructing the paying bank to limit payment on the transferred L/C to the amounts due the vendor or subcontractor and then by substituting export invoices for the balance of the L/C.

This sounds complicated, but it really isn't. It is fairly common practice and banks seldom blink when the exporter initiates the transaction. It does involve more paperwork and, therefore, added cost. Bank fees tend to be reasonable for this service, however, and shouldn't influence the decision to transfer an L/C.

The identity of the foreign buyer can be kept confidential in a transferred letter of credit as easily as with an assignment. Merely include instructions in the documentation that the paying bank should notify the exporter rather than the buyer when both shipment and payment have been made. Again, this is not an unusual request and most banks—and buyers—go along with it. Perhaps a foreign buyer can't raise the capital or credit to place a confirmed, irrevocable L/C as immediate payment. In that case, other financing tools can be used. A "documentary banker's acceptance" is one such tool.

DOCUMENTARY BANKER'S ACCEPTANCE

A documentary banker's acceptance (BA) is a payment device that uses the exporter's credit to allow the sale to be completed. Once the products ship and the sale concludes, the exporter sells the receivable to a bank—at a discount, of course. The process encompasses steps similar to factoring a domestic receivable. The mechanics work as follows:

1. The buyer executes a time letter of credit, referred to in some quarters as a "usance" L/C, for the full amount of the sale price. Instructions included in the L/C authorize payment in a specific number of days after the exporter presents shipping documentation. An exporter should insist on a fixed date not in excess of 180 days from the date of sight, the maximum time frame for a BA.

2. When the exporter presents the shipping documentation, the bank issues a BA in place of cash. The BA consists of the exporter's draft with a bank marking stating "accepted" stamped across its face. This marking means

that the bank promises to pay the exporter, or any other holder of the BA, on the fixed date of the L/C.

3. The exporter presents this BA to the same bank issuing it and requests the bank to discount the document, paying the face value minus the discount interest, which the exporter merely adds to the invoice price. Documentary BAs allow both sides to win. The buyer conserves cash for up to six months, and the exporter gets cash immediately.

The low discount rate charged on BAs makes this process the least costly of practically any trade credit instrument, even if you can't pass the cost on to the buyer. Nothing is as good as it seems, however. To compensate for the low discount rate, the bank issuing a documentary BA charges an acceptance fee for handling the transaction. This ranges between .5 to 2 percent per annum of the face amount of the L/C. Very often foreign buyers will pay this acceptance fee directly—even if they won't allow the exporter to factor it into a higher price for the goods.

CLEAN BANKER'S ACCEPTANCE

A clean BA differs from a documentary BA in that it does not have the buyer's letter of credit as collateral. Instead, the exporter must use its own credit as security. A clean BA applies to a specific transaction or shipment, just like a documentary BA. The BA is discounted with the exporter's bank. The bank then takes this readily negotiable instrument and sells it in the secondary bond market. Banks like this instrument for two reasons: It does not get recorded on the bank's balance sheet, and it is always readily negotiable.

As can be expected, few smaller companies qualify for clean BAs because, once again, the bank must rely on the company's performance on the transaction. Exporters with a good track record of shipping quality products on schedule over a period of time stand a better chance of getting a bank to go along. If you can sell your bank on using a clean BA, however, it provides a low-cost way to finance export working capital.

Clean BAs usually run about $500,000, although they can be as low as $100,000. Clean BAs are the province of very large regional banks or money center banks. Smaller banks prefer other instruments. Interest rates on clean BAs run less than LIBOR (London Interbank Offered Rate), which is nearly always less than prime. Acceptance fees range up to 2 percent per annum on the face amount of the BA.

In some cases shipments against an export order may extend over several years. The sale of equipment and components used in the construction of major foreign projects nearly always covers extended periods. Letters of credit, banker's acceptances, or other trade credit instruments do not normally work for such high value, long-term sales. Forfaiting offers an alternative.

FINANCING WITH FORFAITING

Forfaiting is used as a financing tool throughout the world, although it remains a relatively unknown technique in America. The forfaiting procedure offers a more ingenious financing scheme to handle high value, long-term transactions than straightforward trade credit. With forfaiting, an exporter gives away, or forfeits the right to receive future payments in exchange for immediate cash.

Forfaiting originated many years ago by European corporations for exporting very costly items against orders extending over several years. Now, smaller foreign companies use forfaiting to provide supplier credit for the same type of exports. Although most small and mid-size American exporters have never heard of either the term or the process, forfaiting is gradually becoming acceptable to some of the more progressive international traders.

Forfaiting won't work very well when export transactions have values of less than $250,000. Nor does it work if the transaction runs more than $10 million. The discount rate ranges up to 2 points over LIBOR. Commitment fees run about .75 percent per annum. Forfait transactions range from a period of one to 10 years, although five to six years is most common.

Forfaiting works as follows:

1. The exporter and the buyer, who wants long-term credit for the deal, negotiate a series of notes, drafts, bills, or other instruments. These documents will be used to pay off the balance due the exporter over the term of the transaction.

2. The exporter contacts a forfaiter, and the forfaiter and the buyer negotiate with a foreign bank to provide a guarantee of the buyer's credit as an endorser of the note, draft, or bill. In the parlance of international finance, this endorsement—together with a promissory note or bill from the buyer—is called an "aval." The simplicity of this transaction has great appeal to bankers and buyers alike. No contracts are involved that could require litigation in the event of default.

3. When the exporter presents the forfaiter a complete set of shipping and customs clearance documentation, the forfaiter releases the funds.

Forfaiting has three broad advantages:

1. It provides medium- to long-term financing when short-term credit won't work.

2. It covers the entire sale, not just 85 percent (the maximum under an Eximbank guarantee).

3. It costs less than borrowing from an American bank.

Two major disadvantages dissuade smaller companies from trying forfaiting: It cannot be used for short-term credit, and many American banks just don't understand the mechanics yet. In addition, banks in some developing countries remain reluctant to handle the guarantee portion of the deal for the buyer.

If forfaiting seems like a viable choice, try a foreign bank with offices in the U.S. rather than an American bank. As the years unfold, inevitably more and more American banks of various sizes will begin to support forfaiting. As of this writing, however, the technique remains a mystery to all but a chosen few.

Those chosen few consist mainly of the money center banks and the home offices of certain regional banks. A call for help to one of these banks should result in recommendations of an appropriate forfaiter. It should also entice assistance in arranging the deal. Most of these giant banks have their own internal forfaiting departments, eliminating the need to hire one from the outside. Chase, Citicorp, Bank of America, and Security Pacific represent money center banks experienced in this technique.

If you choose not to deal with one of the giant banks but are still interested in pursuing forfaiting, check out a non-bank bank in St. Louis called British American Forfaiting Company, Inc.; (314)647-8700. This company claims to be the only specialized forfaiting broker in the United States. They offer a wide range of additional export financing services but forfaiting is their specialty.

LEASING

Supplier credit for the sale of capital assets can also be accomplished with lease financing. The lessor may be either the exporter or a recognized leasing company. An increasing number of exporters, recognizing the profitability of foreign leasing, have set up separate companies themselves to handle the leases.

A branch of the Eximbank, the Federal Credit Insurance Association (FCIA), offers extensive coverage against both buyer credit risk and foreign expropriation. With FCIA coverage, the risk of entering into a long-term lease with a foreign buyer diminishes. Minimal risk and an opportunity to increase profits beyond the normal sales transaction, make leasing an easy, safe way to maximize returns.

Another way to structure lease financing involves transferring the ownership of products to an international leasing company as they are shipped. The independent leasing company then has the responsibility for administering the lease and the exporter is immediately off the hook. International Leasing Corp. is one of the largest and best known companies in the international leasing game. They handle foreign leasing for most of the aircraft and other large capital goods exporters. Plymouth Commercial Funding, Inc., in New York is another international leasing specialist. Chapter 11 identifies two excellent sources of listings of additional domestic and international leasing companies.

When exporting to a developing country with soft currency, leasing often provides the only feasible way to finance the sale. Lease payment terms can be very flexible, arranged to suit the needs of both the exporter and the customer. Several large corporations have found leasing so profitable that they finance entire export programs with leases and countertrade arrangements. The use of countertrade to convert lease payments into hard currency or goods is rapidly becoming a popular method for avoiding restrictive currency exchange controls. Descriptions of various forms of countertrade appear later in this chapter.

EXIMBANK

During the past twenty years, entire infrastructures of developing nations were built with imported products and services, many from the United States. Most of these long-term projects were financed through government agencies with little or no funding coming directly from the exporter. In some cases an exporter might initiate the financing scheme, but usually a foreign buyer—many times a foreign government—arranged its own financing, frequently with U.S. government assistance.

The use of trade credits is certainly the least expensive and easiest way to finance export sales. In many cases, however, small and mid-size businesses cannot compete in the world market with trade credit alone. To assist these smaller exporters, the federal government established the Export-Import Bank (Eximbank).

Originally founded by Congress in 1934, the Export-Import Bank has grown into the major federal source of assistance to American exporters enabling them to compete with international firms, subsidized by their own governments. Eximbank is an independent, corporate agency of the federal government. It coordinates its policies with other government agencies to ensure consistency with overall foreign policy and objectives. Normally, it will not support exports to communist countries. Nor will it handle sales of military products or services. Furthermore, to be eligible for financing assistance, exported goods or services must consist of at least 50 percent U.S. content.

For each transaction to be financed through Eximbank the following five questions must be answered in the affirmative:

1. Is a U.S. export involved?
2. What foreign competition exists, and is it officially subsidized?
3. Is the transaction economically feasible?

4. Is there reasonable assurance of repayment?

5. Would voiding the transaction create an adverse effect on the domestic U.S. economy?

A negative response to even one of these questions invalidates a company's application for funding. In the case of small businesses, however, evidence of foreign competition is not required, providing the Eximbank's share of guarantees and loans totals less than $2.5 million.

Eximbank charges application fees for its funding services as well as interest on direct loans. Eximbank bases both charges on its perceived risk of doing business in a specific country. Because it is self-sustaining, Eximbank cannot always compete effectively with the rates and terms offered by foreign export credit agencies. In most cases, however, smaller businesses can get export financing through this agency when private financial institutions back away.

An American exporter of any size and in any industry can avail itself of Eximbank services. Over the years most Eximbank funding went to large corporations. Recently, however, in an effort to brace against increasing foreign trade deficits, Congress has encouraged Eximbank to establish several programs especially helpful to small and mid-size exporters. Part of this effort is a "hotline" counseling service to answer questions about financing and other export assistance; the tollfree number is (800) 424-5201.

Four popular programs are offered by Eximbank:

1. The commercial bank guarantee program.

2. The foreign credit insurance program.

3. A cooperative financing facility with overseas banks.

4. The discount loan program with U.S. banks.

Because federal export assistance remains extremely volatile, verify the current status of programs and country criteria directly from Eximbank before spending time and money making application.

Information leading to the following summaries of these programs was obtained from the most recent pronouncements from Eximbank in 1989 and 1990.

EXIMBANK PRELIMINARY COMMITMENT

The Preliminary Commitment consists of an offer from Eximbank to finance a specific export sale in advance of the transaction. It outlines the Bank's willingness to participate and the terms and conditions for loan or guarantee support. It covers all products and services eligible for Eximbank participation. They must be non-military and have at least 50 percent U.S. content. Any business may file an application for commitment, enclosing with it a $100 fee. The commitment remains valid for 180 days, although Eximbank can extend the date. An exporter, borrower, lender or other responsible party to the transaction can then use this preliminary commitment to establish financing terms and conditions for planning and marketing strategies. Foreign buyers assured of Eximbank support tend to be more willing to buy from a small exporter than if only trade credit had been offered.

EXIMBANK WORKING CAPITAL GUARANTEE

The Eximbank Working Capital Guarantee program was designed specifically to help smaller U.S. exporters obtain short-term bank loans for the production of export products and services. Bank loans are made directly to the exporter, not the foreign buyer. All eligible products and services can be covered. The first step is to get an Eximbank Preliminary Commitment. Then shop for the best terms and conditions from commercial lenders.

Any bank that extends such export-related credit qualifies for an Eximbank guarantee. The guarantee covers up to 90 percent of the principal balance, with interest up to one point over the U.S. Treasury rate. Repayment must fall within 12 months, unless previous arrangements are made with both the lender and Eximbank. Eximbank charges an upfront facility fee of .5 percent of the loan, and quarterly usage fees of .25 percent of the loan's average outstanding balance.

The guarantee provides for recourse to the exporter. This means that the exporter must provide the bank with adequate collateral—usually inventory used to produce the products—so that the loan balance never exceeds 90 percent of the collateral value. The Eximbank Working Capital Guarantee applies to a single export transaction loan, or it can be structured for a revolving credit line. It also can be combined with the SBA's Export Revolving Line of Credit (ERLC) program. Eximbank extends guarantees against loans up to $300,000.

EXIMBANK GUARANTEE FOR MEDIUM AND LONG-TERM LOANS

Eximbank's Medium (1-7 years) and Long-Term (7-10 years) Guarantee Loan program finances buyers of capital equipment requiring credit terms beyond one year. These long-term guarantees apply to exports of products with or without foreign-made components. If the order includes foreign-made components, the guarantee covers up to 100 percent of the American content of the product only. The guarantee carries two restrictive provisions: (1) the U.S. content cannot exceed 85 percent of the contract price of each item; and (2) the total U.S. content cannot be less than 50 percent of the total contract value for all items.

This guarantee applies only for loans made directly to a foreign borrower for the purchase of American goods. The loans may come from either an American bank or a foreign lender. The guarantee cannot be used as collateral for loans made directly to American exporters. A foreign buyer must pay 15 percent of the contract value as a down payment, either in the form of cash or as an irrevocable, confirmed L/C.

Guarantees cover up to 100 percent of the financed portion. For medium-term loans, the guarantee extends to balances up to $10 million. Either the exporter or the lender must counter-guarantee Eximbank for 2 percent of the commercial risk. Eximbank charges interest on fixed-rate loans equal to the lesser of the U.S. Treasury bill rate *plus* .5 percent, or the U.S Treasury note rate *minus* .5 percent. Interest on floating-rate loans is calculated as the lesser of the U.S Treasury note rate *minus* .5 percent, or a preselected rate from the following: prime *minus* 2 percent; LIBOR *minus* .25 percent; or U.S.Treasury bill *plus* .5 percent.

Repayment falls within the following schedule:

Contract Value	Maximum Term
$50,000 or less	2 years
$50,000 to $100,000	3 years
$100,000 to $200,000	4 years
$200,000 or more	5 years

Under exceptional cases Eximbank will go seven years for larger loans. Prenegotiated long-term loans of over $10 million extend to 10 years.

The cost to an exporter for medium and long-term buyer credit guarantees are:

1. A $100 processing fee.

2. An upfront exposure fee based on the term of the loan, country risk, and category of borrower—paid on each disbursement.

3. A commitment fee of 1/8 percent per annum on the undisbursed balance of the guaranteed loan.

Eximbank medium- and long-term loan guarantees are unconditional and freely transferable. The guarantee may also be combined with an Intermediary Loan.

EXIMBANK DIRECT LOANS

Eximbank provides two types of direct loans: (1) loans direct to the foreign buyer of U.S. exported goods; and (2) loans to intermediaries who, in turn, fund the foreign buyer. These intermediaries are usually financial institutions—either American or foreign. The two types of direct loans exhibit similarities, as well as differences.

Intermediary loans are structured as "standby" loans. This means that the lender may draw down on the loan at any time during its term. The lender utilizes this flexibility to take advantage of lower rates than those established by OECD if available. OECD is the acronym for Organization for Economic Cooperation and

Development, an organization of 22 developed nations that sets parameters for interest rates and terms applicable to its members' export credit activities.

Maximum coverages and repayment terms for both categories of loans match the Eximbank guarantee program. Foreign buyer and intermediary direct loans both require a 15 percent down payment by the buyer.

The interest charged on intermediary and direct loans is based on fixed rates established by OECD; however, they do vary between the two programs. Under the direct loan program, the category of the buyer's country determines the interest rate, based on the following:

INTEREST RATES BY COUNTRY CATEGORY

Country Category**	Up to 5 years	Over 5 years
I (Rich)	CIRR*	CIRR
II (Intermediate)	9.15%	9.65%
III (Poor)	8.30%	8.30%

*CIRR stands for the Commercial Interest Reference Rate and is revised monthly.
**Call Eximbank for a current definition of countries falling within each category.

The following summarizes the interest rate charged on intermediary loans, assuming that the intermediary makes the loan to a foreign borrower at the minimum OECD fixed rate:

INTEREST RATES FOR INTERMEDIARY LOANS

Loan Commitment	Eximbank Interest Rate
Less than $1 million	OECD rate less 1.5%
$1-$5 million	OECD rate less 1.0%
$5-$10 million	OECD rate less 0.5%

If an intermediary loan is not combined with a guarantee, Eximbank waives the commitment fee; otherwise, it remains the same as for a direct loan to the buyer—.5 percent per annum.

ENGINEERING MULTIPLIER PROGRAM

According to Eximbank officials, the Engineering Multiplier Program has not received wide use by American exporters. It was designed specifically for two purposes:

1. to provide funding for engineering firms and other preconstruction service companies; and

2. to fund feasibility studies by architectural and design firms.

It also finances the export of goods used in the construction of these projects. Foreign buyers may qualify for direct medium-term loans of up to $10 million.

If the engineering contract results in the export of American-made goods for the project, it can be rolled into a long-term project loan. The maximum qualifying export contract is the greater of $10 million, or twice the value of the engineering contract. Rates, repayment terms, and fees relate to those of other Eximbank programs. Eximbank also funds the costs incurred by American firms for contracts covering the operation and maintenance of foreign projects.

RISK INSURANCE

The Federal Credit Insurance Association (FCIA) provides risk insurance for exporters. Any exporting company qualifies for this insurance. Coverage includes insurance for lease payments, foreign expropriation, foreign currency translation, and export-related foreign currency swaps. The FCIA also offers several specialized coverages.

The entire FCIA program is very extensive. A complete explanation of available coverages and costs can be found in my book, *Going Global: New Opportunities for Growing Companies to Compete in World Markets;* or information may be obtained by writing the FCIA at 40 Rector Street, 11th Floor, New York, NY 10006.

THE PRIVATE EXPORT FUNDING CORPORATION

The Private Export Funding Corporation (PEFCO) was formed by several U.S banks and large corporations to supplement federal long-term financing for foreign buyers of American exports. A private corporation, PEFCO is closely associated with Eximbank. PEFCO extends credit for export projects requiring longer-term financing than a commercial bank will handle, but shorter than provided by Eximbank. PEFCO also structures financing packages with unique interest rate and repayment terms for both parties. PEFCO gets its funding from the sale of Eximbank guaranteed negotiable debt instruments on the open market.

Though not widely used by smaller exporters because of its financing restrictions, the PEFCO facility is available if needed. PEFCO only handles projects exceeding $1 million and restricts foreign buyer loans to periods exceeding five years. Smaller projects do not qualify for PEFCO funding. If the parameters fit, PEFCO provides one more option for making the sale.

U.S. DEPARTMENT OF AGRICULTURE

If your company intends to export agricultural products, the Department of Agriculture (DOA) might be able to help through several specialized financial assistance programs. This assistance varies with specific products. To learn more about program options that may be applicable to your business, contact a local DOA office.

One agency within the DOA—the Commodity Credit Corporation (CCC)–supports universally applicable programs, regardless of product. CCC offers financial assistance in the form of buyer credits based on government-to-government agreements. With a knowledge of how the programs work, the exporter benefits directly.

Two of the most popular programs offered through the CCC are the Export Credit Guarantee program and the Intermediate Credit Guarantee program. Both programs consist of CCC guarantees against a foreign letter of credit for up to 98 percent of the value of the product. The former program issues these credit guarantees for up to three years: the latter extends credit to 10 years. Intended to assist those countries with major economic problems, both programs include unlimited amounts of credit.

A third CCC program, the Bonus Incentive Commodity Export Program (BICEP), comes into play if the CCC determines that to compete with foreign-subsidized companies, your company must be subsidized as well.

This subsidy takes the form of an Export Enhancement Program (EEP) certificate with a value equal to what the CCC deems you need to remain competitive. These certificates can be sold or traded in secondary markets, making them as good as cash. They are redeemable for any surplus commodity held by the CCC. In many cases, the sale or trade value of the certificate exceeds its certificate value by a substantial premium. If you don't mind the extra administrative effort, you can make a profit on this transaction, as well as on the original export sale.

SMALL BUSINESS ADMINISTRATION EXPORT FINANCING

Financing assistance from the Small Business Administration (SBA), though not frequently used, does exist. Although receiving little emphasis from SBA offices, the Export Revolving Line of Credit (ERLC) program has been in effect for years. Lack of publicity probably explains why exporters don't use it. They don't know about it.

Theoretically, Congress enacted provisions in the Omnibus Trade Bill of 1988 to make the ERLC a viable source of export financing. Congress handed the SBA a mandate to support small exporters with the hope that small and mid-size companies would begin taking advantage of the program.

SBA—Eximbank Risk Sharing

Nearly a decade ago, in an effort to reach more small businesses with its Working Capital Guarantee program, Eximbank reached an agreement with the SBA to extend co-guarantees under the ERLC program. The terms of the agreement stipulate that Eximbank and the SBA both guarantee export working capital loans to small businesses. By sharing the risk equally, these agencies support ERLC loans up to $1 million. Thus, if you qualify as a small business under SBA criteria and need working capital funds up to $1 million, both the SBA and Eximbank can help.

The SBA handles amounts below $200,000 exclusively; Eximbank supports the balance, up to $1 million. Other qualification requirements and definitions remain the same as those established by the SBA for domestic assistance.

SBA Capabilities

According to SBA officials in Washington, D.C., the agency continues to experience difficulty in attracting qualified staff personnel with international trade experience for its offices nationwide. This lack of global expertise coupled with slashed budgets over the past 10 years effectively leaves the SBA out of the export financing picture. Conceivably, if Congress loosens its purse strings in the future and qualified staff can be attracted, conditions may change. Until then, the Eximbank, PEFCO, or state and local sources are better choices.

Your local SBA office may be the exception, however, and it can't hurt to at least try. If the SBA can't help, perhaps the office staff can point the way to other sources of assistance. In some states, this could be through the City-State Agency Cooperation program.

EXIMBANK'S CITY-STATE AGENCY COOPERATION PROGRAM

During 1989, the Eximbank began an earnest effort to encourage local financing support for smaller exporters. The outgrowth of this effort was the Eximbank City-State Agency Cooperation program. Initially Tucson, Arizona and Columbus, Ohio participated as cities, and California, Massachusetts, and Maryland participated as states. Agencies formed by these cities and states participate with Eximbank in its loan guarantee and in its foreign credit insurance programs.

The idea behind this program was to open up export working capital funds and long-term financing direct to the small exporter, rather than to the foreign buyer or to large corporations. Traditional avoidance of the financing needs of smaller exporters has brought strong criticism of Eximbank policies from members of Congress and several public lobbies. The City-State Agency Cooperation program is an attempt to rectify a badly skewed export financing system. Since Eximbank has operated at a loss for 10 years, perhaps the powers-that-be recognized that to survive much longer, the agency would have to get more involved in financing smaller exporters.

This new City-State Agency Cooperation program originally began as a marketing tool to make smaller exporters aware of Eximbank programs. City and state agencies market Eximbank guarantees and FCIA credit insurance through direct mailings, calls to local banks and merchants, seminars, and a modest advertising campaign. In addition to advertising Eximbank, these agencies also provide technical support in matters relating to shipping, market research, and joint ventures.

An additional reason for establishing this program was to make the paperwork necessary to arrange export financing easier for banks to handle. Just as with the Eximbank, many larger commercial banks with the ability to manage export transactions have drawn away from smaller customers in favor of large corporations. They reason that the same amount of paperwork is involved in all sizes of export transactions, and they can make a lot more money on the bigger deals. It was hoped that this new Eximbank-sponsored program would encourage commercial banks to look again at financing smaller exporters.

The City of Los Angeles has taken Eximbank's program one step further by forming an agency called L.A.Xport. Not only does L.A.Xport handle the marketing of Eximbank, it also has obtained a separate line of credit from a local bank, specifically set aside for small exporters. The Los Angeles LDC, Inc., functions as the administrative arm for the program.

Eximbank officials report that other cities and a few states have followed the lead of Los Angeles and established similar bureaus to arrange independent credit for small exporters. The best source of information about participation by your city or state is through a local chamber of commerce. Chamber offices keep abreast of these matters and can quickly point you in the right direction if such programs exist.

NON-BANK EXPORT FINANCING

Following the rapid growth in exporting by smaller and mid-size companies and the continued reluctance on the part of traditional mid-sized banks to provide competitive export funding, several private companies outside of the banking industry have been formed that specialize exclusively in creative export financial services.

These non-bank banks operate similarly to European merchant banks. Instead of viewing their roles strictly as lenders, they like to become quasi-partners in the exporter's business, offering administrative and marketing services as well as financing. These new players in global trade finance do not finance the exporting company; they finance the specific transaction. With substantial foreign backing, these transactional financiers can raise capital that smaller and mid-size companies would otherwise find unavailable.

Because of the newness of export transactional financing, very few non-banks have entered the field to date. There can be little doubt, however, that this is an exploding market that will attract many more in the years to come. Currently, two of the most active in transactional financing are Trading Alliance Corporation, (212) 953-0400, and World Trade Finance, Inc., (213) 660-1277.

COUNTERTRADE

Financing exports to Eastern Europe, the Soviet Union, sub-Sahara Africa, and certain Latin American countries—in addition to a number of other nations with soft currency—nearly always involves some type of countertrade arrangement. Countertrade is relatively simple, though somewhat convoluted. One or a combination of six basic techniques are used in countertrade transactions; these are barter, compensation, counterpurchase, offset, buy-back, or co-production.

BARTER

The oldest form of trade, barter means trading a quantity of one commodity for a quantity of another; for example, eight horses for three cows, four gas turbines for 1,000 acres of land, 5,000 bushels of wheat for 40 cases of vodka. Obviously, once you get the exchanged merchandise it must either be used, or sold.

COMPENSATION

Compensation is a modern form of barter. It involves a third party to dispose of the traded merchandise. Compensation involves a single contract, often making the transaction cumbersome to administer. Neither barter nor compensation involve the transfer of cash between the two trading parties.

COUNTERPURCHASE

Counterpurchase is a variation on the barter theme that involves actual cash transfers. The foreign buyer arranges independent financing and pays cash for your products. You concurrently agree to purchase goods that the buyer produces, for cash. The catch is to be able to turn around and sell these goods to recover your cash payment and profit.

OFFSET

Offsets are used primarily by companies manufacturing aircraft, military hardware, or large infrastructure equipment. Frequently, a sovereign government will be the customer and the offset method is used to improve that country's foreign exchange position. An offset deal normally involves a package of transactions, carried out over a defined period of time. Theoretically, at least, it compensates the acquiring or importing country for loss of jobs, currency, and local development of technologies. Offsets are generally too complicated for smaller companies to get involved with and are mentioned here only for completeness.

BUY-BACK

A buy-back is typically used in the turnkey construction of infrastructure projects or manufacturing plants. Buy-back means that you, as the contractor, agree to buy-back a certain percentage of the production of the new facility that you build. It's then up to you to sell the products and, of course, reap any profits.

CO-PRODUCTION

Co-production transactions require you, the contractor, to take an equity interest in the turnkey project or furnish management support to run the facility, as partial compensation. You share the construction with a foreign contractor. Both parties end up sharing in its ownership. Operating the facility is known as co-production since both parties remain responsible for the production of the facility's products and both parties benefit from their sale.

One form or another of countertrade is a way of life when exporting to soft currency countries. Making the deal and administering the contract gets very complex. To try this tack without qualified financial and marketing personnel would be foolhardy. With qualified people, however, countertrade arrangements open new markets that otherwise remain closed. A complete description of how to use countertrade techniques and the type of personnel required to make it work can be found in *Going Global: New Opportunities for Growing Companies to Compete in World Markets.*

SUMMARY

Export financing takes many forms. In order to communicate in global financial circles, a familiarity with certain international trade terms, such as supplier credit, buyer credit, and recourse and nonrecourse loans is necessary. Letters of credit (L/Cs) continue to be the standard form of payment for export sales, and come in many forms. They include a wide variety of special terms and conditions for shipment or collection against an order. Irrevocable, confirmed L/Cs offer the ultimate in collectibility safeguards.

Bank instruments other than letters of credit are also used in international trade. Documentary and clean banker's acceptances have become two of the most popular. Forfaiting is also beginning to be used in America, although it has been popular overseas for many years. Forfaiting in international trade compares to factoring receivables domestically, without the taint of financial difficulty.

Large corporations use leasing as a convenient way to finance the sale of large capital goods. Smaller companies can also use this method, either by forming their own leasing company or by selling the goods to an international lessor.

Several government programs assist companies in financing export transactions. The Export-Import Bank (Eximbank) serves as the master export agency for the federal government. Eximbank offers a variety of programs for direct financing and guarantees to exporters and foreign buyers.

Some of the more popular programs are: the Eximbank Working Capital Guarantee which enables a smaller company to obtain guaranteed bank loans for working capital; the Eximbank Guarantee for Medium- and Long-Term Loans which guarantees bank financing for larger export transactions and for the export of capital goods; Eximbank Direct Loans; and the Engineering Multiplier Program. The Federal Credit Insurance Association insures against credit and political risk losses.

The Private Export Funding Corporation (PEFCO) is a private organization funded by large corporations and banks. PEFCO extends credit for transactions carrying terms in excess of what a bank will do but less than what Eximbank supports.

For companies exporting agricultural products, the U.S. Department of Agriculture supports special financing programs. The Commodity Credit Corporation (CCC) is especially active with smaller exporters.

Although the SBA does have a special program dedicated to financing small exporters—the Export Revolving Line of Credit (ERLC)—its lack of emphasis and under-funding by Congress restricts its use. However, the SBA has now joined forces with the Eximbank to assist in the financing of larger export transactions up to $1 million.

In an effort to bring Eximbank financing assistance down to the smaller exporter, the agency implemented a City-State Agency Cooperation Program. The city of Los Angeles has moved further than others in establishing direct funding for exporters through its agency's direct line of credit with local banks.

A whole new breed of non-bank banks are entering the export financing market. Although higher priced than bank or government financing, they offer transactional funding that doesn't disturb a company's other credit lines or debt to equity ratio; that is, off-balance sheet financing.

When exporting to soft currency countries, some form of countertrade is normally required; the more complex the exported products and the higher the dollar value, the more complex countertrade becomes. Smaller companies must have qualified personnel to effectively use these techniques.

The variety of export financing sources can be intimidating. This chapter provided an overview of many of the major sources and forms of funding available to smaller exporters. All sources are not applicable to all businesses. A company's size, the dollar amount of the export transaction, the type of products or services being exported, the country of destination, and even the company's state of residence all bear directly on where to look for export funding.

Although the choices vary with each combination of these factors, with a little perseverance, every exporter should be able to raise external capital for both working capital needs and special equipment purchases. There is little need to divert internal funds away from domestic business to participate in exporting.

CHAPTER 13

Unusual Financing For Expanding Overseas

Ten years ago few companies other than corporate giants considered establishing a manufacturing, distribution, or sales facility on foreign soil as a viable growth strategy. *Exporting maybe; a foreign location, never!* Most considered the risk too great, the marketing tactics too uncertain, and the financing unattainable. *Going Global: New Opportunities for Growing Companies to Compete in World Markets* describes ways and means to cope with the first two obstacles. This chapter outlines readily available financing techniques to get you over the third hurdle.

In the vernacular of global trade, making a "foreign direct investment" refers to establishing a presence on foreign soil, either with a manufacturing or distribution facility, or by opening sales and administrative offices. Second stage companies normally expand domestically. It seems less risky, easier to manage, and can be done more quickly than going overseas. By the time a company has been in business for four or five years, however, an overseas expansion might be just the ticket to penetrate new markets or sell a new technology or product line.

Financing foreign direct investments can be a gut-wrenching experience; or, it can be accomplished with a minimum of hassle and cost. The difference lies with how much preparatory work you are willing to do. The starting point should be a well-conceived strategic plan to meet your company's long-term objectives. The evaluation of alternative foreign markets becomes an integral part of the planning process. Once sound business reasons justify a specific region of the world or a particular country in which to make the first investment, the sourcing of funds begins.

This chapter describes a variety of methods for raising the necessary captial. Some methods involve more risk than others. Some are more costly. Some more complex. Some relate to investing in specific regions of the world. Matching the right financing with your specific objectives is the difficult part. The following analyses should help make the decision.

Foreign direct investment financing can be arranged through seven channels:

1. Foreign banks
2. U.S. government programs

3. Multinational organizations
4. Foreign government programs
5. Quasi-private funds
6. Joint ventures
7. Public markets

Smaller companies can't count on American banks to finance foreign direct investments, other than as intermediaries, or in some cases as minor participants in a funding group. Although they are needed as depositories and transfer agents, banking industry regulations and lack of global experience keep most American banks on the fringes of global finance. Foreign banks, on the other hand, have actively participated in funding worldwide private investments for years.

FOREIGN BANKS

Foreign banks operate under a different set of rules than American banks. Constrained by archaic accounting practices and the Glass-Steagall and McFadden legislation enacted in the 1930s in response to Depression-related bank closures, American banks remain locked in their traditional roles. Without such restrictions, foreign banks compete worldwide with off-balance sheet financing and a variety of creative loan and equity instruments. Both merchant and clearing banks eagerly participate in financing the overseas expansion of American companies, as well as those from most other nations.

CLEARING BANKS

Clearing banks, the foreign counterpart of American commercial banks, handle short-term working capital loans and other rapid turnover transactions. They also make smaller term loans. Foreign clearing banks with offices in the United States are especially attracted to working with smaller and mid-size companies trying to expand overseas.

If you invest in the bank's home country, a local clearing bank handles the transaction directly. Cross-border financing (funding projects in a country other than the bank's home base) is usually managed by merchant banks. Many of the larger foreign banks bear the label "universal" banks—that is, they have both clearing and merchant banking capabilities. Universal banks engage in both local and cross-border financing.

Regardless of the country you choose, developing a relationship with a local clearing bank is mandatory. In addition to working capital loans, they manage overdrafts (a term used overseas for an open line of credit), performance guarantees, letters of credit, wire transfers, mortgage loans, and construction loans. Clearing banks also get involved with local business acquisition financing.

For smaller requests—say less than $1 million—local clearing banks remain the best source and, in many countries, the only source. Larger multi-national banks or merchant banks won't touch smaller loans, unless of course you already have a personal relationship with a decision-making bank officer.

Foreign banks sport less onerous collateral requirements than those demanded by American banks. Overdrafts are commonly used in place of actual working capital loans. Reputation and references carry more weight than the value of company assets. Customarily, compensating balances provide additional income to the bank. Cross-collateralization is seldom an issue.

The ownership of foreign banks can be confusing and at times an important issue for determining whether or not to use a specific bank. Local governments own or control local banks in many developing countries. Using one of these banks requires a grasp of the importance and intricacies of unwritten "agreements" and "understandings" with appropriate government bureaucrats. It's usually safer to let an intermediary make the arrangements and act as a buffer. This keeps you clear of the Foreign Corrupt Practices Act.

MERCHANT BANKS

Merchant banks provide a broader spectrum of financing choices than clearing banks. At the same time, they prefer larger, more profitable deals. Merchant banking is often referred to as the "granddaddy of cross-border financing," dating back several hundred years. Merchant banks were originally organized by groups of businesspeople—British, French, Dutch, Spanish, and Japanese—to handle credit needs and other financing for merchant customers and suppliers around the world. Eventually their business became more financing and investing and less merchant trading. Further concentration on the money side became a natural evolution. Today merchant banking continues to be the cornerstone of global finance. Even though American investment banks are making inroads, they have a long way to go to catch up.

Merchant banks are an excellent source for larger amounts of long-term capital, either for starting new companies or for acquiring existing businesses or facilities. They provide both equity and debt capital for larger deals. Smaller transactions involve pure debt. Interest rates run higher than clearing banks, but with LIBOR as the base, they continue to be more than competitive with comparable U.S. rates. Merchant banks play a major participatory role with international development banks, either as an equity partner or a coordinating intermediary.

INTERNATIONAL DEVELOPMENT BANKS

In many parts of the world, international development banks (IDBs) play active roles in the solicitation and funding of foreign direct investments. The mission of IDBs is to provide funds for the economic development of a country's infrastructure and its private sector. Some local IDBs are privately-owned by large multinational commercial banks or by local businesses and banks. Host country governments own part or all of other IDBs.

European, Japanese, Taiwanese, and South Korean companies have taken advantage of IDB financing for years. Smaller American businesses have yet to reap the benefit in any magnitude, probably because their advisors have not opened the door.

Local IDBs maintain different eligibility requirements and promote various forms of financing assistance, depending on the country and the current economic climate. However, they are all similar. The best way to contact a local IDB is through a host country intermediary—either an attorney, consultant, or the local office of a "Big-6" accounting firm.

In addition to local IDBs, four "super" or coordinating international development banks serve as central banks for local IDBs. They also offer direct financing to private-sector businesses. The four are: the Asian Development Bank (for Asia and the Pacific Basin); the African Development Bank and Fund (for Africa); the Inter-American Development Bank (for Latin America); and, beginning in 1990, the European Bank for Reconstruction and Development (for Eastern Europe).

The European Bank for Reconstruction and Development was formed specifically to help Eastern European countries rebuild their economies. The Bank will be a "catalyst between the capital and know-how of the West and the businesses of the East," according to French President François Mitterand. It was formed with $12 billion capital contributed by 42 nations, with the United States making the largest contribution. It became fully operable in 1991.

Plans call for 60 percent of the bank's loans to go for private sector businesses in Eastern Europe and the balance for public projects. European Community (EC) countries as a group hold a 51 percent interest in the bank, but the United States remains the largest single shareholder with 10 percent. Eastern European nations hold a 13.5 percent interest.

Although each IDB has slightly different programs, the Asian Development Bank (ADB) maintains the most aggressive and active program for promoting development in the Pacific Basin. Currently, the ADB also seems to be the most receptive to applications from smaller companies. Although each of the four banks has slightly different programs, because it is the most active, the ADB can serve as an example of how they all work.

The following information was provided by the Asian Development Bank in

1990. Further information may be obtained by writing: The Manager, Private Sector Division, Asian Development Bank, P.O. Box 789, Manila, Philippines.

The Asian Development Bank (ADB) was established in 1966 by a consortium of 47 member countries. Its purpose is to accelerate economic and social growth in the Pacific Basin by promoting financial and technical assistance for projects contributing to the economic development of the region. The ADB provides funding indirectly to private businesses and private banks and also directly to the private sector through intermediaries (financial institutions who provide medium to long-term financing such as local development banks, some commercial and merchant banks, leasing companies, and venture capital firms).

Direct financial assistance consists of medium- to long-term loans, without government guarantee, together with the underwriting of, and investment in, a company's equity securities. Private sector companies can also apply grants to project-related feasibility studies. ADB stresses direct assistance to local banks and sponsors of projects involving venture capital, leasing, factoring, investment management, and commercial finance. Indirect assistance to intermediaries consists of credit lines for small to medium-sized new ventures and expansion of existing businesses. ADB also provides equity lines to intermediaries to facilitate equity funding for new businesses.

Eligible projects include new or expansion productive facilities in energy, manufacturing, transportation, forestry, fisheries, mining, tourism, health, and agriculture. Projects providing luxury items might be eligible if products are produced primarily for export. The projects should use domestic raw materials, provide local jobs, and employ modern management techniques. ADB favors export products, or those which stimulate additional foreign investment. The applying company can be locally or foreign owned. Companies may be partially owned by local governments but the business must be run on a commercial basis. ADB also funds the privatization of government-owned businesses.

ADB limits financial assistance, including loans and equity contributions, to 25 percent of the total cost of the project. Loans range from $2 million to $30 million, except under unusual circumstance. If intermediaries participate, loan limits can be increased. ADB equity investment cannot exceed 25 percent of the capital of the business—but neither can it be less than $100,000. The ADB refuses to be the largest single investor. The ADB also assists in structuring syndicated and co-financing arrangements.

ADB insists that adequate collateral be provided for all loans. The bank charges commitment fees of 1 percent per annum on the undisbursed loan balance. It also charges front-end fees and legal fees. Repayment periods may not exceed 12 years. LIBOR-based interest rates vary, as do currency denominations. Upon completion of the project, the ADB sells its equity investment, preferably to nationals.

Non-regional member countries of ADB include Austria, Belgium, Canada, Denmark, Finland, France, Germany, Italy, Japan, South Korea, the Netherlands, Norway, Spain, Sweden, Switzerland, the United Kingdom, and the United States.

OVERSEAS PRIVATE INVESTMENT CORPORATION

Although most of the publicity from Washington relating to American companies involved in international trade concerns exporting assistance, several agencies of the federal government also provide financing assistance to firms interested in foreign direct investment. Some of this assistance comes via indirect means. The Agency for International Development, for example, does not provide direct financial support to American businesses; however, it can be influential in helping to obtain funds from foreign sources. Other agencies, such as OPIC, offer direct assistance.

The Overseas Private Investment Corporation (OPIC) is a self-sustaining agency of the federal government, originally funded with taxpayer money in 1971. It has since repaid its initial capital and now operates on its own funds, much like a private business. The agency must abide by a number or rules and restrictions, however, so it isn't quite like a private company.

OPIC's mission is to promote private-sector economic growth in developing countries by offering assistance to U.S. companies wishing to invest in these nations. Approximately 100 developing countries meet OPIC's investment criteria. To confuse the issue even furthur, OPIC reclassifies these countries several times each year. The current status of development within the country and the conditions of government-to-government trade agreements determine which countries qualify. The only way to be sure which country qualifies is to contact OPIC's Washington office directly when you get ready to move. If you don't intend to invest in one of these countries, don't bother with OPIC.

On the plus side, OPIC targets its assistance to smaller businesses, not large corporations. OPIC's assistance can be invaluable when trying to identify investment or market opportunities. This service is available through OPIC's investor information service and a network of investor missions around the world.

OPIC provides medium- to long-term project loans and political risk insurance (not commercial risk coverage which is handled by the FCIA). The coverage does include protection against currency inconvertibility, insurrection, civil strife, revolution, war, and foreign expropriation.

New foreign ventures of American businesses qualify for both the insurance and finance programs, although they must be commercially and financially sound (OPIC likes a 60/40 debt to equity ratio). OPIC also finances the expansion of existing overseas facilities owned by American companies.

Two caveats apply: (1) the project must contribute to the social and economic development of the host country; and (2) the project must be consistent with the current economic and political interests of the U.S..

OPIC financing may be used only for projects or other ventures in which an

American company has a significant equity and management participation. The company must have a proven record of competence and success in another business the same as, or related to, the one being financed. This automatically excludes OPIC financing for starting up a new business different from that operated at home.

American interests also must have a significant continuing financial risk in the enterprise. "Significant" means 25 percent or more. Political risk insurance coverage is limited to the U.S. equity participation in the venture.

OPIC FINANCING PROGRAMS

If your expansion project meets these standards, one additional set of criteria affects your qualification for OPIC assistance. The investment must relate to one of the following:

1. Energy or energy-related projects (water systems, electric utilities, oil and gas drillings, processing products for local consumption, and alternate energy sources).

2. Projects offering significant trade benefits or development of the infrastructure for the host country.

3. Projects sponsored by small businesses or co-ops in those countries where the per capita income is greater than $3,800 (a measure of the stage of development of the country).

All OPIC loans are nonrecourse. Therefore, OPIC must be assured of the economic and financial soundness of the project. This includes, but is not limited to, evidence of the company's ability to repay the loan. Once OPIC judges a venture financially sound, with competent management, "a company will not be required to pledge any additional general credit," according to OPIC officials. This means that if you want to build a facility in a qualified country and can put up at least 25 percent equity, OPIC coordinates with Eximbank and private foreign and American banks to finance another 25 percent. This debt requires collateral—the building itself or other company assets. OPIC then provides loans for the remaining 50 percent without additional collateral—effectively an unsecured loan!

Occasionally, OPIC considers nonproject financing and takes the role of a secured creditor, but it prefers the other route.

An American company may own 100 percent of the project and still qualify for assistance, but OPIC encourages joint ventures or other participatory arrangements with local corporations or citizens. If a local government or government agency insists on holding a controlling interest—51 percent—chances are very high that OPIC will not finance the deal.

OPIC finances up to 75 percent of the cost of expanding existing facilities. For new projects, OPIC's participation cannot exceed 50 percent. These ratios vary, however, depending on the country, political considerations, and current federal policy.

OPIC provides two types of financing assistance:

- Direct loans to the business
- Bank guarantees

Only smaller projects qualify for direct loans. The current limits set $200,000 as the minimum and $4 million as the maximum. Occasionally, the agency takes an equity position through a variety of convertible bond issues, and then sells its holding to companies or citizens in the host country.

Most guaranteed loans go to major projects. They range up to $50 million, even larger in some cases. Unless you participate with other American companies through joint ventures or by taking part interest in a major construction project, you probably won't qualify for the guarantee program.

OPIC Leasing Assistance

Setting up an overseas leasing company is a natural adjunct to export lease financing (examined in Chapter 11). Not only does OPIC provide political risk insurance coverage for leasing companies, it also participates in the financing. It does this through both direct loans and guaranteed bank loans.

OPIC's loan limit for leasing companies is $1 million, with a medium-term maturity. Any American-owned or -controlled foreign leasing company, defined as a small business by OPIC, qualifies.

OPIC also guarantees foreign bank loans to foreign leasing companies having a significant American interest. These guarantees back loans with up to seven-year terms. The amount varies with the country and the type of leases used. Separate criteria apply to finance and operating leases.

Small Contractor Guarantee Program

Small contractors frequently find it impossible to get a bank guarantee or surety bond to warrant performance against an overseas contract. If they do qualify for surety bonding, the cost can be prohibitively high. This keeps many smaller contractors from even bidding on overseas projects.

OPIC's Small Contractor Guarantee program fills the void. The only requirement is that the contractor must be excluded from the "Fortune 1000." OPIC provides a performance guarantee to banks as collateral to a standby letter of credit. This L/C then serves as a performance bond.

OPIC covers all risks unconditionally up to 75 percent of the credit. Coupled with an OPIC policy under the contractors and exporters insurance program, this percentage may be raised to 90 percent, leaving only 10 percent of the risk open to a bank or surety company.

U.S. AGENCY FOR INTERNATIONAL DEVELOPMENT

Proclamations from Washington state the mission of the U.S. Agency for International Development (USAID) as "to assist foreign governments in economically disadvantaged areas to stimulate economic growth, promote higher standards of living, and improve foreign exchange earnings."

Seventy worldwide offices administer USAID programs. Special private-sector offices offer assistance to private businesses that include:

1. Financial assistance to the host country for short-term stabilization and economic recovery by financing imports of raw materials and intermediate goods for the private sector.

2. Improving the business climate by supporting host country policy reforms and incentives to restore domestic business confidence, rationalize interest and foreign exchange rates, attract foreign investment, upgrade the infrastructure (roads, port facilities, irrigation projects, free zone facilities), and develop new trading programs.

3. Funding programs that upgrade human resource skills and managerial capabilities, overcome technical marketing and export obstacles, and capitalize financial intermediaries that provide credits to businesses in the host country. This includes capital for private sector development banks and other credit facilities for small and medium-sized businesses.

USAID is a government-to-government agency, not directly involved in the private sector. It does not provide any direct financial assistance to American companies, either overseas or domestically. However, there is an indirect way to obtain financial assistance—by investing in an area or a project approved by USAID.

Since the local government receives funding from USAID, American companies bidding for participation in the project receive preferential consideration. In poor, developing countries, where political connections rather than the lowest price determine the successful bidder, USAID influence may be, and frequently is, the only way to get in.

USAID has been very supportive of companies participating in private-sector economic development projects in the Caribbean and Central America under the Caribbean Basin Initiative (CBI) program. Through its Private Enterprise Bureau (PEB), USAID arranges medium- and long-term loans to joint ventures between

American companies and private companies or government agencies from the host country. USAID tailors these loans case-by-case.

Contact the PEB directly for an application and current qualification criteria. Because Washington's political and economic support programs continue their roller coaster ride, the only certain way to get in on USAID or any other government financing program is to stay in touch with your congressional representative or with the USAID, Eximbank, and SBA offices directly. Constant change continues to be the name of the game.

OTHER U.S. GOVERNMENT AGENCIES

Several other federal agencies provide varying amounts of foreign direct investment assistance. Some offer technical or commercial help; others include financial aid. The Departments of Commerce, State, Defense, and several independent agencies maintain their own programs. Most are too specialized to examine in their entirety here, although a few major ones cover a broad enough spectrum to have universal appeal.

Department Of Commerce

The Department of Commerce helps any company with specific procurement needs or proposals for investment in foreign countries. The Department's "Active Match Program" provides direct contacts with either foreign suppliers exporting to the United States, or with potential foreign joint venture partners. This program does not offer direct funding; however, leads and direct contacts with potential partners can be invaluable. This is a free service.

The Department of Commerce is especially active in the Caribbean Basin Initiative program. As an example, the Department established a CBI ombudsman to act as a high-level expediter and facilitator for projects that get bogged down in bureaucratic red tape. The Department also actively pursues investment opportunities for American companies wishing to establish operations in Caribbean locations.

Department Of State

Within the Department of State, the U.S. Trade and Development Program (TDP) funds feasibility studies for Third World development projects. To qualify, these projects must eventually lead to the export of American goods to the host country. Projects include agribusiness development, infrastructure projects (energy, communications, port development, and so on) and mining. This is government-to-government funding; however, TDP also works directly with American companies interested in foreign direct investment by co-financing studies leading to specific investment decisions.

Department Of Agriculture

The Department of Agriculture isn't directly involved in providing financial assistance either. It does, however, assist in identifying overseas agribusiness investment opportunities for private businesses. Write to the Private Sector Relations (PSR) division of the Office of International Cooperation (OICD) in Washington, D.C.

Office Of The U.S. Trade Representative

The U.S. Trade Representative (USTR), part of the Executive Office of the President, is responsible for coordinating U.S. trade policy with other nations. Although not directly involved in financing, USTR assists U.S. businesses invest in host countries through programs negotiated with foreign governments. Two of the most relevant programs are:

1. The Bilateral Investment Treaty (BIT) negotiated with foreign governments to serve as incentives for U.S. companies to locate in the host country.

2. Guaranteed Access Levels for Textiles and Apparel negotiated with foreign governments to provide investment incentives for U.S. firms engaged in the textile and apparel industries.

SECTION 936 FINANCING

Section 936 of the Internal Revenue Code identifies companies doing business in Puerto Rico that leave their earnings on deposit in Puerto Rican banks as "936 companies." Because "936 companies" enjoy significant tax incentives, large deposits remain in commonwealth banks. These "qualified possession source investment income," or QPSII (quipsy) funds, are available for investment in any country qualifying under the Caribbean Basin Initiative, assuming the country has executed a Tax Information Exchange Agreement (TIEA) with the IRS. So far Jamaica, Barbados, Grenada, Dominica, and St. Lucia have signed up for participation in the 936 program. Undoubtedly, more will join the throng in the future.

Using quipsy funds as a base, the government of Puerto Rico—through investment banks—has set up a private Caribbean Basin Initiative Fund (CBIF) for investment in eligible countries. Underwriters raised several millions in investment capital. Loans from this fund must be secured with hard assets, guarantees, and risk insurance. OPIC and the Government Development Bank of Puerto Rico stand ready to assist companies raise this collateral. Because of its tax-exempt status loans from CBIF carry very low interest rates, similar to industrial revenue bonds.

As with other government giveaways, there is a catch. To qualify for these loans, the direct investment project must be located in an eligible country and it must be complementary with Puerto Rico. This means that the project must produce goods or services from which Puerto Rico benefits in some direct or indirect way. The vagueness of this provision drives many companies away from even applying for funds; although if the shoe fits, it's a low cost way to go.

MULTI-NATIONAL ORGANIZATIONS

The United States doesn't have a monopoly on private-sector government financial aid programs. Several multi-national organizations funded by a conglomeration of nations also stand ready to help. The World Bank and the International Monetary Fund are two such organizations that provide financial assistance directly to governments of developing nations. Several agencies within the World Bank also offer financial assistance to the private sector. The International Finance Corporation is the most prominent.

INTERNATIONAL FINANCE CORPORATION

The International Finance Corporation (IFC) manages several assistance programs. Among other activities, it coordinates and assists in arranging financing for U.S. and foreign joint ventures, investing in projects located in developing nations. It also provides equity investment and/or partial debt financing for the enhancement of productive, private enterprise already established in developing nations. Contacts and application should be made through a professional advisor directly to the IFC.

Most IFC projects could be beyond the reach of independent smaller businesses because of their size. However, projects involving a joint venture with a major transnational could very well qualify. (Financing through joint ventures is explored later in this chapter.) Furthermore, conditions change rapidly in the global community. By the time this book gets published, the IFC may have lowered its sights. It certainly can't hurt to ask.

INTERNATIONAL DEVELOPMENT ASSOCIATION

The International Development Association (IDA) offers financing support very similar to that of the IFC, with one major difference. Loans from the IFC extend for a maximum of 10 years; with the IDA, repayment can be amortized over 50 years. Obviously, this make IDA financing very attractive for extremely large development projects. Joint ventures appear to be the only viable way for a smaller company to take advantage of this assistance.

INTERNATIONAL BANK FOR RECONSTRUCTION AND DEVELOPMENT

The International Bank for Reconstruction and Development (IBRD), a hybrid international development bank, lends directly to governments for infrastructure projects and other major development programs. Long-term, low-interest loans finance the construction of roads, power plants, steel mills, and other major infrastructure or capital intensive projects in developing countries. Although the funds flow directly to governments—not the private sector—IBRD helps smaller companies identify foreign projects that qualify for its financial aid.

FOREIGN GOVERNMENT FINANCING ASSISTANCE

All governments of industrialized nations, including those in the Far East referred to as the "newly industrialized countries," offer financing assistance to companies located within their boundaries. Companies from any nation that operate facilities in one of these countries qualify for financial aid.

Financing assistance usually flows directly from the country's government-owned central bank, through agencies similar to Eximbank. Funding is available for exporting products to the U.S. or other nations, for importing products into the country, for making cross-border direct investments, and for foreign credit risk insurance. Programs vary slightly from country to country. Most of the European programs emphasize credit insurance, supplemented by direct financing assistance. In the Far East the reverse occurs. Japan and South Korea, for instance, emphasize financial aid, supplemented by credit insurance.

The following sections describe a cross-section of financing and credit insurance assistance offered by nations in the Far East and Europe. The descriptions of these programs come directly from each of the funding organizations and were operable in 1988 and 1989. Provisions may change in the future.

JAPAN

The Export-Import Bank of Japan (Japan Eximbank) offers yen financing for exports, imports, and direct investments overseas. Japan Eximbank, in parallel with major commercial banks throughout the world, supplies yen loans of medium- to long-term duration. The commercial part of the loan must be arranged through the participating commercial bank. Japan Eximbank adjusts interest charges on its portion of the loan so that the total cost stays within OECD guidelines.

Any qualified company, foreign or domestic, can take advantage of assistance from Japan Eximbank for import-buyer credit and export-supplier credit. Eligibility criteria is based on the type of equipment, resource, service, or raw material involved. Japan Eximbank insists, however, that at least 50 percent of the contract value consist of goods or services with Japanese content. The bank offers the following financing packages:

1. *Import credit.* Energy-related products or resources, raw materials, and manufactured products that Japan Eximbank regards as vital to the Japanese economy qualify for import credit. Applications are received directly by Japan Eximbank.

2. *Export credit.* Major industrial equipment and ships, manufactured in Japan, and Japanese technical services sold abroad qualify for deferred payment export credit. The applicant (foreign importer) arranges the credit with the Japanese exporter who then requests Japan Eximbank to grant the credit in conjunction with a commercial bank.

3. *Overseas investment credits.* Japan Eximbank grants overseas investment credits for the following purposes:
   a. Equity participation in foreign corporations by Japanese corporations.
   b. Long-term equity secured loans to foreign corporations, provided these companies also have equity participation by Japanese firms.
   c. Equity participation in Japanese firms whose sole purpose is to make overseas investments.
   d. Overseas projects directly operated by the borrower.

Japan Eximbank also makes direct investment loans to foreign governments for equity participation in foreign corporations that have Japanese equity participation.

Credits are available only in yen, but can be dollar-denominated by the exporter. Down payment must be 15 percent cash; 20 percent for ships. Supplier credits, including commercial bank participation, cover 75 to 85 percent of the contract value of the export transaction. Japan Eximbank's portion changes periodically but in 1988-1989 it was 60 to 70 percent, with the balance handled by commercial banks. Repayment begins within six months of delivery of the goods and must be made in equal semiannual installments.

Exporting companies are required to obtain insurance from the Japanese Ministry of International Trade and Industry. For private companies, letters of credit, government guarantees, or letters of performance guarantee from a major international bank must secure any unpaid down payment balance or deferred payment arrangement.

SOUTH KOREA

The South Korean Eximbank makes medium- to long-term direct loans to foreign and domestic corporations with participation from major international commercial banks. South Korean content must be 50 to 75 percent depending on the product. South Korea Eximbank extends loans to suppliers and buyers. It also issues guarantees and export insurance.

1. *Export credit.* Credit covers the export of capital goods—including industrial plants, steel structures, machinery, electrical equipment, ships, and vehicles, including spare parts. The installation and operating costs of plants in foreign countries remain heavily subsidized.

2. *Overseas project and investment credit.* Such credit applies to investment in any facility or equipment abroad when most of the parts or materials required for operation are imported from South Korea. Investments in foreign projects can also be covered if they use South Korean materials or exports or promote economic cooperation with foreign countries. South Korea Eximbank determines which projects promote economic cooperation.

3. *Major resource development credit.* South Korea Eximbank provides funds for foreign projects which lead to the stabilization of the supply of natural resources or strengthen economic relationships with a country that supplies needed natural resources such as oil, coal, copper, lumber, and rubber. Studies leading to the acquisition of mineral rights also can be funded.

4. *Direct loans.* South Korea Eximbank loans to foreign importers who purchase South Korean goods and services, but the buyer must have an unconditional guarantee from a commercial bank, central bank, or government.

5. *Guarantees.* South Korea Eximbank provides guarantees for 100 percent of the principal and interest to both foreign and South Korean financial institutions that co-finance loans for periods of more than five years. Foreign importers also get 100 percent performance guarantees and advance payment guarantees.

6. *Export insurance.* South Korea Eximbank provides export insurance to cover political, commercial, and *managerial* risks. The definition of managerial risk varies with each transaction.

All financing is U.S. dollar denominated with the following terms:

- 70 percent of the contract value, less down payment, for contracts exceeding $1 million.
- 100 percent of contract value, less down payment, for contract values of $3 million to $10 million.
- 70 to 90 percent of import value, less down payment, for predelivery export contracts.
- 70 percent of contract value, less down payment, for post delivery export contracts.
- Cash down payment must be 15 to 20 percent of total contract value.
- Terms for export credits are from 180 days to 10 years; major resource development credits can extend to 20 years.
- 100 percent guarantees are required from all buyers.

UNITED KINGDOM

The origins of the Exports Credit Guarantee Department (ECGD) date to 1919. Its programs set the standard around which other countries molded theirs. ECGD remains one of the most successful national export insurers in the world. Compared to most other U.S. and foreign government agencies, it seems to be efficient, timely, and charges reasonable fees for its services. ECGD covers approximately one-third of all exports emanating from Great Britain. The British government provides full financial backing in the event of catastrophic losses.

As the following indicates, credit insurance from ECGD is far more lenient than similar coverage from the FCIA for American exports. Coverages range as follows:

1. *Commercial risk*
   a. Insolvency of the buyer. ECGD covers a full 90 percent of the loss.
   b. Buyer's failure to pay within six months of due date for goods already accepted. ECGD covers a full 90 percent of the loss.
   c. Buyer's failure to accept goods which have been shipped, provided the exporter complied with all the terms of the contract. Exporter bears first 20 percent of loss, ECGD covers 90 percent of the balance. Under certain types of capital goods, this cap is completely eliminated.

2. *Political risk*—ECGD covers 95 percent of any loss after shipment, and 90 percent of losses incurred prior to shipment.
   a. Government action which blocks or delays payment of sterling to the exporter.
   b. Cancellation of a valid import license or imposition of new import licensing restrictions in the buyer's country.

c. Cancellation or nonrenewal of a U.K. export license or imposition of new export licensing restrictions.

d. War between the buyer's country and the U.K.

e. War, revolution, or similar disturbances in the buyer's country.

f. Additional handling, transportation, and/or insurance charges, resulting from an interruption or diversion of the ocean shipping vessel if these charges cannot be recovered from the buyer.

g. Any other cause of loss occurring outside the U.K. and not within the control of the exporter or the buyer.

h. Repudiation of the contract in cases where ECGD agrees that the buyer has government status.

Premiums vary depending on whether a seller insures all export business or only specific transactions. Exporters wishing full coverage must agree to insure all export shipments for one or three years with the latter resulting in substantially reduced premiums.

In addition to covering all goods exported from the U.K., ECGD credit insurance includes a variety of other features:

1. Political risks of shipments to overseas subsidiaries and affiliates.

2. Exports to intermediaries.

3. Re-export of imported goods after packaging or value added processes.

4. Non-sterling invoices.

5. Overseas stocking of a U.K. company's inventory.

6. Erection costs of exported capital equipment.

7. Construction goods and services.

8. Services, including technical or professional assistance, repair work, technology transfers, and so on.

9. Arbitration award where the buyer refuses to comply. ECGD also covers that portion of a contract involving a U.K. exporter and a foreign subcontractor jointly contracting with a customer.

ECGD also offers financial assistance to companies and joint venture partners located in Great Britain. The most widely used form continues to be guarantees to banks that make direct loans to exporters. The department ties this assistance to credit insurance by insisting that participants must have taken comprehensive coverage with ECGD for at least 12 months.

ECGD also offers a buyer credit guarantee for transactions in excess of 250,000 pounds sterling. The importer must make a 20 percent down payment and pay the balance direct to the exporter or to a local bank handling the financing. Terms extend to five years. Finally, ECGD guarantees lines of credit from British banks to overseas buyers.

FRANCE

The French export credit agency is called the Compagnie Française d'Assurance pour le Commerce Extérieur, or COFACE. COFACE provides credit insurance but, unlike the ECGD, stays away from direct financing or guarantees. As described later, however, insurance can in effect become interest-free financing.

COFACE works closely with the French banks—Crédit National, Banque Française de Commerce Extérieur, and Banque de France. It splits its commercial and political coverage, insuring 85 percent commercial risk to the U.S. (80 percent to other countries), and either 80 or 90 percent of political risk depending upon how much the exporter is willing to pay in premiums.

Under its definition of consumer goods, COFACE covers the export of raw materials, semi-finished products, metals, foods, chemicals, pharmaceuticals, electrical appliances, and small tools. It also covers the export of light machinery and other capital goods sold under contracts with credit up to three years. For large projects, COFACE extends coverage up to 10 years.

When an exporter or contractor is required to put up a "good faith" or performance deposit, it can get exchange risk guarantees. Such guarantees extend directly to the bank financing the deposit. Exchange coverage also applies when invoicing is required to be in a foreign currency and the exporter has no other way to cover the fluctuation risk.

The French go one step further than ECGD or the FCIA. As a means of supporting French companies entering new markets in foreign countries, COFACE insures the coverage of all fixed costs of marketing studies, office administration, publicity and advertising, and so on, incurred by that company in a foreign country while trying to develop new sales. If these sales do not materialize, COFACE pays between 50 and 70 percent of these expenses, depending on the duration of the marketing effort and other risk classifications. It also reimburses 50 percent of the expenses of participating in an international trade fair if additional sales do not materialize. For projects that don't work out, this insurance is essentially an interest-free grant.

GERMANY

Beginning in 1962, the West German government was authorized to extend credit and political risk insurance. Two private companies administer the program —Hermes Kreditversicherungs-AG and Deutsche Revisions-und Trehand AG. Exporters submit applications to Hermes, which performs an examination and a review. Hermes then forwards the documents to the International Committee for Export Guarantees for approval or rejection. For approved applications, Hermes issues the actual guarantee with the full backing of the German government.

Hermes offers only credit guarantees. Although no direct financing is involved, Hermes does issue bank guarantees.

One policy includes both political and commercial risks. Political risks are defined as:

1. Nonpayment due to general moratorium on repayment debts and other government payment prohibitions.

2. Currency convertibility and transfer restrictions or the freezing of balances deposited in the local currency of the importer's country.

3. Losses from seizure, damage, or destruction of goods that result from political causes and not otherwise covered by private insurance.

Commercial risk coverage for sales to private buyers includes the buyer's insolvency or proven inability to pay the exporter. Sales to government customers may be insured against a flat nonpayment in six months. Pre-shipment risks are also covered when equipment cannot be delivered due to the deteriorated financial condition of the foreign buyer. Hermes covers 80 percent for commercial, 85 to 90 percent for political, and 85 percent for pre-shipment risks.

Special coverages may also be arranged with Hermes for:

1. Currency convertibility and transfer.

2. Inventory kept abroad.

3. Guarantees for bank loans to carry this inventory abroad.

4. Foreign exchange risk if the invoice is in U.S. dollars, English sterling, or Swiss francs, but only for two years. Losses beyond two years in excess of 3 percent are covered. If gains in excess of 3 percent are realized, they must be turned over to Hermes.

QUASI-PRIVATE VENTURE FUNDS

The whirlwind development of new, free-market economies has stimulated the formation of U.S. government-supported private venture capital funds. One of the first to begin operating was a venture fund started by 40 American corporations to provide funding for the privatization of Polish industries and the development of Polish infrastructures. This fund assists American companies start-up new businesses in Poland as well as invest with Polish and other joint venture partners in previously nationalized companies. The venture program is structured after the African Growth Fund currently supporting investments in poor countries in sub-Sahara Africa.

Utilizing the administrative mechanisms of OPIC, the U.S. government guarantees the political risk of these ventures. If the Polish free-market experiment fails and the country reverts to a nationalization policy, OPIC covers all losses from the venture group. During 1990 and 1991, similar quasi-private venture funds were planned to accomplish the same aims in Hungary and Czechoslovakia. Some have already been formed.

As free-market economies begin evolving in the Balkans, the Soviet Union, China, and certain African and Latin American nations, it seems inevitable that additional U.S. government-supported programs and venture funds will be announced. Close contact with OPIC's Washington, D.C. office remains the best way to stay on top of these new sources. OPIC also keeps close tabs on what projects are coming up for bid or other direct investment in each country.

JOINT VENTURES

In addition to other overseas expansion advantages with either a local or a U.S. partner, financing is frequently the overriding reason for joint ventures. Host country partners can arrange financing with local banks or government agencies when an American company would be stone-walled. A larger U.S. partner might bring financial resources to the table in exchange for your operating expertise and risk-taking.

JOINT VENTURES WITH FOREIGN NATIONALS

Financing assistance is available from nearly every industrialized country. Germany, France, the United Kingdom, Sweden, Norway, the Netherlands, Italy, Spain, Japan, and Taiwan all have government-sponsored financing schemes to assist new or existing companies fund expansion. The lack of national production capability for specific technologies stimulates assistance from developed countries. Money is seldom a roadblock. Teaming up with a local company in one of these countries virtually assures local financing assistance.

Similar conditions warrant joint ventures with local partners in developing, or redeveloping nations. Here, the lack of technology continues to be a serious problem and many governments support American direct investment as long as a local partner is available to learn the ropes.

In Eastern Europe, the Soviet Union, most of South and Central America, the Middle East, Southeast Asia, sub-Sahara Africa, and China, local financing assistance is virtually impossible to arrange without a local partner. Foreign clearing banks and merchant banks also target financial aid for business development with a local partner in preference to full American ownership. Many of the larger, private-sector foreign companies provide the funding themselves if allowed to participate in the project's ownership.

If a joint venture with a foreign partner holds any interest, the Department of Commerce, the CBI ombudsman, OPIC, international development banks, and the larger merchant banks all offer assistance for locating appropriate foreign companies and individuals.

JOINT VENTURES WITH U.S. COMPANIES

Joint ventures with American companies either already established in a foreign country or eager to give it a try provide an alternative way to go. Many smaller companies find this route less risky than joining up with a foreign company. U.S. partnerships work well if you are already selling patented technology or proprietary products to a customer with overseas branches.

Frequently, the larger partner provides the financing in exchange for the marketing rights to your product in designated countries. This shifts operating risk to your company while giving your partner a market entry with product lines not otherwise available. Joint ventures structured this way are probably the fastest and least expensive way for a smaller company to finance a direct investment in foreign markets. It remains one of the most widely used methods in manufacturing and distribution businesses.

PUBLIC MARKETS

In addition to financing foreign direct investments through government and private sources, public financial markets offer unusual opportunities to companies large enough to employ qualified financial managers. The following brief descriptions, though certainly not inclusive, serve to illustrate what can be done.

BANK LOAN DEBT-EQUITY SWAPS

During the 1970s and early 1980s, American banks—as well as many other global financial institutions—extended enormous sums of credit in the form of long-term loans to Latin American governments. Mistakenly believing that governments wouldn't default, the banks did not require any collateral. History proved them wrong and large and mid-size banks across the country have since reserved billions of dollars against these defaulted loans; but they have not written them off.

In the mid-1980s, a few American banks tried to swap their defaulted loans for equity investments in Latin American companies and properties, expecting a lesser loss through this method than by selling the debt instruments in the secondary markets. This didn't work because the banks wanted only sound investments (which were practically non-existent) in return, and debtor nations would not issue new currency to buy the debt for fear of adding to an already impossible inflation problem. Consequently, banks turned to the secondary market, and a new financing tool was created for American businesses.

This is the way it works. A company first purchases a bank instrument in the secondary market evidencing one of these loans, at a substantial discount from its face value—for example, 50 percent. The company then offers to exchange this debt with the debtor government for local currency. The rate of exchange might be, for example, equivalent to 75 percent of the debt. This soft currency is then used to build or purchase a plant or other facility in the host country for one-half the cost of an investment with U.S. dollars. Of course, companies must use their own funds to acquire the debt instrument in the first place.

Although not used extensively, swapping activity continues. Federal officials estimate that through 1988, debt-equity swaps reduced total Latin American debt by about 5 percent. The figure is higher by now.

DEBT AND EQUITY FINANCING ON THE WORLD'S EXCHANGES

Companies that already have publicly traded stock or are considering an initial public offering, might also look at using a foreign exchange to float stock and bond issues. Capital raised through this means can be either in Eurodollars on European exchanges or local currency on other world exchanges. Either larger American investment banks or foreign merchant banks handle the details.

Once entering this realm, other financing options open up—currency and interest swaps and zero-coupon bonds, for example. Swapping debt obligations in global financial markets is not a new creation. As related in *Going Global,* the classic case occurred 10 years ago between the World Bank and IBM. When the World Bank wanted to borrow low-interest rate Swiss francs to lend to developing countries, Swiss investment bankers, skeptical of the repayment ability of these nations, wanted to charge an interest rate of .2 percent above their government bond rate.

On the other hand, the Swiss were eager to accommodate IBM. IBM was trying to raise funds in U.S. markets but had been quoted a rate of .4 percent over the U.S. Treasury rate. This amounted to .05 percent higher than comparable financing offered to the World Bank from U.S. markets. The World Bank and IBM engineered a currency swap; IBM taking the Swiss francs and the World Bank taking dollars.

With competition mounting between the world's financial markets, even a mid-sized company can balance one market against the other to achieve the best financing terms.

SUMMARY

The opportunities for financing an overseas expansion are indeed limitless. In many respects financing foreign direct investments continues to be far easier and less expensive than domestic expansion. Funding for foreign projects comes from seven sources.

1. *Foreign banks.* Clearing banks provide loans in amounts under $1 million. They also arrange guarantees and export financing. Merchant banks handle larger amounts of long-term capital. "Super" international development banks (IDBs) and local IDBs help finance projects in the Pacific Basin, Africa, Latin America, and recently, Eastern Europe.

2. *U.S. government programs.* The Overseas Private Investment Corporation (OPIC) provides guarantees, direct loans, and leasing assistance for investments in developing countries. The Agency for International Development (USAID) extends government-to-government aid to developing nations but companies benefit indirectly by political pressure from the Agency. USAID also identifies investment opportunities for American companies. The Departments of Commerce, Agriculture, and State, and the U.S. Trade Representative assist companies finance specific projects and identify financing sources and investment opportunities. Financing for Caribbean projects can be accomplished through the Government Development Bank of Puerto Rico and the IRS Section 936 program.

3. *Multi-national organizations.* The International Finance Corporation (IFC) helps arrange and finance joint ventures and provides direct equity and debt funds for up to 10 years. The International Development Agency makes loans extending to 50 years. The International Bank for Reconstruction and Development (IBRD) offers long-term loans for major infrastructure projects and assists in identifying qualified foreign opportunities.

4. *Foreign government programs.* Direct off-shore investments and exports from several Far Eastern and European nations can be financed locally through central bank programs. Export-Import banks from Japan and South Korea serve as examples of Far East programs, and ECGD (England), Hermes (Germany), and COFACE (France) illustrate similar assistance from European countries.

5. *Quasi-private venture funds.* Venture capital funds have been formed to support investment in Eastern Europe and sub-Sahara Africa. These venture funds are funded by private businesses but guaranteed by OPIC. More will probably originate to serve Latin America and other regions.

6. *Joint venture financing.* Joint ventures with foreign nationals pave the way for funding from local banks, government agencies, or directly from the venture partner. Both parties benefit from joint ventures between U.S. companies. One provides the financing, the other manages the risk.

7. *Public markets.* Larger companies already trading their securities or those anticipating an initial issue benefit by floating Eurodollar stock and bond issues on foreign exchanges. Purchasing Latin American debt instruments on the secondary market and swapping them with debtor nations provides another low-cost way to invest in these countries.

CHAPTER 14

Refinancing Start-Up And Second-Stage Debt

By the time a company has been in business for five or six years, it has moved through the sequence of first- and second-stage development and matured to the third stage. Not infrequently, third stage companies find that the short and long-term debt and equity arrangements negotiated in earlier years have become outmoded. Operating needs change. Venture capitalists must be paid off. High interest rates add unnecessarily to debt service obligations. Overseas expansion looks strategically viable, but current partners or banking relationships put a damper on the move. These and many other reasons arise in a maturing business that lead owners and managers to think seriously about achieving a more flexible capital base by restructuring earlier financing arrangements.

Inertia blocks such decisions more than any other factor, even though evidence clearly indicates the need for action. In the heat of battle, it's easy to justify postponing refinancing until time permits a thorough investigation of alternatives. Solid relationships with existing lenders and investors make it more difficult to venture into greener pastures. Meeting loan covenants without much difficulty lends an air of complacency. Owners and managers continue to draw increasing bonuses. Payable and receivables may be stretched, but cash flow remains sufficient to keep the company going.

Smaller companies typically shy away from concerted strategic planning. This makes creeping viruses difficult to spot. Yet, given the time and opportunity, viruses can kill, and in smaller companies, they often do. Those with the foresight to restructure, and refinance if necessary, to maximize liquidity and, hence, flexibility before tough times hit are usually the companies that survive and grow. Complacent owners and managers, more often than not, look for new jobs.

Of course, if relationships with lenders or investors are strained to the breaking point, refinancing may be a necessity, not a choice. Refinancing occurs for a variety of reasons. Many companies refinance current debt to decrease debt service payments and increase the amount of operating cash available for discretionary uses. Others need to raise substantial sums of capital for a specific purpose such as a business acquisition or a major overseas expansion. Many companies go the refinance route to improve their tax position. Owners who want to retire strive to liquidate as much debt as possible to improve the book value of their company. If a company is on the skids, refinancing might be necessary for survival.

I won't insult your intelligence by suggesting that your company should be refinanced now. You certainly know your own company better than anyone else. However, many clients have found the following checklist helpful for beginning the thinking process that might or might not lead to a refinance decision.

It's time to consider refinancing when:

1. The monthly sales trend is declining, leveled off, or not accelerating as rapidly as planned.
2. More than 2 percent of receivables have slipped beyond 60 days.
3. Trade payables are stretched longer than receivables.
4. Inventory is increasing faster than sales.
5. Personnel are not fully occupied with productive work.
6. Bank relationships have deteriorated beyond repair.
7. Published financial statements show your bank's profits and ratios deteriorating.
8. Your debt to equity ratio exceeds 3 to 1.
9. The value of collateralized assets has increased.
10. Lease payments are higher than debt service would be—or the reverse.
11. Expansion requires additional capital but all assets are already pledged.
12. Additional capital is needed to develop a new product and bring it to market.
13. The acquisition of another business makes strategic sense.
14. A management incentive program needs major improvements.
15. You want to sell the company or retire.
16. Either debt service or dividend payments are draining too much cash.
17. Your bank is about to call its short- or long-term loan.

Even if internal indicators point to a refinancing decision, the external timing may be way off. Time and again companies embark on a refinancing expedition only to learn after spending thousands of dollars some uncontrollable circumstance prevents or delays completing the job. The main external reasons killing refinancing plans seem to be:

- A national happening—war, presidential election, and financial market crisis (i.e., the breaking of the S & L fiasco)
- Stock market jitters—roller coaster averages trending downward
- Stock market collapse—i.e., October 1987

- Rapidly declining industry—i.e., machine tools and semiconductors in the 1970s
- Out-of-control inflation—rapidly rising prices, interest rates, and unemployment
- Country or region in a hard recession—but only as long as economic indicators continue trending downward

Of course many more reasons exist, but these indicate the type of circumstances under which it becomes increasingly difficult and costly to raise large amounts of either new debt or new equity. Capital may be available, but the cost will be higher than necessary. Companies are usually better off waiting until conditions improve.

If your reason for considering refinancing is to reduce debt service payments or to inject new capital for operating needs, the quickest and least expensive ways to go are:

1. Renegotiate existing term loans
2. Foreign term loans or guarantees
3. Sale/leaseback of major hard assets

When refinancing for major business acquisitions or expansions, or for restructuring the company in anticipation of selling it, equity capital makes the most sense. Raising large amounts of equity capital takes more ingenuity than refinancing with debt or leasebacks. It also takes a lot longer. On the flip side, a significantly greater amount of capital can be raised. This chapter examines three ways to raise large amounts of equity capital:

1. Public stock issues
2. Private placements
3. Employee Stock Ownership Plan (ESOP)

Raising capital through a limited partnership requires steps similar to a private stock placement. Chapter 9 described the use of limited partnerships for second-stage expansion needs.

REFINANCING TO RAISE OPERATING CASH

Substituting new debt obligations for old doesn't make any sense, unless the new debt results in one or more of the following benefits:

- Lower interest rates
- Better terms (i.e., lower debt service payments)
- Cash infusion

Refinancing financially troubled companies often takes one of these routes. Short-term cash shortages resulting from a decline in the general business activity, the loss of a major customer, disagreements with a bank, competitive market pricing, and a variety of other causes easily create a need to restructure debt obligations. The amount of capital raised by substituting new debt for old is normally quite modest. Cash infusions help in the short run, but it doesn't take long to dissipate discretionary cash if business conditions don't turn around.

Refinancing troubled companies can be a difficult, tedious task. Trying to interest a new lender in a business experiencing difficulties takes a great deal of creativity and perseverance. Ideas for restructuring financially distressed companies can be found in two of my other books: *Recession-Proof Your Business* and *When The Bank Says No!*.

Whether your company is in trouble or not, if you decide to go this route, your first stop should be the bank or other lender holding your current debt obligations.

RENEGOTIATE CURRENT LOANS

If you still have an excess of short-term loans on the books by the time your company reaches its third-stage development, it usually makes sense to try to convert as much of the balance as possible to long-term debt. Assuming bank relationships rest on solid ground, most larger banks, as well as asset-based lenders holding working capital loans, should consider transferring at least part of the outstanding balance to a term loan. Obviously, the longer the term the better. Five years is a good place to begin negotiatiing.

To the extent that such a conversion can be made, soft collateral previously securing the short-term debt can now be used for operating needs. True, monthly principal and interest payments must be made against the term note, but at least you have pushed substantial cash outflow into the future. Two drawbacks make this tactic risky. Inevitably, interest on the new debt will be higher than the old. Few banks will wait longer for their money and still charge the same rate. Second, a bank or other lender will certainly want additional collateral to secure the term loan. If hard assets already are securing the loans, the only choices are non-business assets and personal guarantees.

FOREIGN TERM LOANS/GUARANTEES

If your current bank isn't interested in converting to long-term debt, a foreign bank might be. Major players in the global banking arena continually open new branches in smaller cities around the country. They are usually not full service banks, but they do entertain loans placed through their main U.S. offices. This tactic works especially well when a branch has just opened and the foreign bank is eager for new business. They demand the same security as American banks; but foreign banks tend to be more creative in the definition of acceptable collateral.

If a foreign bank won't actually make the loan, it might consider a guarantee, which can then be used as collateral to a term loan with your own bank. A "standby" letter of credit usually evidences this guarantee. You can't draw against the L/C; it serves only as collateral to a loan from another lender. If you default on the new loan, the lender then draws against the L/C. Most American banks accept such collateral.

Of course, there is a catch. Some type of collateral must be given to the foreign bank to secure the standby L/C. Since most of these banks have branches all over the world, assets located off-shore easily serve the purpose. An American bank won't touch off-shore assets, but foreign banks are quite comfortable with them. A second home in the Caribbean, investments through a Swiss bank, gold holdings in Hong Kong, and trust assets in a tax-haven country are a few examples of off-shore assets you might pledge.

SALE/LEASEBACK OF MAJOR HARD ASSETS

A sale/leaseback arrangement is another method for refinancing both short- and long-term debt. Chapters 9 and 11 briefly mentioned sale/leasebacks as a method to finance the expansion of production capacity. Sale/leasebacks apply even more to refinancing arrangements, especially for troubled companies.

Not all companies have sufficient hard assets to employ this method, however. Assets may already be pledged to existing loans. Unless the loan balance has been paid down enough to create a spread between the value of the asset and the balance of the loan, this tactic won't work. If you do have hard assets, either free of liens or with market values in excess of outstanding loan balances, a sale/leaseback could be a viable refinancing tool. With the cash infusion, you can liquidate unwieldy loans and simultaneously increase operating cash.

Renegotiating new debt with your current bank, using foreign bank term loans and standby guarantees, and arranging sale/leasebacks all work reasonably well as refinancing methods for modest amounts of capital. None of these schemes raise sufficient capital to make a business acquisition or a major capital expansion. Those ventures require equity capital.

REFINANCING FOR MAJOR PROJECTS

Third-stage capital requirements in excess of $1 million nearly always involve new equity rather than debt. The higher the amount needed, the greater the necessity to go the equity route.

Large corporations have another option that smaller companies do not enjoy—raising debt capital through public bond issues. The infamous junk bonds of the 1980s used for large acquisitions are one example of a public debt issue. If public bond issues appear to be a viable alternative, any reputable underwriter can offer advice about how, where, and when to make the issue. Typically, smaller companies find this route too expensive and potential investors few and far between. Therefore, the balance of this chapter is devoted to an examination of refinancing with equity capital, not bonds.

A PUBLIC STOCK ISSUE

Under the right circumstances, a public stock issue can dramatically increase a company's capital base. A company's first public stock issue is called an "initial public offering," otherwise known as an IPO. Equity capital raised through an IPO may be used for any purpose but is most effectively applied to long-term projects—liquidating long-term bank debt, expanding plant and equipment, acquiring a company, or financing a major research project.

Refinancing loans with equity capital remains the single most effective way to increase operating cash. Public equity also is one of the best sources to finance large projects. Typically, IPOs range between $5 million and $20 million. An issue for less than $5 million becomes prohibitively expensive. Of course, the maximum amount is, in the end, controlled by the investing public.

To make an IPO cost-effective, a company should be generating annual sales of at least $5 million, and preferably over $10 million. An IPO is very expensive. Issues of less than $7.5 million, defined as small issues by the Securities and Exchange Commission (SEC), will be less expensive than larger issues, but even then issuing costs of $250,000 to $500,000 are the rule rather than the exception.

Once the issue is sold, on-going administrative costs also increase significantly. Costs to produce periodic SEC reports and proxy statements, as well as substantial outside printing and mailing expenses, must be borne by the issuing company. In addition, accountants, lawyers, registrars, and transfer agents charge extra fees.

New shareholders also look for a return on their investment. Although interest expense does not apply, shareholders expect annual dividend payments. Non-deductible dividends must be paid with after-tax rather than pre-tax dollars, thereby increasing operating costs even more.

Other than cost, three potential problems face companies making an IPO. SEC approval (state securities commission approval for intrastate issues) must be obtained before the issue can be sold. Because market timing is frequently such a crucial ingredient, the actual issue date requires careful planning. More than one issue has flopped because the SEC or state commission took too long to give their approval and the market window closed before the issue was ready. You may decide to proceed in spite of the delay, but chances are high the price per share will be substantially lower than anticipated.

After selling the issue a second problem crops up. Will the market support active trading in your stock? In addition to being an excellent vehicle for raising large amounts of capital, publicly-traded stock provides a convenient method for rewarding management employees with non-cash, stock option incentives. You also might want to acquire another company by using stock rather than cash. Both circumstances require an actively traded security to establish its value. However, what if the market doesn't have any interest in trading your stock? Share value could plummet and make the stock unusable for either incentives or acquisitions.

A third problem relates to a company's management. It doesn't take long to realize that the trading price of a company's shares relates directly to its earnings trend. Management personnel spend more time worrying about keeping the earnings per share up than they do about running the company efficiently. Short-term decisions that favorably affect earnings for this quarter or this year may in the long run do more damage than good. This short-range view is a malady suffered by large and small public companies alike. And very often such shortsightedness signals the end of strategic growth.

Probably the most aggravating issue confronting private businessowners when they take their company public is their loss of privacy. SEC regulations require complete disclosure of the most intimate and proprietary company matters such as officers' compensation, personal histories, incentive programs, forecasts of future earnings, planned new product developments, and strategic operating plans. Not only must this information be revealed when making an IPO, it also must be continually updated in quarterly and annual reports; all of which become public information.

How Expensive Is an IPO?

Both issue costs and continuing compliance expenses must be considered when evaluating an IPO. Theoretically, the upfront costs should be covered by the proceeds of the issue, just like a real estate agent's commission when you sell a house. But what if the market buys only part of the stock offered? Or worse still, what if the issue fails completely? Either way, a company stands the upfront costs; and these costs can have a major detrimental impact on both cash flow and profits.

The following examples indicate the types of up-front costs that must be incurred for a public stock issue. The amounts vary depending on the company's circumstances and the market timing, but those shown are fairly normal for most initial issues.

1. *Legal and filing fees.* Lawyers perform three functions. They assist in the writing of the prospectus, coordinate the preparation of the registration

statement, and issue legal opinions in compliance with SEC regulations. Larger law firms charge more, smaller ones less. The range of legal fees run from a minimum of $75,000 to a maximum of $150,000 for a small issue. Large issues command fees in excess of $250,000. Filing fees with the SEC add another $50,000 to $100,000. States also want their share and filing fees; here add another $40,000 to $60,000.

2. *Public accounting fees.* A stock registration statement requires audited financial statements: two years for a small registration, three for a standard one. Audit fees from "Big-6" accounting firms easily stretch from $30,000 to $150,000 per year, depending on the complexity of the audit. They charge additional fees in the same magnitude for assisting in the preparation of the registration statement, the compilation of pro forma forecasts, and the calculation of various statistical tables required by the SEC. On an hourly basis, fees of $150 to $250 per hour are not uncommon for special IPO work. Smaller CPA firms charge less, but not by much.

3. *Printing registration statements and other documents.* Once everything is prepared, the registration statement, proxies, offering prospectus, and official notices must be printed and bound. Printing costs vary significantly in different regions of the country, but an average of $40,000 to $100,000 for typesetting, printing, collating, and other clerical preparation costs is not unreasonable.

4. *Underwriters.* You can't make an IPO without using an underwriter, at least with any assurance that it will be a success. Underwriters assist in the preparation of the prospectus and registration statement. They also coordinate with lawyers, accountants, and the SEC. An underwriter's primary tasks are to sell the stock issue and then to provide a trading market for the shares. Initial fees run 1 to 2 percent of the issue value. On top of that, underwriters get a commission of 7 to 10 percent of the actual value of the stock sold.

An underwriter is the key to a successful IPO. A good one can make things happen. Without an underwriter's constant attention and dedicated efforts, issues very often fail. The accounting firm or lawyer that helps with the registration represents the best source for locating a competent underwriter. These professionals know which underwriter will do the best job for your company.

It doesn't take long for these costs to add up. Smaller public issues typically cost up to $500,000, with larger issues much more.

After the issue is on the street, an assortment of administrative duties (and associated costs) must be performed on an on-going basis. Quarterly and annual SEC reports must be prepared. Annual certified audits must be performed. Proxy statements must be prepared and distributed to shareholders. Quarterly financial reports and annual reports must be prepared, printed, and distributed. Shareholder meetings must be announced and held. For a listed stock, special stock exchange reports must be filed periodically. Dividend notices, checks, and tax reports must be handled. Most companies find that they must hire additional financial personnel to manage these compliance requirements.

Does a Public Issue Make Sense?

In an effort to assist clients evaluate the reasonableness of going public, I prepared the following set of guidelines. Clients seem to like them because they take a lot of the guesswork out of the evaluation. These same guidelines appeared in *When The Bank Says No!*.

GUIDELINES FOR GOING PUBLIC

Company Structure

1. The company must already be incorporated.
2. If an S corporation election has been made and the new shareholders will total more than thirty-five, the company must convert back to a C corporation.
3. The company must be large enough to have professional management such as a controller, sales manager, chief engineer, and so on.
4. At least some of the products or services offered by the company should have high-growth potential over the next five years.
5. This potential growth must be demonstrable, not the owner's dream.
6. A commanding market share or unique market niche is highly desirable.
7. The company must have three years of progressively improving profitability (two years if a small IPO under $7.5 million).
8. Projections for the next five years should show continued improvement.
9. The prior three years financial statements (two years for a small issue) must be audited by a reputable CPA firm.
10. The CPA firm must have issued a clean certificate for each of the years.

The Economic Picture

1. Stock exchange averages should be rising.
2. Per share averages should be running above 10 times earnings.
3. General optimism should prevail in the national economy.
4. Regional economic indicators should be at least stable, preferably rising.
5. Interest rates, national unemployment statistics, and inflation projections should be at modest levels.

6. Industry trade statistics should indicate favorable growth projections for the next three years.

7. Federal international trade policies should not be detrimental to the company's product lines.

PREPARATIONS FOR GOING PUBLIC

Going public is not a decision to be made on the spur of the moment. A successful IPO requires extensive planning started long before the actual issue. Most entrepreneurs who have been successful with an IPO began the process up to three years in advance. Obviously, with a two or three year certified audit requirement, a company not regularly audited must begin at least that far in advance.

Here are some tips for getting your company ready for a public issue.

1. If the market your company serves is mundane, unglamorous, and perhaps declining, try to develop a complementary market with the reverse characteristics.

2. Get your management team in place and functioning. Don't leave any key slot open. Replace those managers not performing.

3. Clean up all contingent liabilities such as lawsuits, insurance claims, tax audits, pension liabilities, and so on.

4. Implement a five-year strategic plan.

5. Get a hot new product through the initial development stage. Nothing attracts investors like a chance to get in on the ground floor with a snappy new product introduction.

6. Develop a conscious, public relations campaign. Get your company known in the community and the industry. A good image in the financial community doesn't hurt either.

7. Try to get a "name" personality to join your board of directors. Anyone from the financial community is a big plus.

8. Get a good feel for the economics of your industry. Try to plan the issue to coincide with a rising stock market.

DO YOU LOSE CONTROL WITH AN IPO?

Many private businessowners fear that they will lose control of their company if they take it public. Other than the loss of privacy and restricted freedom of action discussed earlier, this fear is groundless.

You have the option of issuing as many shares as you want, assuming the underwriter can sell them. Few IPOs ever exceed 25 percent interest in the company, however. The most successful issues for smaller companies tend to be under 20 percent. If the issue gets into the 30 to 40 percent range, it becomes increasingly difficult to sell. The investing market prefers a small minority interest to a controlling share.

ADVANTAGES AND DISADVANTAGES OF GOING PUBLIC

A public stock issue may be the only way to raise enough growth capital for third-stage internal expansion or business acquisitions. Most companies reach a point where additional growth cannot be financed internally. Debt becomes too expensive. They find that going public adds financial stability to the company and increases additional borrowing capability for later needs.

To summarize, in addition to the above, most owners and managers of companies that have taken the public route find the following to be the most beneficial and the most troublesome elements:

ADVANTAGES

1. Greater amount of capital raised than with debt financing.
2. No interest payments. Company unilaterally determines what, if any, dividends to pay.
3. Company's owner keeps control.
4. Ready market to sell company when it's time to retire.
5. Valuable incentive compensation program for key employees with stock options.

DISADVANTAGES

1. Very high cost, both for initial issue and on-going compliance
2. Restricted freedom of action from SEC regulations.
3. Wrong economic or market timing.
4. Loss of privacy for owner and officers.
5. Management effort diverted from long-term strategic actions.

If a public stock issue doesn't fit, perhaps a private placement offers a better alternative for refinancing first and second stage debt.

A PRIVATE PLACEMENT

Private placements are used to raise a limited amount of equity capital in a relatively short period of time at the least cost. Because the SEC considers private placements exempt offerings, the cost of issuing the stock stays substantially less than a public offering. Although anti-fraud securities regulations must still be followed, a company does not have to file a formal registration statement. State laws might require a filing, but this is much easier and less expensive than going through the SEC.

Reasons other than cost influence the decision to opt for a private placement. The economic or market timing to make an effective public offering may be way off. Your company might not have two or three years of steadily increasing earnings (usually required to make a successful IPO). Perhaps you don't mind losing a little privacy but won't go all the way with public disclosure.

WHO ARE THE INVESTORS?

A private placement involves a limited number of investors. They can be relatives, friends, business associates, or strangers. If you have enough personal contacts with ready cash to invest, then sell the stock yourself. Otherwise, use a securities broker. Certain brokers specialize in keeping tabs on private investors anxious to make equity investments in closely-held companies.

Four types of individuals or companies invest in closely held companies:

1. Customers, suppliers, commissioned sales personnel, employees, and other individuals and companies with whom the company does business.
2. Professional investors who specialize in getting in on the ground floor of a potentially high-flying company.
3. Private investors looking for investments in small companies that can be taken public within a reasonable time frame.
4. Venture capital funds expecting a public issue in the future.

A competent securities broker specializing in private placements knows where to find investors in each of the last three categories. You might have some ideas for the first.

TYPES OF PRIVATE PLACEMENTS

There are several types of private placements, or exempt offerings. Their designation relates to the section of the securities regulations to which they apply.

Regulation D is an attempt to establish uniform requirements for private placements between the SEC and states. Most states allow Regulation D filings; a few do not. Regulation D provides exemption for small issuers selling securities under certain conditions. Such exemptions are designated as "Rule 504," "Rule 505," and "Rule 506."

Rule 504

Rule 504 stipulates that privately-held companies may sell stock in a total amount not to exceed $1 million. The sale must be completed within 12 months. Stock may be sold to an unlimited number of investors. However, the rule forbids a general solicitation of investors. It also imposes restrictions on the resale of shares by investors. These constraints do not apply in those states requiring the filing of a disclosure document, similar to a very brief registration statement.

Rule 505

Rule 505 allows a stock issue up to $5 million. This rule limits the number of investors to 35, unless they fall into the "accredited investor" category, in which case the number becomes unlimited. Accredited investors are defined by Regulation D as:

1. Institutional investors (banks, brokers, insurance companies, ERISA plans) with total assets in excess of $5 million.
2. Private business development companies defined in the Investment Advisors Act of 1940.
3. Tax-exempt organizations under IRS Code Section 501(c)(3), with total assets over $5 million.
4. Insiders of the issuer (directors, executive officers, general partners).
5. Any person whose individual or joint net worth (including that of a spouse) exceeds $1 million.
6. A person with income in excess of $200,000 in each of the two most recent years.
7. A trust with assets exceeding $5 million (with certain provisions).
8. An entity in which all the owners are accredited investors.

Rule 506

Rule 506 includes the same provisions as Rule 505 *plus* one additional provision for the 35 nonaccredited investors. These investors must meet a definition of financial and business expertise. This definition requires a statement that the investor is capable of evaluating the merits and risks of the investment.

The following conditions also apply under both Rule 505 and Rule 506:

1. Disclosures must be provided on SEC Form 1-A for issues up to $2 million. Offerings from $2 million to $7.5 million must use Form S-18. Those over $7.5 million are considered public offerings and must comply with full SEC disclosure requirements as if the securities were registered.

2. Disclosures may require two years financial statements, one of which must be audited. If this cannot be accomplished reasonably, only a balance sheet need be audited.

Intrastate Offering

To qualify for an intrastate offering exemption, all securities must be offered and sold to persons residing within the state in which the issuing company is incorporated, and in which it does a significant portion of its business. These securities, once issued, must remain in the state. No instructions govern how these provisions should be monitored. Caveat emptor!

Regulation A

Regulation A offerings must be for less than $1.5 million. A formal Offering Circular must be filed with disclosures similar to those required for registering securities. One advantage exists, however; the included financial statements need not be audited.

Wide variations in securities laws relating to private placements exist between states. Many have adopted common regulations, but many others insist on remaining unique. If a private placement seems like a viable alternative for refinancing, or for use in any expansion move, a competent attorney can fill you in on your state's requirements.

EMPLOYEE STOCK OWNERSHIP PLANS

An Employee Stock Ownership Plan (ESOP) is another vehicle for raising equity capital, either for refinancing existing debt or for funding a major expansion. The major benefit from an ESOP, aside from being an added employee benefit, is that Uncle Sam helps raise the capital. Either of two types of ESOPs can be employed—an unleveraged ESOP or a leveraged ESOP.

UNLEVERAGED ESOP

An unleveraged ESOP is funded entirely with company money, which on the surface doesn't seem to bring in additional capital. Indirectly it does, however. Contributions by the company to the ESOP are tax deductible. Since the funds are immediately returned to the company's coffers, no cash goes out the door. In effect, the IRS makes a contribution of about 35 percent!

For example, assume annual payroll is $1 million. The company contributes 10 percent, or $100,000, to the ESOP. The amount of taxes saved by the transaction totals 35 percent of $100,000, or $35,000. The company would not have this cash without the ESOP; therefore, the IRS has actually put $35,000 into the company.

LEVERAGED ESOP

A leveraged ESOP works the same way, except now even more money flows in. In addition to contributions made by the company, the ESOP borrows from a bank or other lender to buy shares in the company. Employees get company stock, the company gets the bank's money without taking out a loan and with practically no collateral!

The bank will probably want guarantees from the company, but should not require additional assets to be pledged. Annual contributions by the company pay the principal and interest on the loan.

The leveraged ESOP has grown in popularity as a way for the sponsoring company to borrow money at a significantly lower interest rate than it could with a straight bank loan. The effective rate stays lower because of the tax treatment of the loan repayment. Annual contributions to an ESOP used to repay the principal of the loan to the ESOP are tax-deductible, up to a limit of 25 percent of payroll. This means that the company repays the ESOP loan out of pre-tax earnings, an impossibility with a bank loan. Furthermore, contributions to an ESOP for interest payments are fully deductible, without limit.

On top of all this, dividends paid on ESOP shares are deductible if used to retire the ESOP loan or if distributed to ESOP participant accounts. This also applies when selling convertible preferred shares to the ESOP rather than common stock.

An extra feature kicks in when the ESOP owns more than 50 percent of the company's stock. At that point, the lender of funds to the ESOP may exclude from taxable income 50 percent of its interest earned. This should encourage the lender to charge significantly lower interest rates.

REFINANCING WITH AN ESOP

Although the ESOP has developed as a popular employee-benefit plan and as a convenient way to structure a management buyout, its greatest benefit to a company is as a refinancing tool. Figure 14-1 shows a comparative calculation of the after-tax cash effect of using an ESOP compared with a conventional term loan. The assumptions are a $1 million loan, interest at 10 percent, annual payments for seven years, an effective tax rate of 35 percent, an annual payroll of $600,000, and maximum contributions of 25 percent of payroll or $150,000 per year.

Figure 14-1

COMPARISON OF AFTER-TAX CASH EFFECT OF CONVENTIONAL VS. ESOP LOAN

Year	Principal	Interest	Conventional Loan		ESOP	
			Tax Savings	After-Tax Cash Effect	Tax Savings	After-Tax Cash Effect
1	$142,857	$100,000	$35,000	$207,857	$85,000	$157,857
2	142,857	85,714	30,000	198,571	80,000	148,571
3	142,857	71,429	25,000	189,286	75,000	139,286
4	142,857	57,143	20,000	180,000	70,000	130,000
5	142,857	42,857	15,000	170,714	65,000	120,714
6	142,857	28,572	10,000	161,429	60,000	111,429
7	142,857	14,285	5,000	152,143	55,000	102,143
	1,000,000	400,000	140,000	1,260,000	490,000	910,000

With an ESOP, the actual cash cost of the loan is nearly 28 percent lower than with a conventional loan. This savings of $350,000 results because with an ESOP, company contributions to the plan used to repay the principal of an ESOP loan are deductible. Even more cash benefits result when the ESOP owns more than 50 of the outstanding shares, or if instead of common shares, the company uses convertible preferred stock and then pays dividends.

If your payroll is high enough to make an ESOP worthwhile and if you plan to refinance with equity capital, ESOPs are hard to beat. Given the right circumstances, an ESOP remains one of the least expensive and most beneficial ways to do the job.

ESOP Restrictions

Neither the IRS nor the SEC regulates how much stock or what percentage of ownership can be sold to an ESOP. When used in management buyouts, 100 percent of the ownership changes hands. On the other hand, two restrictions do affect the size of the ESOP indirectly.

1. That portion of a company's contribution used to repay the principal of an ESOP loan is limited to 25 percent of annual payroll. However, the deductiblity of contributions for interest payments is unlimited.
2. The ESOP loan cannot extend beyond 15 years. Banks prefer a maximum of 10 years, although some go further.

Assuming that 10 years is the best you get, the maximum amount of capital that can be raised through an ESOP amounts to 25 percent of your annual payroll multiplied by 10 years, or 2½ times your annual payroll. If full tax deductions are not important, or if a bank will go beyond 10 years, no maximum applies.

A few restrictions relate to the tax-qualified status of the ESOP.

1. The primary purpose of the ESOP must be for the benefit of its participants, namely an employee fringe benefit.
2. The primary investments of the plan must be in the employer's stock—common or convertible preferred for leveraged ESOPs, any other type of securities for non-leveraged plans.
3. Each employee must have voting rights equal to allocated shares.
4. Employees must have the right to receive plan distributions of company stock.
5. Closely-held companies may exclude terminated employees from retaining ownership.

Although an ESOP won't work for every company, if the circumstances warrant, it can be a convenient, inexpensive way to refinance conventional bank debt.

SUMMARY

As a company reaches maturity, further expansions and other strategic moves frequently require replacing earlier loan balances with longer term debt or equity capital. Replacement is seldom dollar for dollar.

Raising large amounts of capital to pay off old debts and leave enough for major projects continues to be the primary purpose of refinancing. Companies suffering financially might restructure their debt obligations, but this usually involves smaller amounts of residual capital. It doesn't make sense to refinance for the sake of refinancing.

Although any number of reasons might make refinancing a desirable move, two circumstances remain critical to the success of any program; the form and amount of capital to be raised should match a company's long-range strategic objective, and, the timing of a capital-raising program must be right.

REFINANCE TO RAISE OPERATING CASH

Companies pressed for immediate cash can refinance old loans through three primary avenues. The first step should be an attempt to negotiate a conversion of short-term to long-term loans. Foreign banks offer an alternate approach, either for new long-term loans or for guarantees as collateral to secure new loans from your current bank. Sale/leaseback arrangements work for companies with unencumbered or appreciated hard assets.

REFINANCE TO RAISE MAJOR PROJECT CAPITAL

Buying a business or making major capital expansions requires large amounts of new capital. This normally means restructuring the company's balance sheet by substituting new equity capital for old debt. Either a public stock offering or a private placement brings good results. Private placements are much less expensive, quicker to implement, and less restrictive.

USING AN ESOP

Employee Stock Ownership Plans (ESOPs) represent another refinancing vehicle. Loans raised through leveraged ESOPs are much less expensive than conventional debt. Tax savings free up internal cash for expansion purposes, although restrictive rules must be followed.

Appendices

Appendix A
TOP 20 U.S. BANK HOLDING COMPANIES*

by Bank For International Settlements Tier 1 Capital Components

	Total Capital	Tier 1 Ratios BIS	Fed. Reserve
Citicorp	7,319	2.76	3.14
Bank America Corp.	4,764	5.06	5.72
J.P.Morgan & Co.	3,997	3.93	4.17
Chase Manhattan Corp.	3,813	3.38	4.13
Security Pacific Corp.	3,575	3.94	3.94
Manufacturers Hanover Corp.	2,780	4.05	4.75
PNC Financial Corp.	2,705	8.12	8.27
NCNB Corp.	2,275	4.92	4.45
Chemical Banking Corp.	2,199	3.19	4.26
Bankers Trust New York Corp.	2,166	3.23	3.60
First Chicago Corp.	2,153	3.23	3.60
Bank of New York Company	2,124	3.93	4.34
Wells Fargo & Co.	2,103	5.34	5.91
BancOne Corp.	2,041	9.84	9.95
Fleet/Norstar Financial Group	1,934	7.75	8.26
Suntrust Banks	1,917	9.16	9.16
First Union Corp.	1,858	8.88	8.88
Bank of Boston Corp.	1,758	4.82	5.39
First Wachovia Corp.	1,705	9.46	9.46
Sovran Financial Corp.	1,575	8.10	8.10

*A U.S. bank holding company owns banks and other subsidiaries involved in such regulator-defined "non-banking activities" as mortgages, consumer credit cards, leasing, and securities.

Source: *The Banker,* 1990, published by Financial Times Business Information Ltd., London.

Appendix B

U.S. HOME OFFICES OF "BIG-6" ACCOUNTING FIRMS

Arthur Andersen & Co.
69 West Washington St.
Chicago, IL 60602
(312) 580-0069

DRT International
1114 Avenue of the Americas
New York, NY 10036
(212) 790-0500

KPMG Peat Marwick
345 Park Avenue
New York, NY 10022
(212) 758-9700

Coopers & Lybrand
1251 Avenue of the Americas
New York, NY 10020
(212) 536-2000

Ernst & Young
200 National City Center
Cleveland, OH 44114
(216) 861-5000

Price Waterhouse & Co.
1251 Avenue of the Americas
New York, NY 10020
(212) 489-8900

Appendix C
STATE GOVERNMENT FINANCING PROGRAMS

For complete, up-to-date descriptions of programs in all states contact:
National Council of State Legislatures
1125 - 17th Street
Denver, CO 80202
(303) 292-6600

Note: Many cities have financial assistance programs in addition to the following state agencies.

Alabama Development Office
State Capitol
Montgomery, AL 36130

Alaska Office of Enterprise
Department of Commerce
Pouch D
Juneau, AK 99811

Arizona Office of Business and Trade
Department of Commerce
1700 West Washington Street
Phoenix, AZ 85007

Arkansas Small Business Development
  Center
University of Arkansas, Library
  Building
Little Rock, AR 72204

Colorado Business Information Center
Office of Regulatory Reform
1525 Serman Street
Denver, CO 80203

Connecticut Small Business Services
Department of Economic Development
210 Washington St.
Hartford, CT 06106

Delaware Economic Development
  Office
99 King's Highway
Dover, DE 19903

District of Columbia
Office of Business and Economic
  Development
1350 Pennsylvania Ave. NW
Washington, DC 20004

Florida Small Business Development
  Center
University of West Florida, Bldg. 8
Pensacola, FL 32514

Georgia Small Business Development
  Center
1180 East Broad St.
Athens, GA 30602

Hawaii Small Business Information
  Service
250 South King St.
Honolulu, HI 96813

Idaho Division of Economic and
  Community Affairs
Department of Commerce, State
  Capitol
Boise, ID 83720

Illinois Bureau of Small Business
Department of Commerce and
  Community Affairs
620 Adams St.
Springfield, IL 62701

Indiana Division of Business Expansion
Department of Commerce
1 North Capitol Avenue
Indianapolis, IN 46204

Iowa Small Business Division
Iowa Development Commission
600 East Court Ave.
Des Moines, IA 50309

Kansas Small Business Development
Center
Wichita State University
Clinton Hall
Wichita, KS 67208

Kentucky Business Information
Clearinghouse
Commerce Cabinet
Capitol Plaza Tower
Frankfort, KY 40601

Louisiana Small Business Specialist
Office of Commerce and Industry
1 Maritime Plaza
Baton Rouge, LA 70802

Maine Small Business Development
Center
University of Southern Maine
246 Deering Ave.
Portland, ME 04102

Massachusetts Small Business
Assistance Division
Department of Commerce
100 Cambridge St.
Boston, MA 02202

Michigan Local Development Service
Department of Commerce
Box 30225
Lansing, MI 48909

Minnesota Small Business Assistance
Office
Dept. of Energy and Economic
Development
150 E. Kellogg Blvd.
St. Paul, MN 55107

Mississippi Small Business
Clearinghouse
3825 Ridgewood Rd.
Jackson, MS 39211

Missouri Small Business Development
Office
Dept. of Community and Economic
Development
Box 118
Jefferson City, MO 65102

Montana Business Assistance Division
Department of Commerce
1424 North Ave.
Helena, MT 59620

Nebraska Small Business Division
301 Centennial Mall South
Lincoln, NE 68509

Nevada Small Business Development
Center
Univ. of Nevada
College of Business Administration
Reno, NV 89557

New Jersey Office of Small Business
Assistance
Department of Commerce and
Economic Development
1 West State St.
Trenton, NJ 08652

New Mexico Business Development
and Expansion
Dept. of Economic Development and
Tourism
Bataan Memorial Bldg.
Santa Fe, NM 87503

New York Small Business Division
Department of Commerce
230 Park Ave. - Rm. 834
New York, NY 10169

North Carolina Small Business
Development Division
Department of Commerce
Salisbury St.
Raleigh, NC 27611

North Dakota Small Business Specialist
Economic Development Commission
Liberty Memorial Bldg.
Bismarck, ND 58505

Ohio Small Business Office
Dept. of Development
Box 1001
Columbus, OH 43266

Oklahoma Small Business
Development Center
517 West University
Durant, OK 74701

Oregon Economic Development
Department
595 College St.
Salem, OR 97310

Pennsylvania Small Business Action
Center
Department of Commerce
483 Forum Bldg.
Harrisburg, PA 17120

Rhode Island Small
Business Development Division
Dept. of Economic Development
7 Jackson Walkway
Providence, RI 02903

South Carolina Business Assistance
Services and Information Center
Industry, Business and Community
Services Division
State Development Board
Box 928
Columbia, SC 29202

South Dakota Small Business
Development Center
University of South Dakota
414 East Clark St.
Vermillion, SD 57069

Tennessee Small Business Office
Dept. of Economic and Community
Development
320-6th Ave. No.
Nashville, TN 37219

Texas Small and Minority Business
Assistance Division
Economic Development Commission
410 East 5th St.
Austin, TX 78711

Utah Small Business Development
Center
University of Utah
Business Classroom Bldg.
Salt Lake City, UT 84112

Vermont Small Business Development
Center
University of Vermont Extension
Service
Morrill Hall
Burlington, VT 05405

Virginia Small Business Coordinator
Dept. of Economic Development
1000 Washington Bldg.
Richmond, VA 23219

Washington Small Business
    Development Center
441 Todd Hall
Washington State University
Pullman, WA 99164

West Virginia Small Business Division
Governor's Office of Community and
    Industrial Development
Capitol Complex
Charleston, WV 25305

Wisconsin Small Business Ombudsman
Department of Development
123 W. Washington Ave.
Madison, WI 53707

Wyoming Economic Development
    Division
Economic Development and
    Stabilization Board
Herschler Bldg.
Cheyenne, WY 82002

Appendix D

FEDERAL DEPARTMENTS AND AGENCIES GRANTING FUNDS UNDER SMALL BUSINESS INNOVATION RESEARCH PROGRAM

Department of Agriculture
Department of Commerce
Department of Defense
Department of Education
Department of Energy
Department of Health & Human Services:
    Office of Public Health
    Office of Service/Health
    Office of Care Finance
    Office of Administration
    Office of Human Development Services
    Public Health Service
Department of Transportation
Environmental Protection Agency
National Aeronautics & Space Administration
National Science Foundation
Nuclear Regulatory Commission

Appendix E
SAMPLING OF FOUNDATIONS AWARDING LARGER GRANTS AND LOW-COST LOANS

Foundation	*Type of Businesses*
Butler Manufacturing Company Foundation BMA Tower P.O.Box 917 Penn Valley Park Kansas City, MO 64141	Agribusiness
The Edna McConnell Clark Foundation 250 Park Avenue, Room 900 New York, NY 10017	Education Related
Financial Executives Research Foundation 10 Madison Avenue P.O.Box 1938 Morristown, NJ 07960	Research in Finance
The Xerox Foundation P.O.Box 1600 Stamford, CT 06904	Science & Technology
The Joyce Foundation 135 South LaSalle Street Chicago, IL 60603	Conservation
The Ford Foundation 320 East 43rd Street New York, NY 10017	Urban development, Public policy, International economic issues
Charles Stewart Mott Foundation 1200 Mott Foundation Bldg. Flint, MI 48502	Environmental
Adrian & Jessie Archbold Charitable Trust Chemical Bank Administrative Services Department 30 Rockefeller Plaza, 60th Floor New York, NY 10012	Health Care

The Robert Wood Johnson Foundation
P.O.Box 2316
Princeton, NJ 08543

Personal Health Care

Rockefeller Brothers Fund
1290 Avenue of the Americas
New York, NY 10104

International Trade &
International Finance

Appendix F
SELECTED FOREIGN BANKS WITH OFFICES
IN THE UNITED STATES

Banca Serfin, S.N.C.
8 Pine Street
Wall Street Plaza, 24th Floor
New York, NY 10005

Banco Popular de Puerto Rico
7 W. 51st Street
New York, NY 10019

Banco De Santander
375 Park Avenue, 29th Fl.
New York, NY 10152

Bank of East Asia, Ltd.
450 Park Avenue
New York, NY 10022

Bank Leumi Trust Co. of New York
579 Fifth Avenue
New York, NY 10017

Banque Indosuez
1230 Avenue of the Americas
New York, NY 10020

Banque Nationale de Paris
499 Park Avenue
New York, NY 10022

Barclays Bank of California
111 Pine Street
San Francisco, CA 94104

Chicago-Tokyo Bank
40 N. Dearborn Street
Chicago, IL 60602

The Fuji Bank and Trust Co.
1 World Trade Center, Suite 8023
New York, NY 10048

Hong Kong & Shanghai Banking Corp.
5 World Trade Center
New York, NY 10048

Israel Discount Bank of New York
511 Fifth Avenue
New York, NY 10017

Kansallis-Osake-Pankki
575 Fifth Avenue
New York, NY 10017

Lloyds Bank of California
612 S. Flower Street
Los Angeles, CA 90017

Mitsui Manufacturers Bank
515 S. Figueroa Street, 4th Fl.
Los Angeles, CA 90071

National Westminster Bank USA
175 Water Street
New York, NY 10038

Appendix G
COORDINATING INTERNATIONAL
DEVELOPMENT BANKS

African Development Bank and Fund
B.P. No. 1387
Abidjan,
Ivory Coast

Asian Development Bank
2330 Roxas Boulevard
P.O.Box 789
Manila, Philippines 2800

Inter-American Development Bank
808 17th Street NW
Washington, DC 20577

Appendix H
SELECTED LISTING OF FEDERAL AND PRIVATE SOURCES OF INFORMATION

National Association of Small Business Investment Companies
1156 15th Street NW, Suite 1101
Washington, DC 20005

National Venture Capital Association
1655 N. Fort Myer Drive, Suite 700
Arlington, VA 22209

Overseas Private Investment Corp.
1615 M St. NW, Fourth Floor
Washington, DC 20527

Private Enterprise Bureau
U.S. Agency for International Development
Washington, DC 20523

Securities and Exchange Commission
Office of Small Business Policy
Division of Corporate Finance
450 Fifth Street NW
Washington, DC 20549

U.S. Department of Commerce
Economic Development Administration
Credit and Debt Management Division
14th and Constitution Ave. NW, Room 7839
Washington, DC 20230

U.S. Export-Import Bank
811 Vermont Ave. NW
Room 1229
Washington, DC 20571

U.S. Small Business Administration Office of Business Loans
1441 L Street NW, Room 804
Washington, DC 20416

U.S. Trade and Development Program
Room 301 - SA - 16
U.S. Department of State
Washington, DC 20520

Western Association of Venture Capitalists
3000 Sand Hill Road, Bldg. 2, Suite 215
Menlo Park, CA 94025

Index